Time and Education

Also Available from Bloomsbury

Wonder and Education, *Anders Schinkel*
Cherishing and the Good Life of Learning, *Ruth Cigman*
Althusser and Education, *David I. Backer*
Pedagogies of Taking Care, *Dennis Atkinson*
Capitalism, Pedagogy, and the Politics of Being, *Noah De Lissovoy*
Knowing from the Inside, *edited by Tim Ingold*
Deweyan Transactionalism in Education, *edited by Jim Garrison, Johan Öhman and Leif Östman*
A New Perspective on Education in the Digital Age, *Jesper Tække and Michael Paulsen*
Philosophy and the Metaphysical Achievements of Education, *Ryan McInerney*
Hopeful Pedagogies in Higher Education, *edited by Mike Seal*
Posthumanism and the Digital University, *Lesley Gourlay*
Politics and Pedagogy in the "Post-Truth" Era, *Derek R. Ford*

Time and Education

Time Pedagogy Against Oppression

Petra Mikulan and Nathalie Sinclair

BLOOMSBURY ACADEMIC
LONDON • NEW YORK • OXFORD • NEW DELHI • SYDNEY

BLOOMSBURY ACADEMIC
Bloomsbury Publishing Plc
50 Bedford Square, London, WC1B 3DP, UK
1385 Broadway, New York, NY 10018, USA
29 Earlsfort Terrace, Dublin 2, Ireland

BLOOMSBURY, BLOOMSBURY ACADEMIC and the Diana logo are trademarks of
Bloomsbury Publishing Plc

First published in Great Britain 2023
This paperback edition published 2024

Copyright © Petra Mikulan and Nathalie Sinclair, 2023

Petra Mikulan and Nathalie Sinclair have asserted their right under the Copyright,
Designs and Patents Act, 1988, to be identified as Author of this work.

For legal purposes the Acknowledgements on p. viii constitute an extension
of this copyright page.

Cover design: Grace Ridge
Cover image © Hans Neleman/ Getty Images

All rights reserved. No part of this publication may be reproduced or transmitted in any
form or by any means, electronic or mechanical, including photocopying, recording, or
any information storage or retrieval system, without prior permission in writing from the
publishers.

Bloomsbury Publishing Plc does not have any control over, or responsibility for, any third-
party websites referred to or in this book. All internet addresses given in this book were
correct at the time of going to press. The author and publisher regret any inconvenience
caused if addresses have changed or sites have ceased to exist, but can accept no
responsibility for any such changes.

A catalogue record for this book is available from the British Library.

A catalog record for this book is available from the Library of Congress.

ISBN: HB: 978-1-3503-3486-1
PB: 978-1-3503-3490-8
ePDF: 978-1-3503-3487-8
eBook: 978-1-3503-3488-5

Typeset by Deanta Global Publishing Services, Chennai, India

To find out more about our authors and books visit www.bloomsbury.com and
sign up for our newsletters.

Contents

List of Illustrations	vi
Acknowledging	viii
Introducing	1
Troupe	17
1 Remediation	22
2 Revelation	56
3 Rupture	86
4 Repetition	118
5 Refusal	150
Reprise	183
Notes	187
References	194
Index	206

Illustrations

Figures

1.1	The number line	23
1.2	Energizing the origin into multiplicity	24
1.3	Data points showing the number of bird chirps in relation to temperature	26
1.4	A straight line of regression to fit the data	27
1.5	A broken line	27
1.6	A curved line	27
1.7	Different spatial imaginaries	37
2.1	The geometry of perspective painting	57
2.2	Juan Gris, *Nature morte à la nappe à carreaux (Still Life with Checkered Tablecloth)*, 1915 (public domain)	58
2.3	Fort logic	60
2.4	Indigenous Métissage	60
2.5	A one-sided band	61
2.6	Past in front, future behind	71
2.7	Two contrasting representations of time as a vector field	82
3.1	Detail of *Father Time* in the *Rotunda Clock* (1896), by sculptor John Flanagan (1865–1952). Photographed in 2007 by Carol Highsmith (1946–), who explicitly submitted the photograph in the public domain. Library of Congress, Prints & Photographs Division, LC-DIG-highsm-02121	87
4.1	The Koch curve: iterative process (left), and the result after many iterations (right)	126
4.2	Vincent van Gogh, *A Pair of Shoes*, 1886; Paris, France. https://www.wikiart.org/en/vincent-van-gogh/a-pair-of-shoes-1886 (accessed 28 February 2022)	129
4.3	The Frog Life Cycle	143

5.1 Baba Yaga, the witch from Slavic folklore. She lives in the forest in a hut on chicken legs and flies in a mortar, covering her tracks with a broom. Natalia Mikhalchuk / Alamy Stock Photo. DOI: 10.1080/09518398.2019.1597210   172

Exhibits

2A	A Conversation about Bells	66
2B	How Children Understand Time	73
3A	The Grizzlies, and Biidaaban (The Dawn Comes)	90
3B	Time and Transdisciplinary Research on Touch in Education	111
4A	Cycle/Frog/Child	142

Acknowledging

'What reprise is required by your wager?'

In this river of time, familiar ghosts of the past reassure and the strange ones of the future frighten us, but they all hunt us in the lazy rhythms between daydreamings. You will not find time laid out in these pages, as it is in schools, hospitals, museums, prisons and our daily lives, carefully separated by the tick and the tock of habituated hopes and desires. What, if anything at all, you will find reading these pages we cannot say, but we invite you to hold and pull back time to read several possible paths at once, some unintended, some lost in the loopholes uncharted.

We would like to thank our readers Asilia Franklin-Phipps and Taylor Webb for their deep engagement with these pages. Their comments haunt us. We thank Adam Rudder and Elizabeth de Freitas for their intellectual proddings and affections. We thank Leo Yamanaka-Leclerc for thinking with us about school bells. Finally, we also thank Kelly Paton for her incredibly nuanced and precise work with our words, citations, ideas and missing links. We thank the beautiful words gifted to us by the many writers we cite. Their words probe deep into the flesh of the quintessential afterthought of 'completing' a book; could the paths conjured in this book have been different? Yes, just as Time could have been different.

pm and ns.

Introducing

If time and reason are functions of each other, if we are creatures of time, then we had better know it, and try to make the best of it.

(Ursula Le Guin)[1]

The Problem

When you consider all the structures that are used to organize schooling – the years that make up the K-12 system; the number of hours of 'contact time'; the bells of the school day; the minutes allocated for tests, exercises, group work – it may seem that education has everything to do with time. But what could the study of time itself possibly bring to our understanding of education? What is there to say about time? It passes. It goes too quickly, or not quickly enough. So what? In writing this book, we have come to believe that our assumptions about time say a lot about who we are and how we understand the educational enterprise. If you think that time is like an arrow, steadily advancing forward, you might see the educational enterprise as the continuous development of learners towards ever better human beings. But what if you think that time is cyclical, as is the case in many Indigenous cultures? What would constitute development? What would 'better' even mean? And what if time does not even really exist, which is what theoretical physicists are now telling us? Does that mean we have organized schooling in a completely arbitrary way? Can we even speak of 'better' in the absence of a linear sense of *before* and *after*?

Temporal conceptualizations are implicit and constitutive of school life, but they are also not neutral. Furthermore, time is habitually naturalized in daily pedagogical practices, except perhaps in moments of crisis. That is, school life formalizes unreflective or unthought presuppositions of temporality by continually narrativizing homogeneous time, linear narrative and progressive teleology as tropisms of before and after, past and futurity. Here, we focus on dramatizing the tension between established time tropisms in organized education on the one hand and rhythm and tempo as certain capacities of time to bear on educational alternatives on the other.

Our aim in this book is threefold. First, we want to show the embeddedness of assumptions about time in our theories, be they academic or folk. In examining the assumptions of time made in a wide variety of contexts – from ancient Greek fiction to nineteenth-century theories of evolution; from twenty-first century physics to eighteenth-century mathematics; from twentieth-century Indigenous stories to twentieth-century afro-futurist fiction – we find time being mobilized in very different ways that are relevant to the way we have been thinking and might yet think of education. We have arranged these in the following 'tropisms': time as remediation, times as revelation, time as rupture, time as repetition and time as refusal. You can probably quite easily associate these tropisms with things we have all said as teachers (we leave it to the reader to make the one-to-one associations!): 'It will all become clear when you get to grade 10'; 'We'll have to go back to the basics'; 'There's now a completely different way of understanding this phenomenon'; 'If you stick it out, it will pay off'; 'You'll see this over and over again.'

Our second aim is to show how pervasive a certain image of time has been, gathering steam over at least two millennia. This image of time – which we call *time-as-arrow* – has emerged as being abstract, one-way, singular and teleological. Abstract in its lack of association with space, with place – time proceeds no matter where you are or who you are. One-way in that you neither go back in time nor skip forward. Singular in that there is one axis of time that gathers all phenomena into a single organizational principle. And teleological in that it is going somewhere; it encodes progress, meliorism. These assumptions may seem quite reasonable – and in many respects, they are – until we realize some of their repercussions, many of which are engendered non-intentionally. For example, if there is one temporal axis, then that must mean that we all adhere to it, which makes it difficult to account for the different temporalities of lived experience – and even if we recognize that your experience of time is different from mine, the power of abstract time colonizes phenomenological time. If there is a teleology of time associated with progress, then everything that is learned in time must be read as moving towards or achieving a goal – or falling behind it – but then how do we understand how learning is associated with forgetting or preserving or even refusing? As we survey the different forces that have contributed towards this dominant image of time, we will also be offering others, providing counterpoints that should help you see the very contingent nature of any set of assumptions about time.

Finally, our third aim is to show how different conceptions of time might intervene in our thinking about education. By evoking other sets of assumptions about time, we do not intend to argue that any one of them is the best way of thinking about time. Instead, our hope is that we can expose some of the potential complexity that exists in seemingly trivial or obvious decisions around time and education, and provide alternatives to problems that we already recognize as being pressing and thorny. For example, as Canadian philosopher of education Kieran Egan (2002) has argued, our current educational systems are somewhat shackled by a desire to satisfy three goals that often contradict each other: we educate in order to preserve cultural achievement; in order to ensure children's personal growth; and in order to prepare future workers. Loosely speaking, these goals relate to the past, the present and the future, which are timescales that are impossible to address simultaneously in a strict time-as-arrow concept of time. If the present is understood as a particular actualization of the past, then new possibilities might arise. If the future is not so insistently teleological, then 'preparing for the future' might actually mean re-living the past well.

We are Balkan and French–Canadian women; literature, ethics and mathematics scholars; teachers and mothers; past cross-country skiers and basketball players; possible bakers and farmers; potential quantum fabulists; and interested in the ways that (often implicit) philosophical assumptions shape the most mundane perceptions, actions and beliefs. These assumptions abound in education. However, the strong saviour complex that drives so much educational research – to help students and teachers, to guide and empower – often offers a kind of philosophical immunity. We can say this because we are not outside the ecosystem of Education theory and research. The more we read, the more we interacted with students and teachers and researchers and the more we understood the modulating effects of (often implicit) historical, cultural and material commitments to time. These are macro-scale concerns that are sometimes articulated in curriculum documents and perhaps even sometimes at play in teachers' actions in the classroom. But time is relevant to more meso- and micro-level concerns as well.

> **time (n.)²**
>
> Old English *tima* 'limited space of time', from Proto-Germanic **timon-* 'time' (source also of Old Norse *timi* 'time, proper time', Swedish *timme* 'an hour'), from PIE **di-mon-*, suffixed form of root **da-* 'to divide'.

> When we observe the environment, we necessarily do so only on a limited range of scales; therefore, our perception of events provides us with only a low-dimensional slice through a high-dimensional cake. (Levin 1992: 1945)

Think of all the ways that we as teachers try to fill time or make more time; where we feel that we lose time or gain time; where we wish we could go back in time to do something differently or step out of time to do what we think is important. A few months into the global coronavirus pandemic, we remember reading an article about how a small country had decided to just set the clock back one year – how that would solve all the problems about students having lost classroom time or the economy having lost fiscal growth time. Setting the clock back one year is fine for the sun, the crops, the animals; why can't it be fine for humans? Because it doesn't honour time-as-arrow; instead, it honours *time-as-cyclic* (rhythm). We are interested in how different ways of conceptualizing time can offer creative, disruptive and even liberating ways of doing education, in how time-as-cyclic, for example, and the slowing down of time across educational dimensions (tempo), can get us out of filling and killing time; away from racing against time; protected from official time.

Our commitment to agonizing time in education is manifested here not only in our style of writing, provoking discomfort by allowing this text to pattern dense frequencies, textured volume, jagged rhythm and a writing flow that is choked by the lack of air. We hoped to also, in part, achieve this by giving voice to the scholars and literary artists whom we cite in long, perhaps too long, citations, often in virtual conversation with one another. We call this a feminist citational pedagogy, a humble proposal that strives to keep up with the rhythms, velocity, voids and tempos of the writers we cite. This leaves their voices intact and refuses the colonial and masculine academic demand for paraphrasing – a mimetic practice of extractive inclination towards performing this said or that unsaid; an exhibition of one's professional and certified ability for deep levels of knowing what the authors cited are really saying, interpreting what is being said and unsaid in her texts.

A certain unbecoming of schooling is called upon if the future pasts are to be hospitable to humanity. 'Sustainability' calls for epistemological, axiological and curricular strategies of untimeliness that depend on both a deep engagement with time, timing, pacing, tempo *and* thinking against time, the segregated and stratified times we live in. What is being called upon is a certain reimagining of what will be possible, when, how much and for whom? While discussing these questions with a colleague, one of his comments stood out with a poetic clarity worth repeating:

> It is a little strange, perhaps, when you think about it, that schooling may not truly be interested in education, if education is a far more slow and deliberate movement of thinking, across collective lifetimes, generations, and across space and time. (Neil Bassan, personal correspondence, 2021)

In schools – as autopoietic sites of cultural reproduction and interpretation – epistemologies, axiologies and ontologies are created and reproduced based on certain regimes of time. In 1995, American anthropologists Fred Myers and George Marcus advocated for the acknowledgement of art-writing in the field of art as 'quintessentially part of art's own constitutive narrative(s) and signifying practices, particularly enabling art to *have a history*' (1995: 27; *emphasis added*). Similarly, as participants in educational research and publishing economy, we repeatedly interpret and contribute to the production of educational history. The production of solid, factual and objective historic timelines is an essential means for legitimizing the field of education through continuous 'enabling' of its potential to *have a history* and, on a progressive continuum, parcelling out its potential to having a legitimate future.

> Autopoiesis is the process through which we repeat the conditions of our present mode of existence in order to keep the living-system – our environmental and existential world, our humanness – living. The living-system is normalized and inconspicuous and comfortable (our attachment and allegiance to the system keeps it living). Here, too, the processes of repetition and replication fold into each other demonstrating the correlational workings of how we *know* our human life and, simultaneously, do not notice the process of recursion: the practice of being human, and the enactment of social life replicates itself with the analytic, affective, and material talisman of *realization* inducing the replication of how things

already are and therefore normalizing the system as imperceptibly quotidian. (McKittrick 2021: 133–4)

> *artifice (n.)*[3]
>
> 1530s, 'workmanship, the making of something by craft or skill', from French *artifice* 'skill, cunning' (14c.), from Latin *artificium* 'a profession, trade, employment, craft; a making by art; a work of art', from *artifex* (genitive *artificis*) 'craftsman, artist, master of an art' (music, acting, sculpting, etc.), from stem of *ars* 'art' (see **art** (n.)) + *facere* 'to make, do' (from PIE root ***dhe-** 'to set, put'). Meaning 'crafty device, trick' is from 1650s.

While the various disciplines in humanities and social science interrogate time as the location of power and struggle within Western societies (there is even a journal called *Time and Society*), in the field of educational studies, there is little attention paid to the history and discourses of time. Schools, as a micro-scale of relations in wider society, are governed by the universal language of time and clocks. As students, teachers and administrators, policy-makers, curriculum researchers, etc., we have become so accustomed to organizing our thinking, doing and knowing by the tick-tock of hours, minutes, seconds and the five-day school-week, that for most of us, the alternative ways of organizing school rhythms seem inconceivable. Our suggestion is that radical decolonization of school organization, policy, practices and research might be unthinkable, because we continue to resist (via explicit refusal or simply lack of attention) to imagine alternative epistemologies, axiologies and ontologies of time.

> *Time is the substance I am made of. Time is a river which sweeps me along, but I am the river; it is a tiger which destroys me, but I am the tiger; it is a fire which consumes me, but I am the fire.*
>
> (Borges)[4]

Many have shown that organized schooling in the West promotes a colonial discourse and material relations of power that continue from the European-American imperial and colonial era. We suggest that colonial discourse in schools continues its extractive, eliminating and expanding projects through and with the persistent colonial and biblical vestiges of linear, homogenous, causal and universal time-as-arrow in at least three ways:

1. the progressive discourse of civilizing both the children and the profession of education,
2. the production and promotion of universal, ordered, standardized hierarchies of knowledge and value systems and
3. the interconnectedness of neoliberal educational policies (i.e. evidence-based curriculum), medicalization/remediation of child 'deviation', (i.e. cognitive, sexual, behavioural) and persistent 'segrenomic' (Rooks 2017) logic of the different modes of temporalities (school to prison pipeline).

> In fact, if there is a feeling of unreality in contemporary Europe, just as it tries to create itself, this is not because of the well-known torments that one feels at the end of a century, but because of the enormous multiplicity in which History is now going astray, and the pain caused by the lack of power or control over this History, felt by those who had conceived it as an origin projecting itself towards an end. (Glissant [1997] 2020: 64)[5]

The next time you sit down to plan your weekly curriculum, breaking it down to days, hours and minutes – as you begin to feel the pressure of accountability to temporal structures and the demands of the yearly programme – steal a moment to pause, lean back and lean into the long history of monastic, industrial and colonial efforts to command, order and own time in order to extract value and to discipline the minds, bodies and souls of those who 'have no part', that is, slaves, children, women and the working class.

If, on the one hand, philosophers since ancient times have pondered about the being of time, European imperial, geographic expansion has always been steeped in the cultural and ideological conquest of time. As Italian-Australian historian and writer Giordano Nanni shows in his terrific book *The colonisation of time: Ritual, routine and resistance in the British Empire* (2012), the belief that the 'primitive' societies the world over were 'not attentive enough' to time and its passage 'functioned as a powerful legitimising discourse for colonial and missionary projects and therefore European hegemony' (2). In the European imperial and colonial spatial expansion, time became the tool with which the European civilization began to imagine 'itself as a time-conscious civilisation in opposition to a time-less Other', and thus 'western Europe staked its claim to universal definition of time, regularity, order; hence also to definitions of knowledge, religion, science, etc.' (3). For Nanni, there is a 'very real sense' in which this 'temporal hubris, together with the mathematically abstracted idea of time which distilled into the mechanical clock, created the necessary culture of time for building empires' (3).

In this book, we seek metaphors and sources of inspiration from music, myth, math, art, cinema and anthropology, to draw attention to educational research and writing practices as sites of disciplining knowledge production, and to avoid the risk of these texts becoming self-referential. Here we thus develop an ethical stance towards temporality; a new sense-ability and response-ability that those of us working in education will have to answer for and bear. School productions of inextricable temporality of daily acts, experience and practice 'make' the time we are 'in' through the critical features of governing school rhythms. But these rhythms as established regimes of biocentric temporality have in them contemporaneously embedded, repetitious and stratified inequalities of temporalities. Our humble goal is to undo our reader's sense of time, by breaking up narrative continuity, progress and resolution through the stacking up of textual layers like geological strata, superimposing thoughts and voices on different scales and from various fields and timelines. We do this in order to create beautiful contrasts everywhere, in the spirit of the British philosopher and mathematician Alfred North Whitehead.

We break with the linearity of time by offering a series of chapters that can be read in any order, forwards or backwards, skipping to and fro (or you can read the same one twice!). None of the chapters are prerequisites; none sum up the argument – we avoid conditions and foundations. The names of the tropisms – remediation, revelation, rupture, repetition, and refusal – set up a rhythmic encounter, gesturing towards cyclicity, rhythm and reverberation. Alongside this written text, we also use sketches to evoke spatial imaginaries and affects. We see these as cinematic stills, teetering between the dynamic and static, enabling – once again – a rhythmic tempo rather than a continuous duration. Sketches are used to provide a tempo for each tropism. The series of sketches in Rupture was drawn to accompany the text, but also in response to the Ishmael Reed poem, *The Diabetic Dreams of Cake*, whose stanzas we had distributed as poetic stills in our text. While we were unable to secure permission to include the poem in this book, readers may wish to experiment with a side-by-side reading, to engage in the virtual conversation we had with the poem and then realized in images – images that operate as a poem in absentia.

As non-textual elements, we see the sketches as modes of freezing the affective. They are not representations of an external event or object – they do not freeze something out there, but instead freeze the affective response to what is out there. They are not, either, research creations, a concept that focuses on product, on solutions that can then be plucked up and used elsewhere, on definitive origins, on intentional ex nihilo mental production – all of which reproduce the linearity and pragmatics of time. It is for this reason that we do not attempt to 'apply' or make 'useful' our problematizing to education. Instead, we stick closely to the problem of how to think about time in and alongside education. Our modes of thinking, sketching, imaging, writing and reading, as well as our citational pedagogy, model ways of posing the problem in a variety of educational contexts, including ones taken from our own experiences, but to offer ready-made or speculative solutions would be to shirk our response-ability, to not take adequate care of our abstractions, as per Whitehead's injunction. For that, we need a community of readers, like yourself, to be able to respond to any or all of the provocations/abstractions in the book, and see their various instaurations in your own specific pedagogical milieu.

Instead of applications and solutions, we aim to provide provocations for the reader. These provocations, we hope, will function in different ways for different readers, whose own problems and temporalities will vary. But for most of us, the worldwide pandemic has changed our awareness of time. It has made time visible anew. Time was felt. The habits through which time normally functions were halted. We have wondered about the time of *before*. We wonder about whether there will be an *after*. Speculation in both tenses – of *future* and *past* – sprout from the unease of the present. The fabulations we pursue in this book are meant to pick up on and rework this attention to time, to work with time rather than allow it to lapse into its invisible machinations.

We write/draw/feel in the spirit of Timothy Clark (2012), inviting you to read at several scales at once as 'a way of enriching, singularizing and yet also creatively deranging the text through embedding it in multiple and even contradictory frames at the same time (so that even the most enlightened seeming progressive social argument may have one in agreement on one scale and reaching for a conceptual brick on another)' (163).

> The word works on itself, arises each time from its own birth, its own contradiction, its internal Relation, the enormous duration accumulated from so many revelatory dispersals. The mass that emerges from this is a dizzying Whole-World, which involves us. (Glissant [1997] 2020: 124)

Five Tropisms of Time

Education is all about time. The structure of the day, the week and the year; the curriculum, the lesson, the unit; the development of cognitive, moral and physical capacities. And yet, few scholars have discussed time explicitly, other than to urge the slowing down of teaching and learning, or the speeding-up of curriculum change. This book aims to think about time in education, to inquire into the ways that images of time have affected assumptions about what it means to learn, to teach, to know, to be, to care. In each of the five tropisms – a word we've chosen in order to reduce the temporally ordered, hierarchical expectations of chapters – we explore one specific mode of orientation towards time to show how it operates in education, and how it has evolved, been responded to and sustained through philosophy, literature, mathematics and the arts. Our aim is not to privilege one tropism over the other, but to intensify them all, both as a way of studying their consequences and as a means of fabulating new temporalities of education.

We have conjugated each tropism with two named scholars whose work provided, as we wrote, strong pulses, beautiful contrasts and fertile concepts. This method may resonate with the diffractive approaches of scholars such as American feminist philosopher of science Karen Barad, who reads French philosopher Jacques Derrida alongside the Danish physicist Niels Bohr. We see, with our pairs of scholars, some forceful stones, dropping in the water and producing diffractive wave patterns, but we also embrace the many pebbles complicating, breaking, antagonizing and amplifying those waves. Pebbles in one reading might become stones in another. In other words, feel free to swap out or add to the names we've chosen for now.

> *tro·pism* | \ ˈtrō-ˌpi-zəm [6]
>
> 1. a: involuntary orientation by an organism or one of its parts that involves turning or curving by movement or by differential growth and is a positive or negative response to a source of stimulation
>   b: a reflex reaction involving a tropism
> 2. an innate tendency to react in a definite manner to stimuli
>   *broadly*: a natural inclination: PROPENSITY
>   // encouraged his *tropism* toward the theatrical
>   – John Updike

Remediation: Queering Time-as-Arrow with Giordano Nanni and Valerie Rohy

The very idea of remediation depends on the assumption that time flows like an arrow: heading along a single path, in one direction. This image is distilled in the mathematical number line, which starts at the origin (at zero) and stealthily advances with no end in sight. Remediation involves going back in time to recover, relearn and remember that which should have occurred before, but did not. It structures the past as the ground that must be covered before moving forward. And, by direct analogy, it describes the path from primitive to civilized, from child to juvenile, from deviant to normal. The Italian historian Giordano Nanni shows how time-as-revelation functions as a tool and channel for incorporating subjects into the master narratives of colonialism. We show how educators from Herbert Spencer to Jean Piaget have used the trope of time as remediation to chart out their developmental lines. And with queer scholars such as American literature professor Valerie Rohy, we follow the destructive consequences of such rigid, universal lines as they pertain to education.

With Rohy, we show how time is implicated and what it might mean to recompose spatio-temporal time-as-arrow images, which are dominated by straight, upward-tending lines – lines that desire continuity and constancy. Other paths exist: dotted lines of discrete jumps, in which time itself has changed speed; multiple simultaneous lines of schizophrenic quantum existence, in which we are forced to speak of time in the plural; circular lines, knotted lines, lines that stop, lines that reverse direction. In each of these mathematical fabulations, remediation itself transforms, no longer requiring a fix or correction. The student who failed high school mathematics is no longer *assumed* to require remediation before pursuing post-secondary education; the blind student is no longer assumed to require remediating technologies that enable them to read the exam; the female student is no longer assumed to need to develop a thicker skin so that she can participate in the science labs.

Revelation: Diverting Time-as-Deferral with Édouard Glissant and Sara Ahmed

As the saying goes, 'only time will tell'. The Christian idea of redemption happening in heaven structures time as the opening towards a final, euphoric opening of the curtains, revealing in time (a) its atavistic condition in the origin myth; and (b) the predestination of all being and becoming as essentially temporal. We read this idea of redemption with Édouard Glissant, a Martinique writer (of novels and poetry) and philosopher, who calls out its colonial roots and suggests alternate, anticolonial myths. We call this trope revelation and show how it is used in schools, when students are told – especially in mathematics classes – that 'you'll need this later'. School, like life, becomes a waiting game that will provide an unknown, but certainly fabulous, future. Time itself becomes lived *through* rather than lived *in*. It's the Aristotelian transcendental path. And this makes the 'getting there' all the more desirable. Quickly, if possible or rather, quicker than others.

What if we loosen our thinking about time as being given and static? We might, as British geographer Doreen Massey (2005) suggests, reconceive it as 'the product of interrelations' (55) of multiple trajectories, some of which might reveal (yes, I *do* need to understand fractions in my job!), while others bury, cover and hide. This would thwart facile assumptions of progress, which have infiltrated schooling both in its traditional instantiations and its modern ones (in which reflection, sharing and explaining operate as revelatory mechanisms). With Sara Ahmed, an Australian–British feminist and queer scholar, we explore how the trope of time-as-revelation gives shape to the ongoing utilitarianism of schools, to their techniques of using usefulness as modes of deferral. We use (!) Ahmed's notion of queering use to interrogate the trope of time-as-revelation.

Rupture: Discretizing Time with Denise Ferreira da Silva and Luce Irigary

Western epistemology (grounded in reason, science, bifurcation of nature and culture) and its grammar of thought (Subject-predicate logic) is conditioned on a very particular colonial regime of Time and Space. As such, decolonizing pedagogies, if they are going to be successful, have to go all the way, meaning that as teachers, we cannot stop at choosing Black and Indigenous literature and/or rituals, queer and feminist films and celebrating festivities from various different cultures, without accounting for how Time and Space are the privileged and Unthought sites where colonial epistemologies reproduce themselves (e.g., here in Canada's British Columbia, the new curriculum would look much different if the conceptual starting point was Place, as theorized by many Indigenous scholars,[7] instead of the now-implemented triad 'know-understand-do'). *Celebrating* difference in One-ness benefits and corresponds with the multicultural and neoliberal juridico-economic system that demands integration according to a logic where All implies Sameness, while *respecting* the Other in their Difference/Pluri-ness ruptures, disobeys this Logic.

We explore feminist experiments of rupturing time, drawing on the French feminist scholar Luce Irigaray, and Brazilian Black feminisms scholar Denise Ferreira da Silva, who excavate indeterminacies that show how time as contingency can upset abstract time, and therefore create the non-dialectical time required to release current regimes of patriarchy, whiteness and ableisms. Inasmuch as abstract time also conditions assumptions of part-whole relation, which in turn structure assumptions around causality and theories of change (which are currently either top-down flowing, or bottom-up – both conditioned on the requirement that the whole contains the part), we show how Whitehead's mereotopological structures of the philosophical/mathematical can condition the general on the particular *and* the particular on the general. If time can also be a function of space, the very idea of curre becomes contingent on place, on the flows gushing and drying up, or being rerouted by dams, condominiums and burial grounds.

Repetition: Escaping the Fugitive Present with Henri Lefebvre and Saidiya Hartman

Formal education in its spatial image of time is represented by a metaphor of a stream – *curre* – flowing forth in successive events. We make use of the concept of curre to represent an objective counterpart in the world, namely the passage of time in the world beyond human mind/experience. With curriculum conceived as a programme with history, temporal and causal order of successive developmental stages and change, students and teachers adhere to time-frames decided in advance, repeating the pre-established epistemological and axiological regime of signification, enacting the patterned division of time into the slotted periods, measured, operationalized, managed. This scientifically predetermined time regime is conditioned on and justifies the repetition of subservience, discipline and compliance. The notion of school time as both the repetition of predetermined successive learning stages and the cyclical repetition of the passage of time 'out there', governs the power configuration of schools because it institutes moral zones and ethical ideals of the 'already established', 'tested and objective' regimes of schooling. With French philosopher Henri Lefebvre, we explore a different way of thinking time-as-repetition, working with his notion of rhythm, which does not isolate time from space (or energy), in keeping with Einsteinian scientific thought.

From Nietzsche to Lewis Carroll to Deleuze, repetition also obtains, but is no longer grounded in, the continuous flow of human consciousness. Thinking repetition with these scholars changes the assumptions we make about traditional practices such as memorization and choral changing, which are often eschewed in progressive movements that value conceptual understanding and individual accomplishment. Instead of merely repeating the past, such practices can, if we follow African-American studies scholar and novelist Saidiya Hartman, also be seen as swelling the present and creating futures and even altering the past. Indeed, habits and rituals that operate through thinking, doing and feeling, both individually and collectively, mark out different measures – rarely, actually, achieving synchronicity.

Refusal: Fabulating Time with Bonnie Honig and Michael Taussig

The recent calls to refuse, among feminist, Indigenous and Black scholars and activists, are calls to stop participating, to stop action and hence, to stop time – changing not just the present and the future, but also the past. But such refusing does not effect change. Hence American philosopher Bonnie Honig's proposal for a tripartite arc of refusal that may begin with the inoperativity of not-doing, but then seek new inclinations that disrupt the categories of given space-time: refusing to make students write the standardized test but then having them take it in pairs, thus disrupting the individuality of being and knowing. These new inclinations – practised within the walls of a single classroom, in a refuge that is free from outside gaze – can fortify the move to refusal-as-fabulation, when refusals of individuality break out across the school.

In addition, we examine the ethical premises that are constitutive of refusal of the temporal in addressing education's colonial relations; if the aim is to disrupt the seductive workings of colonial power in its most intimate dimensions, then it is crucial to invent practices and strategies that engage with the affective (dis)investments of students and educators in colonial relations. We work with Australian anthropologist Michael Taussig's feminine notion of mimeses to show a different way of thinking time. We address time as refusal in education as a viable political ethics that wagers in the name of future possibles not already governed by extractive politics of colonial progress and oppressive regimes of knowing and doing, and contribute to ongoing debates about the implications of our theoretical choices for enriching educational study and pedagogies.

Reprise

The thoughts on the final pages reverberate an ethic of reprise, whereby we place our passion for/from the other not to the test of the past or the future possibles, but to other dreamers and fabulators, also dreaming up impossible worlds, densities and dimensions of time. The ethical obligation to 'respond . . . ' to the other is here replaced by the question: 'what reprise is required by your wager?' Such a question affirms and presupposes the continuity of discontinuity, a being out of phase with the others' dreams; it asks of us to be ok with that.

:

Troupe

Sara Ahmed (born 1969); Australian-British feminist and queer scholar.
Mikhail Bakhtin (born 1895 – died 1975); Russian philosopher and historian.
Karen Barad (born 1956); American feminist philosopher and physicist.
Tina Campt (born 1964); American historian, modern culture, media studies, feminist and Black studies scholar.
Michel de Certeau (born 1925 – died 1986); French scholar of history, psychoanalysis, philosophy, and the social sciences.
Claire Colebrook (born 1965); Australian feminist philosopher.
Dwayne Donald; amiskwaciwiyiniwak and Papaschase Cree educational studies scholar.
Kieran Egan (born 1942); contemporary educational philosopher, focusing on classics, anthropology, cognitive psychology, and cultural history.
Denise Ferreira da Silva; Brazilian feminist philosopher, focusing on critical race and ethnic studies, critical legal, political and moral theory.
Asilia Franklin-Phipps; American educational research, indigenous, race, and ethnic studies scholar.
Édouard Glissant (born 1928 – died 2011); Martinique philosopher, literary critic and writer (of novels and poetry).
Elizabeth A. Grosz (born 1952); Australian feminist philosopher.
Saidiya Hartman (born 1960/1961); American writer and Black studies scholar.
Georg Wilhelm Friedrich Hegel (born 1770 – died 1831); German philosopher.
Bonnie Honig (born 1959); American political, feminist, and legal scholar.
Luce Irigaray (born 1930); Belgian French feminist philosopher, linguist, psycholinguist, psychoanalyst.
Julia Kristeva (born 1941); Bulgarian French feminist philosopher, literary critic, semiotician, psychoanalyst.
Henri Lefebvre (born 1901 – died 1991); French Marxist philosopher and sociologist of everyday life.
Giordano Nanni; Italian-Australian historian, writer and satirist.
Friedrich Wilhelm Nietzsche (born 1844 – died 1900); German philosopher and classical philologist.

Jean William Fritz Piaget (born 1896 - died 1980); Swiss psychologist and theorist of child cognitive development.

Plato (born 428/427 or 424/423 – died 348/347 BCE); Greek philosopher.

Valerie Rohy; American scholar of nineteenth- and twentieth-century American literature, queer, feminist and psychoanalytic theory.

Carlo Rovelli (born 1956); Italian physicist and philosopher.

Gilbert Simondon (born 1924 – died 1989); French philosopher.

Hortense J. Spillers (born 1942); American literary critic, Black Feminist scholar.

Michael T. Taussig (born 1940); Australian anthropologist and ethnographer.

Alfred North Whitehead (born 1861 – died 1947); British philosopher and mathematician.

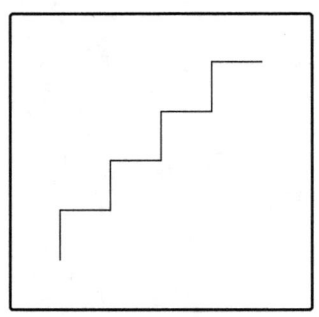

Lies 3: The difference between the past and the future is that one has happened while the other has not.

(Jeanette Winterson)[1]

1

Remediation

Queering Time-as-Arrow with Giordano Nanni and Valerie Rohy

remediation (n.)[2]

1818, noun of action from stem of Latin *remediare*, from *remedium* 'a cure, remedy'. In educational jargon by 1966.

remedy (n.)[3]

c. 1200, *remedie*, 'means of counteracting sin or evil of any kind; cure for a vice or temptation'; late 14c., 'a cure for a disease or disorder, medicine or process which restores health'; from Anglo-French *remedie*, Old French *remede* 'remedy, cure' (12c., Modern French *remède*) and directly from Latin *remedium* 'a cure, remedy, medicine, antidote, that which restores health', from *re-*, here perhaps an intensive prefix (or perhaps literally, 'again'; see **re-**), + *mederi* 'to heal' (from PIE root ***med-** 'take appropriate measures').

Negative numbers – the ones we see on thermometers, such as −10° Celsius – came very late in the history of Western mathematics. The Ancient Greeks didn't use them, since their mathematics was geometric in nature, and the geometric shapes they worked with only involved positive measurements. However, in their commercial and tax calculations over 2,000 ago, the Chinese worked with a rod system in which colours represented positive (red) and negative (black) quantities. Red rods were used for incoming money (sales) and black rods for negative quantities related to outgoing money (purchases). About 1,400 years ago, negative and positive quantities were also used in India, representing debts and fortunes.

Eventually, some rules for describing what happens in arithmetic operations involving negative numbers were developed, this time referring to numbers more abstractly – not necessarily tied to commercial situations. For example, 900 years ago, Al Samawal stated that the product of a negative number and a positive number is negative. It was not until the fifteenth century that negative numbers appeared in Europe, along with the double entry bookkeeping system. It is in the invention of the number line, roughly 400 years ago, that the 'meaning' of negative numbers – that is, their spatial metaphor – was given. That is to say, while negative quantities were previously associated with certain types of objects (like purchases), the number line made possible the idea of a negative number as being a continuation, in the 'backwards' or reverse direction, of the positive numbers. If the positive numbers march us forward in time, the negative ones could take us backwards.

The number line confers a particular spatial meaning of number that provides not only a sense of bi-directionality and continuity, but also symmetry – where the negatives are a shadow twin of the positive numbers. −2 is not 2, literally 'naught – 2', perhaps even naughty 2 (why else the use of the word 'negative'?). In mobilizing a new continuity between I and not–I, the possibility of more or less I arises, of the right, red (the colour always used to represent positive numbers in school manipulatives) and the left, black (the colour always used to represent negative quantities). With all (numerical) values lying on one same line, objective comparisons can be made; the movement back and forth that might be sinning and repenting, can be tracked; there is no jumping off the line. If you are at −5, you can improve, move up to 2 or even 10.

As can be seen in Figure 1.1, 0 becomes a sort of pivot – rather than being the existential void of nothing, the number line tames it down into the company of other numbers and therefore merely *a(not)her* number. The number line also creates infinity – actually, two infinities, one for each direction. There is therefore no beginning, which forecloses a few questions about origins.

But it makes many new ideas possible. First, there's the idea that between any two 'points' on the line, there must be another number. This other number is of a different kind – rather than being a whole number or an integer (both words

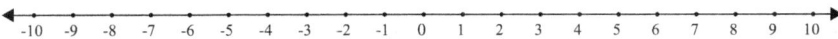

Figure 1.1 The number line.

indicating intact, discrete quantities), the new number is called rational, which derives from the Greek word for ratio, which means 'to reason, to reckon'. In between the whole numbers 2 and 3, there is a ratio 5:2, which we can express as the fraction 5/2 or decimal number 2.5. If we continue zooming into the number line, there will be another number, say, 2.51, and we can continue zooming as much as we want and still find other rational numbers. Another infinity at play.

The taming of negative numbers into the number line speaks to the desire to make meaning by fitting with that which is already known (sinning and repenting; the bad and the good; losing money and making money), into the spatial configurations that already exist, into relation by counterpart, by opposition, by dialectical negation. But things could have been different. In the diagram in Figure 1.2, there is little spatial support for thinking of negative numbers as continuations or shadows of positive ones. The French philosopher of mathematics Gilles Châtelet ([1993] 2000)[4] uses this image to show how to recast 0 as the bringing into existence of nothing. The question of origins returns.

In this sense, 0 is not just what happens when you subtract a quantity from itself, when you are about to slip into debt, but as the energetic, creative nexus from which two branches can grow. From passive mediator of + and –, 0 becomes a font of multiplicity, of different kinds that are not necessarily collinear or even coplanar. This 0 evokes new and unscripted directions that you yourself could draw. (Try it. Draw another line – make up a new mathematics!) This matters to our thinking about time inasmuch as it invites different spatial possibilities that challenge the ubiquitous Time-as-Arrow spatial imaginary. In the classical number line, the past-present-future lay contiguous one to the other, with the present – which we can take as the zero –

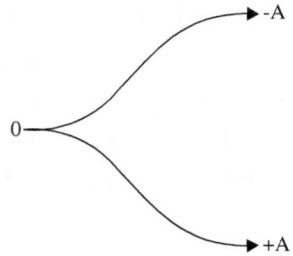

Figure 1.2 Energizing the origin into multiplicity.

being that which is passed over in moving from the past to the future. In the wishbone, the present gains potency and the causal relation between the past and the future is upended.

Consider how such a space-time image would upend the curriculum; it would change the narrative about students not being adequately prepared, or being behind. We might ask, for example, how moving forward remakes the past. How does learning about the Second World War in Grade 10 repeat, refuse, relegate that which was learned in Grade 9? In Grade 4, children learn about negative numbers, which certainly repeats some of Grade 3 (the focus on arithmetic operations), refuses what happens in Grade 3 (when you could subtract a number from one bigger than it) and relegates Grade 3 to the naïve past. Our habit of doing negative numbers in Grade 4 rests on the number line approach of phylogeny recapitulating (Western) ontogeny. It rests on the centripetal attractant of sequentiality that makes plurality and simultaneity seem developmentally wrong.

> Once again we see evidence for the ontological priority of phenomena over objects. If one focuses on abstract individual entities the result is an utter mystery, we cannot account for the seemingly impossible behavior of the atoms. It's not that the experimenter changes a past that had already been present or that atoms fall in line with a new future simply by erasing information. The point is that the past was never simply there to begin with and the future is not simply what will unfold; the 'past' and the 'future' are iteratively reworked and enfolded through the iterative practices of spacetimemattering – including the which-slit detection and the subsequent erasure of which-slit information – all are one phenomenon. (Barad 2007: 315)

In education, the word 'remediation' is only ever applied to children who are experiencing a difficulty of one kind or another. They are not developing in the expected way so there is therefore a need to remedy them, to heal or smooth over presumed disabilities. Remediation always refers to a return to basic skills, almost always in reading and arithmetic. It involves diagnoses (identifying where along the negative side of the number line a learner might be) and then specialized training, to smooth the passage back towards the positive side. But healing is one thing; restoring health is quite another.

The force of the line in Western thought cannot be underestimated (Ingold 2015). Lines act as basic metaphors for how we move, how we think and how we relate to each other and the world. In mathematics, the line is, in geometrical terms, defined by two points. On the plane, it marks the path that is the shortest distance between those points, and it extends in both directions. This is quite different from the line that emerges from 'taking a point for a walk'. One is straight and the other not necessarily so. Mathematics covets those straight lines, which can be described so succinctly, without requiring any drawing, by a simple algebraic equation: $y = mx + b$, where m describes the slope of the line – that is, how slanted it is. A slope of 1 is an inclined plane of 45°. A slope of 100 is quite steep and a slope of 0.1 is almost flat.

The line is coveted because there are many mathematical techniques for working with lines, for moving them, intersecting them with other lines, figuring out where they might start and stop. These powerful techniques produce desires, desires to find lines everywhere, and to sometimes treat things that aren't really lines as if they were, which makes the calculations easier – and what begins as pretending things are straight so quickly turns into forcing them to be. For example, the regression line is the imposition of a straight line on a group of points in the coordinate plane, as shown in Figures 1.3 and 1.4. Try to draw a line that passes as close to as many of those points as possible. If you can, then you have a model for the relation between the number of chirps that a bird will make in fifteen seconds as a function of the temperature.

It is called a regression line since it is formulated in terms of how far you have to 'walk back' from each data point to the line. The mathematical regression

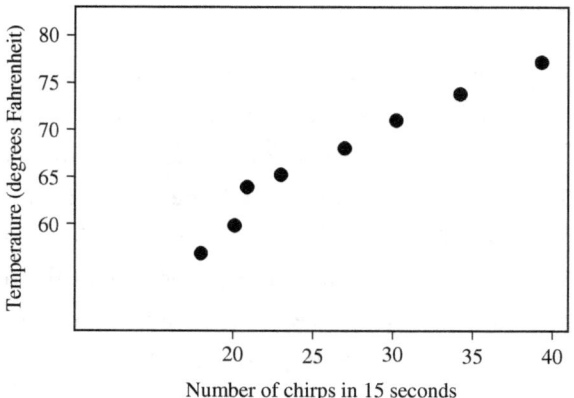

Figure 1.3 Data points showing the number of bird chirps in relation to temperature.

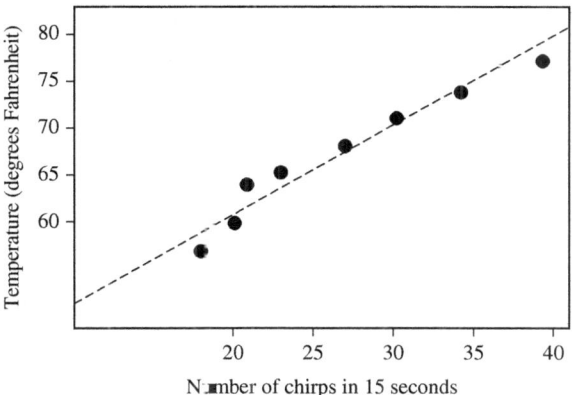

Figure 1.4 A straight line of regression to fit the data.

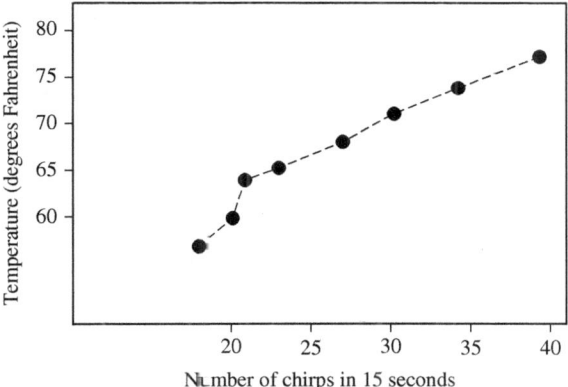

Figure 1.5 A broken line.

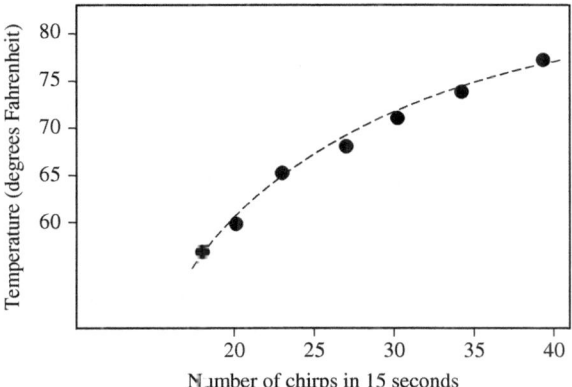

Figure 1.6 A curved line.

line minimizes the total number of 'walking backs' – mathematicians like efficiency. It is also called the 'line of best fit'. But there are many other lines that could fit the data, like the broken one that goes from data point to data point, or the slightly curved one that hits more of the points.

But the straight line offers so much predictive power (what will happen at higher and lower temperatures); it satisfies the fantasy of correlation and uniformity, of a rule that can perhaps even apply to all chirping birds, and not just the ones that produced the data (on that day, in that location, by that scientist . . .). How do we stop seeing straight lines everywhere?

:

Remediation of the Primitive and the Savage

In reading the following passage, remember the three goals of education we sketched out in the introduction, following Canadian education philosopher Kieran Egan: transmission of culture; personal growth of a child; and preparing children for the future workforce. That a certain image of time is the organizing principle of these educational aims, becomes apparent when we consider the 'civilizing mission' of schools. Not only in colonies, but of children as 'underdeveloped' human beings on their progressive journey to fully formed rational subjects in general.

> But whether it was a case of securing regular and disciplined labourers for farms, mines and plantations, legitimating the dispossession and displacement of nomadic populations, or advancing 'savages' along the scale of civilisation or securing souls for the kingdom of heaven, all such projects relied on forms of temporal conversion and the establishment of a specific language and consciousness of time. In assuming the authority to determine when other societies could work, rest and play, the emissaries of the clock worked daily, and hourly, in their quest to bring about a sense of worldwide 'order', by exporting their ways of structuring the flow to distant lands, and by preaching to their inhabitants new ways of thinking about what time itself is. Such efforts were driven by significant cultural, as well as concrete economic, imperatives. . . . At the most fundamental level, therefore, time was both a tool and a channel for the incorporation of human subjects within the colonisers' master narrative; for conscripting human subjects within the

matrix of the capitalist economy, and ushering 'savages' and superstitious 'heathens' into an age of modernity. (Nanni 2012: 4)

The Italian historian Giordano Nanni's analysis of the historical colonization of time shows two important things for our discussion of time and education. The first is the importance of thinking of the Western temporal discourse of 'remediation' and 'regression' in conjunction with the history of its European imperial power and colonialism. The mission of civilizing the 'savages' was, first and foremost, conditioned on a particular progressive, monastic and industrial conception of time (straight lines), disrupting and purposely eliminating Indigenous temporalities. Second, it was in places such as the factory, railroad, mine, plantation and missionary/residential school that the colonial missionaries/teachers, administrators, officers and slave owners exercised, practised, solidified, perfected and justified their ideological conception of timetables, the clock and the bell, as the organizing principle and material embodiment of Western moral values attributed to time. Nanni gives an example of how the moral and the temporal reform were part of the same colonial method by looking at the time discipline at Lovedale, a missionary school in Cape Town. Imbued with the Victorian moral charge ('echoing' contemporary values 'aimed at the English masses'), and converging the concepts of 'time, money, and God', *Lovedale News* asks its readers:

> HOW MUCH HAVE YOU IN THE BANK? Not the Savings Bank, though it would be a good thing to have a little there too. This Bank is a better one. Perhaps you have nothing to put in the savings bank, and think you have nothing to put in any other. You are wrong. You may be putting money in every day. Did you ever count up how much or how little you had got there – in the Bank of which God is the manager, and over whose counter pass the well used moments of each day and all the good things a man thinks or says or does. We speak of spending time. Time *spent* does not go into the Bank, any more than money spent. But every moment you use well, for God, you put into the Bank . . . . I would advise you all to put something in – to put in all you can. For the bank gives good interest. (Nanni 2012: 198)

In schools, we experience an *image*[5] of time, Time-as-Arrow (from 'primitive' to rational, from 'savage' to human, from 'juvenile' to adult, from 'concrete' to abstract, from 'cosmological' to technological, from 'nature' to culture, from 'queer' to heterosexual), that functions as a naturalized, institutionalized and presupposed order of being and doing. It operates as a racially coded, biocentric artifice that (a) continually reproduces, conditions and materializes western neoliberal hegemonic discourses of knowledge, information, progress, order, abstraction, and universality; and (b) structures the affective experiences of Black, Brown and Indigenous students.

For theorists of education determined to sustain educational studies into the future, it is important to acknowledge, as Black feminist scholar Kara Keeling (2007) suggests, the 'recurrent violence of colonization and enslavement and the configuration of (neo)colonial temporality authorized by that violence', because only then will the efforts to decolonize educational studies and White-centric curriculum be 'relieved of their quest to locate and identify more accurate (somehow less problematic) representations of blacks, whites, and so on, and charged with the daunting task of understanding, articulating, and challenging (in ways that must hold open the possibility of the impossible) the socioeconomic relations and the spatiotemporal configurations made visible by images' (34–5). As White women researchers, one of us Balkan and the other French–Canadian, we also recognize that writing about the colonization of time and history from our privileged positionality requires that we acknowledge that the project of decolonization 'requires that every recognition of the Black and the White entail an acknowledgment of the violence that authorizes such recognition. Each appearance of the Black and the White conserves that violence' (Keeling 2007: 35).

> The examples of creolization are inexhaustible and one observes that they first took shape and developed in archipelagic rather than continental situations. My proposition is that today the whole world is archipelagizing and creolizing itself. In these circumstances, it has become necessary for us to distinguish between two forms of culture: Those that I will call atavistic, whose creolization took place a very long time ago, if it did take place, and which have meanwhile armed themselves with a corpus of mythical narratives aiming to reassure them as to the legitimacy of their relations with the land that they occupy. These mythical narratives usually take the form of a Creation of the world, of a Genesis. Those that I will call composite, whose creolization is happening so to speak before our very eyes. These cultures do not generate a Creation of the world, they do not consider the founding myth of a Genesis. Their beginnings proceed from what I call a digenesis. (Glissant [1997] 2020: 119)

For example, Nanni is careful to sustain Indigenous agency by showing that while the colonization of time by the European imperial expansion was violent and unidirectional, the Indigenous and the enslaved systematically resisted and refused the colonial imposition of timetables, seven-day weeks and the Sabbath. This became a contentious issue, wherein the failure of missionaries to ideologically indoctrinate and interpolate the 'native' into the temporal order of the colonizer was not perceived as 'a radical condemnation of the methods and of the regime' (Fanon, cited in Nanni 2012: 206) by the colonized. Rather, such agency was 'denied' by colonialism, promoting instead a certain image of 'irregularity and compulsive "lateness" as innate racial defects' (Nanni 2012: 212), immortalizing stereotypical views of the racially innate deviance and the inability of Black and Indigenous subjects to uphold time-consciousness. Not toeing the line.

Nanni asserts acts of resistance and refusal as enactments of Indigenous agency to avoid the 'conservation of violence' present in so much of the recent neocolonial discourses and practices of representation and recognition of the Other as a passive receptacle of Western violence and hegemony. Acknowledging this is important to keep in mind in any discussion of time and temporalities in the field of educational research and study, because, as Keeling (2007) suggests, 'if the Black conserves the originary violence of colonialism' deployed in part by the violent expansion of European pastoral, monastic and industrial temporal imaginary, 'and redeploys it', we also need to acknowledge that the Black 'might function simultaneously (as Fanon explains about "the native" in *The Wretched of the Earth*) as "the corrosive element" within colonial and neocolonial reality' (35).

> Influenced by the formidable powers of persuasion of the Western linear time that was conceived in this half-shadow, a time that we tend to consider a definitive result, we find ourselves almost adapting, in our exploration of this period, the attitudes and formulations of the sorcerer's apprentice – convinced that we can easily gain an overview of it and that, as with modern chaos theory, we grasp its principal themes. Illusions that are emphasized by our innocently pedantic exposition of our knowledge, which will certainly irritate specialists in the subject. (Glissant [1997] 2020: 56)

The ethical challenge the Time-as-Arrow poses to those of us working within education is twofold. One, who is the time of education for? Who or what does it serve? And two, how do educational planning, writing, reading and speaking practices reproduce, maintain and commit further temporal violence to those who 'have no part' (Rancière 2010), including the inhuman (animal, geologic, cellular, etc.)?

⁝

British Columbia is one of the ten provinces in Canada. Its curriculum has recently undergone significant changes, evidently responding to the sociocultural and economic changes we face in the twenty-first century. On the home page of the redesigned curriculum, a reader (perhaps a teacher, parent, policy maker?) is invited to ponder the following parochial view of the present speed of change:

> British Columbia has one of the best education systems in the world. Teachers are skilled, facilities are sound, and students are performing near the top of international assessments. Yet it is an education system modelled on the very different circumstances of an earlier century – when change was much more gradual than it is today. Conditions in the world are changing greatly and rapidly. Today's students will grow into a world that is very different from and more connected than that of generations before. . . . Today we live in a state of constant change. It is a technology-rich world, where communication is instant and information is immediately accessible. The way we interact with each other personally, socially, and at work has changed forever. Knowledge is growing at exponential rates in many domains, creating new information and possibilities. This is the world our students are entering. (Province of British Columbia 2021)

There are a number of temporal presuppositions embedded in this curriculum exposition that imply explicit consequences in terms of the before-mentioned ethical challenges:

1. Newtonian Time

In Newtonian imagination, time is empty, universal, a homogenous vessel *in which* change happens at different speeds. Even if nothing changed, there would still be time.

2. Historicism

Just as in the Newtonian universe, in the historical imagination of educational systems, events happen in a continuous, disenchanted, homogenous and empty time. As Indian historian Dipesh Chakrabarty (1997) suggests in 'The Time of History and the Times of Gods', the idea of history is a 'code' for 'natural, homogenous, secular, calendrical time' without which a story of a universal, evolutionary history of 'single human' cannot be told (37). If neoliberal goals of education for the twenty-first century present school to be an equalizing factor in the just distribution of economic and cultural gains, educational programmes depend on the idea of history as a 'code' for a single humanity. For this ideology to be successful, schools condition their curriculum on the idea 'that independent of culture or consciousness, people exist in historical time', in which it is 'always possible to discover "history" (say, after European contact) even if you were not aware of its existence in the past. History is supposed to exist in the same way as the earth does, for instance' (Chakrabarty 1997).

Time-as-Arrow continually reproduces this mandate and, as such, it enables educational planners to produce statements such as 'Today we live in a state of constant change. It is a technology-rich world, where communication is instant and information is immediately accessible' (Prov. of B.C. 2021). Such statements do not, however, ask: what and whose image of time operates in such lofty goals? Who has the privilege to experience this 'constant change' and who continually owns its fruits?

In his account of the Crow way of life before and after their land was stolen by settlers, American philosopher Jonathan Lear (2008) shows that in the after-life of colonial displacement and dispossession of Black and Brown bodies, 'Nothing happened after that. We just lived' (57). When happening/time breaks down.

> But what doesn't count as a happening is the breakdown of the concepts in terms of which people understand things to be happening. Concepts get their lives through the lives we are able to live with them. If nothing any longer can count as dancing a Sun Dance or planting a coup-stick, then the tribe has lost the concepts Sun Dance and coup-stick. This is how I interpret Plenty Coups's witness: to a loss that is not itself a happening but is the breakdown of that in terms of which happenings occur. (Lear 2008: 37–8)

As Petra Mikulan shows in *Ethics of Refusal* (forthcoming), 'it is possible to see how these values are put forth as a response to a very particular historic, cultural and geographic *continuum* that was being built anew by settler colonists in the New World, one built on the subjugation and possession of the inhuman', a continuum conditioned on disrupting and eliminating Indigenous temporalities. Lear further shows that continuity of time, and time itself, were stolen from the Crow: 'It is a time when there were heavy snows, a time when we were preparing to fight against the Sioux, a time when Plenty Coups counted his first coup. Aristotle says that time is a measure of change and rest. We mark that change with a now – a now that divides the change into a before and an after' (Lear 2008: 48). School reproduces the discipline of the industrial and colonial regime of Time-as-Arrow epistemologically and axiologically, but while such discipline represents a successful convergence of values, rights and beliefs for some, Time-as-Arrow's colonial discipline will have always presented a divergence for others:

> But to grasp this now we need to understand it as a now-when: a now when this change is occurring. But in the situation as we are envisaging it, the Crow ran out of whens: the categories that would normally have filled in the blanks lost their intelligibility. It could no longer be a now-when-we-are-hunting buffalo. And nothing could any longer count as now-when-we-are-preparing-for-such-a-hunt. Similarly for battle. But all Crow temporality had fitted within these categories – everything that happened could be understood in these terms – and thus it seems fair to say that the Crow ran out of time. Obviously, the members of the Crow tribe still inhabited some minimal form of temporality. They could of course grasp that nomadic life was in their past; and they were aware of such moments as now-when-we-are-struggling-to-get-our-rations. But this was not a category in their way of life. It was a description that arose as a symptom that that way of life was devastated. Above all, it didn't amount to anything: there was no larger framework of significance into which it could fit. One can now see how a witness to the demise of that way of life might nevertheless declare his allegiance to it by insisting that the breakdown of Crow temporality does not itself count as a happening. (Lear 2008: 42)

Growing up in Socialist Yugoslavia, time was something *we all* seemed to have plenty of. But this *having* time was not experienced as a commodity you can store in a bank (godly or corporate). Our first encounter with the concept of time as a commodity was when, in our early twenties, we met our future partner from Canada, who, then living with us in post-socialist Slovenia, (but also post many other colonial invasions, such as Turkish, Austro-Hungarian,

French, Italian etc.), was constantly frustrated with how slow and irrelevant time seemed to run there, and who would repeatedly say things like 'time is money'. We could not understand why anyone would want to think and live like that. But as we now live and work in settler colonial Canada, we are beginning to understand that our sense of time is deeply shaped by being exposed to a particular kind of historicism of struggle, where neither the Newtonian universal time, nor the Aristotelian time as a measure of change, took hold; rather, time only endlessly repeated itself as if in a loop:

> György Konrád wrote that trains and movies run slower here, because time runs slower. I think it runs differently. As layers and layers of illusions are peeled away – the illusion of beauty, the illusion of power, the illusion of importance, even the illusion of meaning – time profoundly changes our view of life itself. The Austro-Hungarian Empire built up its signs of wealth and power for four hundred years. They slowly decayed, fading away. Then for almost half a century the communists tried to destroy the past and replace it with their own symbols – they faded even more quickly. Now the new governments are again changing the names of streets and squares, destroying old monuments and replacing them quickly with new ones, taking history and memory as their own little playground. But the cities are remembering and showing it, and the people, too. The nostalgia and hopelessness of the Central European soul, its sadness and cynicism – the inner sepia, if you wish – all stems from this. So, I guess, we are something else, after all, something visibly different. In our cities, 'renewal' does not renew, it only points out the passing of time, the fact that there is no progress, that history repeats itself endlessly. (Drakulić [1992] 2016: 166–7)

3. Syntax of Change

In everyday speech, Time-as-Arrow (commodified artifice) participates in a general economy of exchange made possible through historical emergence of literary abstraction. The idea that history is layered and coeval (captured in the expression 'simultaneity of the non-simultaneous', coined by the German historian Reinhart Koselleck, and applied by Marxists such as Ernst Bloch and historicists such as Heidegger), is possible only when time is abstracted away from events. The dichotomy between time as the becoming of events (a belief held by ancient philosophers before Plato and revived by Whitehead and Leibniz) and time as a universal being, has been documented (and is worth quoting at length) in the *Preface to Plato*, wherein the British literature of antiquity scholar Eric A. Havelock (1963) shows that in the ancient oral tradition of Ionic Greece,

> 'knowledge' (we place the term deliberately in quotation marks) is compelled to be obedient in these ways to the psychological requirements imposed by the memorised saga, it becomes possible to define its general character and content under three separate aspects, none of which agree with the character of 'knowledge' as it is assumed to exist in a literate culture. First of all, the data or the items without exception have to be stated as events in time. They are all time-conditioned. None of them can be cast into a syntax which shall be simply true for all situations and so timeless; each and all have to be worded in the language of the specific doing or the specific happening. Second, they are remembered and frozen into the record as separate disjunct episodes each complete and satisfying in itself, in a series which is joined together paratactically. Action succeeds action in a kind of endless chain. The basic grammatical expression which would symbolise the link of event to event would be simply the phrase 'and next . . .'. Thirdly, these independent items are so worded as to retain a high content of visual suggestion; they are brought alive as persons or as personified things acting out vividly before the mind's eye. In their separate and episodic independence from each other they are visualised sharply, passing along in an endless panorama. In short, this kind of knowledge which is built up in the tribal memory by the oral poetic process is subject precisely to the three limitations described by Plato as characteristic of opinion (doxa). It is a knowledge of 'happenings' (*gignomena*) which are sharply experienced in separate units and so are pluralised (*polla*) rather than being integrated into systems of cause and effect. And these units of experience are usually concrete; they are 'visibles' (*horata*). (180)

A very particular conception of historical time is at play when we use the word *change* in curriculum and educational ethics and policy. Following Chakrabarty (1997), we can say that there is a 'gesture of exclusion built into the use of the word' (87) *change*. For example, for some (i.e., colonized, Indigenous, women, people with neuro-atypical modes of reasoning, people experiencing schizophrenia, etc.), change either does not 'happen', no longer happens or happens in a plurality of different speeds, tempos and rhythms. Change, being expressed in these various modes, can go 'many different places at the same time' (Chakrabarty 1997: 50). If *change* was understood outside Time-as-Arrow ('metanarrative of progress', as Chakrabarty would have it), as something that has the potential to narrate many different futures, in a plurality of modes, then school policy, research funding and curriculum planning could not claim legitimacy as things that can positively flow along into the speedy future.

How do we stop seeing everything in terms of line(ar) progress?

> We must pay due attention to our *imaginaries*, aware that '[t]he imaginary comments with a dirge, or it just giggles' (Glissant [1990] 1997: 199)[6]

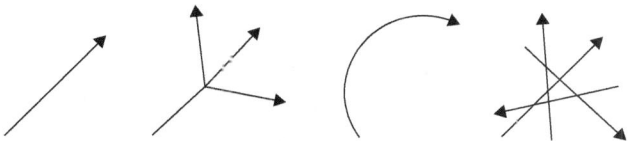

Figure 1.7 Different spatial imaginaries.

The 'gesture of exclusion' splits the force of *change* as an event into a teleological and causal process on the continuum from past to future. In the new British Columbia provincial curriculum, the temporal expression of speed as slow change '– when change was much more gradual than it is today' (Prov. of B.C. 2021) can now be safely relegated into the past stages of its progressive education.

> I am talking about millions of men in whom fear has been cunningly instilled, who have been taught to have an inferiority complex, to tremble, kneel, despair, and behave like flunkeys. (Césaire [1955] 2000: 43)

Temporal discourses are discourses of power and resistance. Any thought of educating children for the future in which access to 'a technology-rich world, where communication is instant and information is immediately accessible'[7] (Prov. of B.C. 2021) is just and equitable, will have to account for how particular colonial forms of temporality reproduced in schools are naturalized to operate successfully for the White, bourgeois class. If many educational researchers are struggling to promote radical change, perhaps it is because radical change would first and foremost entail decolonizing White, neoliberal, utopian Time-as-Arrow, in curriculum design, policy and pedagogy. In this book, ours is a modest ethical proposal, that we might begin by dramatizing the tension between, on the one hand, historicism of colonial passage, progress, hope, optimism and, on the other, its underpass: dissonance, violence, negation, extraction and desolation. The political power of infantilizing/anachronizing the Black-Child-Queer modes of (non)being and (un)becoming of variously situated students on a school trajectory *towards* (rational, adult, heteronormative political maturity) continues to play out as a dystopic continuity of discontinuity of effective and affective present:

> Waiting is a sensation made ever more insufferable when fused with a sense of inferiority that percolates beneath the unmistakable impression that someone else's time is more valuable than your own. After all, your time is your life. Following this logic, it is but a momentary lapse before the realization hits that you inhabit a time and space in which other lives are more valued than your own. At best, the accelerating frequency of these experiences might proffer a range of affective points of departure from which to build bridges stretching between those more or less accustomed to prevailing timescapes to the chronospheres of the untimely others who make relatively privileged epochs possible. For populations on the underside of segregated temporality, waiting is not merely an episodic rite of passage. Waiting is an articulation of structural inequality that functions as an indefinite denial of any passage whatsoever. (P. J. Brendese in Shulman, Reinhardt, and Coles (2014: 103))

:

Remediation of the Child and the Juvenile

It is well documented in the educational studies of the history of childhood, that until far in the Middle Ages, the school was serving adults and children together. This is because the sentiments we hold around children today did not exist before the Middle Ages. The main evidence for the non-existence of the concept of a 'child' in that period is the absence of explicit childlike elements in medieval art (such as portrayal and sculpture). Historians also agree that in that period, one cannot find books, tools, games and clothes tailored specifically to children. But it wasn't until French historian Philippe Ariès's publication in 1962 of his *Centuries of Childhood*, that historians started to argue (and many disagreed[8]), that the concept of 'le sentiment de l'enfance' was a modern invention, one that developed during the process of modernization in the late Middle Ages, with Humanism as its main force. What was new in Ariès's central concept of the 'sentiment de l'enfance', as Colin Heywood (2001) suggests, was 'both an awareness of childhood and a feeling for it' (19). However, in Ariès's view, the 'sentiment de l'enfance' was not entirely a new phenomenon, but a rebirth of sentiments that can be found much earlier, indeed, perhaps as far back as in the world of the ancients.

Ariès suggested that change in sentiments around children could be observed in the thirteenth century, but the process became explicitly represented in fifteenth and sixteenth-century European art, with the first traces of 'la découverte de l'enfance'. According to Ariès, the transformation of the medieval family and school contributed to the 'sentiment de l'enfance', with families now embracing the behaviour of 'mignotage', which means that children were approached by adults as funny human beings, to be coddled and laughed at. The new sentiments around childhood in family, art and literature necessitated educating the child to become an adult, something that was absent until then. The school began increasingly serving mainly children, arranged into the same age groups:

> Learning at school now increasingly became a typical children's activity, with the school itself becoming specifically an environment for children, which not automatically meant a child-oriented environment, as will be seen below. A growing group of moralists, humanists, and school reformers from the 16th century on strived to make clear to parents and schoolmasters that children, now considered as still imperfect human beings, should be prepared carefully and in a regulated and disciplined way for adulthood. This 'sentiment de l'enfance', emerging at the end of the 15th century among the upper bourgeoisie, became widespread in those countries with an expanding school system and a broad bourgeoisie, such as parts of France, Germany, Italy and England, and the Northern Netherlands. (Dekker and Leendert 2012: 136)

It is interesting to observe that the 'sentiment de l'enfance', as well as the emergence of the sentiment of child innocence, was reserved for the leisured, upper bourgeois class. As Ariès suggested, these sentiments did not develop in the working and lower classes until the nineteenth century, while the notion of adolescence as a special developmental stage had to wait even longer, until the twentieth century, when the introduction of compulsory schooling postponed the start of labour careers for children.

As children were 'now' perceived as 'imperfect', and in need of discipline and control of their basic instincts in the process of progressive development to fully formed and rational adults, so too did the cultural imaginary of European philosophers, scientists, missionaries and moralists ingress a certain belief in the equation of individual development of the human and the development of civilizations. Freud, for example, was adamant that:

> When, however, we look at the relation between the process of human civilization and the development of the educative process of individual human beings, we shall conclude without much hesitation that the two are very similar in nature, if not the very same process applied to different kinds of object. The process of civilization of the human species is, of course, an abstraction of a higher order than is the development of the individual and is therefore harder to apprehend in concrete terms, nor should we pursue the analogies to an obsessional extreme; but in view of the similarity between the aims of the two processes – in the one case the integration of a separate individual into a human group, and in the other case the creation of a unified group out of many individuals – we cannot be surprised at the similarity between the means employed and the resultant phenomena. (Freud [1930] 1961: 86)

Unconscious processes recapitulate stages in the development of civilizations, from infancy (ancient Greece), to adolescence (Middle Ages), and adulthood (modern industrial and colonial expansion). This progressive temporal development has for its mythical origin both the Genesis and a primal father who was murdered by his sons because he kept all the women to himself. Then He established the Law to redress their guilt. Apart from Freud, Plato and many other ancient thinkers used similar analogies, and we can find this narrative structure of temporality in many modern thinkers as well. Hegel, in speaking of consciousness and self-consciousness in the *Phenomenology of Spirit* ([1807] 1977), systematically obfuscates any distinction between the individual and society, or between maturation and history. In his geographical story of the development of *geist*, Hegel suggests that '[s]ince the original American nation has vanished – or as good as vanished – the effective population comes for the most part from Europe, and everything that happens in America has its origin there' (Hegel [1861] 1975: 165). By the geographical *there*, he means Europe as the most advanced stage of human development for which America, as an empty land, offers nothing but further resources. The resources he has in mind are not those of human intellect as '[t]he Americans, then, are like unenlightened children, living from one day to the next, and untouched by higher thoughts or aspirations' (Hegel [1861] 1975: 165), but those of Black slave labour in order to extract energy from plants and minerals because '[t]he weakness of their physique was one of the main reasons why the negroes were brought to America as a labour force; for the negroes are far more susceptible to European culture than the Indians' (Hegel [1861] 1975: 165).

Then comes German philosopher Karl Marx (1973) who understands ancient Greek civilization as the youthful stage of humanity when men were like gifted children:

> Why should not the historic childhood of humanity, its most beautiful unfolding, as a stage never to return, exercise an eternal charm? There are unruly children and precocious children. Many of the old peoples belong to this category. The Greeks were normal children. The charm of their art for us is not in contradistinction to the undeveloped stage of society on which it grew. It is its result, and is inextricably bound up, rather, with the fact that the unripe social conditions under which it arose, and could alone arise, can never return. (111)

As Harry Redner (2015) shows in *The Tragedy of European Civilization: Towards an Intellectual History of the Twentieth Century*, this civilizing process becomes a basic methodological principle for many who saw civilizations as bounded organisms which go through the stages of life from youth to elderliness. German philosopher Jürgen Habermas (1984), for example, suggests that:

> In discussing Weber's sociology of religion in the next chapter, I shall attempt to make the development of religious worldviews comprehensible from the aspect of a development of formal world-concepts, that is, as a learning process. In doing so I shall be making tacit use of a concept of learning that Piaget expounded for the ontogenesis of structures of consciousness. (67)

Habermas here explicitly uses Piagetian temporal narrative – the 'law' that phylogenesis recapitulates ontogenesis. Both phylogenesis and ontogenesis are foundational learning processes in the Piagetian stages of a child's cognitive development, a structure that much dominates educational approaches to curriculum and pedagogy to this day. Importantly, this temporal developmental process is practised in relation to American psychologist Lawrence Kohlberg's 'levels of moral consciousness', which many thinkers, including Habermas, apply in the fully Hegelian manner both to children and societies (Habermas 1984: 174). The single, monomaniacal point of view gathers strength, proving itself (trivially) as it is applied to one domain after another. It begins making it difficult to imagine another point of view, or others' points of view.

> One could only watch the extraordinary efforts made by those tiny legs against an oncoming doom which could, had it chosen, have submerged an entire city, not merely a city, but masses of human beings; nothing, I knew, had any chance against death. Nevertheless after a pause of exhaustion the legs fluttered again. It was superb his last protests, and so frantic that he succeeded at last in righting himself. One's sympathies, of course, were all on the side of life. Also, when there was nobody to care or to know, this gigantic effort on the part of an insignificant little moth, against a power of much magnitude, to retain what no one else valued or desired to keep, moved one strangely. (Woolf [1942] 1974: 6)

The simultaneous process of civilizing the presupposed innate, regressive, infantile[9] characteristic of 'children', indigenous 'savages' and the clinically 'deviant', is bound up with power relations in very particular discourses of time and abstract (mathematical) time-consciousness. Time-as-Arrow is produced, narrativized and upheld as the condition and a result of human evolutionary development towards White, rational, literate Subjects. This image continues to be used as a biocentric and biosocial tool, justification and explanation of modernist, patriarchal, imperial and colonial mentalities. For example, in schools today, both (a) the failure to fully embrace and comply with the various pressures of time (five-day school-week, rigid timetables, Piagetian developmental stages, Kohlberg's moral development, time-constrained tests); and (b) the resistance and refusal of the enforced White and bourgeois temporalities (i.e. school drop-out) are continually managed by biosocial and racial explanations (i.e., the school-to-prison pipeline[10]), often resulting in student medicalizations (i.e., ADHD) and learning disabilities designations (i.e., including all neuro-atypical students without an official medical diagnosis of genetic or cognitive impairment[11]).

At a different scale, the policy narratives surrounding evidence-based education also perpetuate a colonial discourse of civilizing. The field of education has always struggled with legitimizing its public and professional existence, and nowhere is this clearer than in demands to provide scientific evidence (about teaching, learning, administration, policy) in order to support the field's public and academic respectability and accountability. In other words, and as suggested by Riyad Ahmed Shahjahan (2011), through employing a civilizing colonial discourse, as well as constructing and highlighting the chaos looming over the functionality and production of evidence, proponents of evidence-based education operate from a particular colonial ideology that wishes to counter the barbarous disorder in educational practice and policy-making by instilling scientific-based education. This colonial discourse is also tied to particular epistemology of control. (188)

Since the nineteenth century, children have been routinely confined to designated spaces of schools and playgrounds in the local neighbourhoods. In the narrative syntax of Time-as-Arrow, children and various indigenous temporalities have come to function as regressive, unconscious, rhythmic, local and concrete Other (micro-scale) to the mathematical, abstract, universal and linear time-consciousness of the rational Subject (macro-scale). Educational scholarship and practice, heavily influenced by state- and privately funded research in the field of psychology, continues this teleological focus on children's mental and emotional linear development over time in their individual, intimate, local, familial and concrete agency of everyday rhythms. This focus on the parochial and micro-scale temporal lives of children in educational research, curriculum, pedagogy and educational policy (including the affective and relational or agential turn in educational theory), leaves unchallenged the question of Time as already presupposed and predetermined scale in terms of which the political, global and deep time macro-scale social processes receive little attention. By focusing on the micro-scale intimate (rhythmic, daily, individualistic, mindful) temporalities, school research and institutional practices deny any possibility for radical thought of coevalness of the geologic and the biocentric racial code, spanning over centuries (just think of the ongoing child slave labour for sexual, capitalist, and wartime gain), and are thus complicit in maintaining the status quo.

By contrast, as American feminist philosopher Elizabeth Grosz (Grosz, Yusoff and Clark 2017) argues that 'the geological is always moving, always transforming, even if it is not always impacted by catastrophic events, it is continuously marked by the events that occur below and near the surface of the earth' (133). Pàlsson and Swanson (2016) also invite a thought of 'geosocialities' as the 'co-minglings of the geological and the biologic and the sensibilities involved' (150). Such thinking through geosocialities pays attention to scale, recognizing the 'intertwining of bodies and biographies with earth systems and deep time histories' (Pàlsson and Swanson 2016: 155). Our humble provocation in this book, for the field of educational studies, involves precisely the thought of thinking ethically (response-ably) with and within different scales (each with particular spatio-temporal modes of composition) in order to usher a pedagogy of thinking and reading different scales side-by-side, caring for the force of contrasts, without choosing foundations or starting points or slopes.

In discussing the effects of what he calls 'derangements of scale', British philosopher Timothy Clark (2012) gives an example of such inability to read various scales parochially (in which he understands scale to be that which 'usually enables a calibrated and useful extrapolation between dimensions of space or time' (148)):

> Scale effects in relation to climate change are confusing because they take the easy, daily equations of moral and political accounting and drop into them both a zero and an infinity: the greater the number of people engaged in modern forms of consumption then the less the relative influence or responsibility of each but the worse the cumulative impact of their insignificance. As a result of scale effects what is self-evident or rational at one scale may well be destructive or unjust at another. Hence, progressive social and economic policies designed to disseminate Western levels of prosperity may even resemble, on another scale, an insane plan to destroy the biosphere. Yet, for any individual household, motorist, etc., a scale effect in their actions is invisible. It is not present in any phenomenon in itself (no eidetic reduction will flush it out), but only in the contingency of how many other such phenomena there are, have been and will be, at even vast distances in space or time. Human agency becomes, as it were, displaced from within by its own act, a kind of demonic iterability. (Clark 2012: 150)

Insisting on an anachronistic image of a child (mostly White, mostly male, mostly heterosexual) as only locally, familially agential (because they are primitive in terms of temporally progressive cognitive, sexual and moral development) continually reproduces the politico-affective sentiment of children's temporal/developmental 'innocence'. The macro-scale effects of the biopolitics of sentimentality – in this instance the 'innocence' promoted pedagogically and axiologically within the micro-scale environment of the present-oriented family, school and playground – are intensely destructive in their trans-temporal cumulative geological impact on the earth strata and the biosphere (children's daily rhythms are governed by their participation in the consumption/waste of energy, raw materials and capitalist goods in these local environments).

The ethico-political effects of refusing to *image* children within the scale of deep time as geological agents that participate fully in the extractive logic of neocolonial appropriation of energy, lands, minerals and labour, are (a) an inability to think and read 'everything at once', *alongside* Time-as-Arrow; and (b) 'an implosion of scales, implicating seemingly trivial or small actions with enormous stakes while intellectual boundaries and lines of demarcation fold in upon each other' (Clark 2012: 152). Because organized education is conditioned on and conditions (solidified by psychology research in the nineteenth century) the anachronistic biopolitical sentimentality of the (White, male, straight) child's bourgeois 'innocence', 'the horror of many probable future scenarios' (Clark 2012: 152), including species extinction, is successfully kept at a distance by the deranged insistence on children's proper, authentic, individual, meaningful 'future' responsibility within the micro-scale rhythms of such innocent daily practices as learning to garden, caring for worms and recycling. Time is not a privileged term of research in education because the micro-scale psychological, local, intimate, and concrete (space, place) became the organizing onto-epistemological principles privileged over and above the macro-scale, abstract concepts (deep-time, ancestral timelines) and micro-scale quantum, resonant and yet-to-be-actualized timelines and densities.

> The light of the Enlightenment was not to be blue – not full of misplaced and otherwise abused objects, displaced spectators, short-wave blurred edges of historical lament. It was to be the white light that as we know, but cannot see except refractively, contains the entire spectrum – the light of programmatic optimism: Utopian light. The light of hope, with its dependence on undependable pleasant surprises, is, on another hand-to-mouth, blue. It arises out of a strangely luminous pessimism, late in the day. Blue light to be perceived as light at all requires an oblique angle of vision, an averting of the eyes from the glare of our cultural foreground toward the silent periphery that is our future. Blue – last and first color visible at twilight. (Retallack 2003: 77)

In education, reading and thinking take on meaning at scales that are naturalized; that privilege one universal measure (male, White, heterosexual, abled), supported by the myth of universal, progressive, sequential and durational Time-as-Arrow, to the point of being intuitively used to discipline, shape and govern bodies, as well as the intellectual, material and ethical commitments as contained in particular racialized and sexed biopolitics of sentimentality; for example, innocence, happiness, hope, optimism, growth, sustainability, etc. Or in French philosopher Henri Bergson's poetic language, 'life is like a current passing from germ to germ through the medium of a developed organism. It is as if the organism itself were only an excrescence, a bud caused to sprout by the former germ endeavouring to continue itself in a new germ. The essential thing is the continuous progress indefinitely pursued, an invisible progress, on which each visible organism rides during the short interval of time given it to live' (Bergson 1911: 27).

:

Remediation of the Queer and Deviant

What time is it in the unconscious? Is it too early or already too late?
(Malcom Bowie)[12]

A concern with histories that hurt is not then a backward orientation: to move on, you must make this return. If anything, we might want to reread melancholic subjects, the ones who refuse to let go of suffering, who are even prepared to kill some forms of joy, as an alternative model of the social good. (Ahmed 2010: 50)

In this chapter, we trace notions of linear time as dependant on a certain fantasy of Time-as-Arrow assailed by colonial and scientific regimes of racist and bourgeois notions of evolutionary progress and development from primitive (childlike, backwards, regressed and in need of remediation/civilizing) to advanced (rational Subjects responsible for civilizing/saving those in need of remediation). Our project, however, aims to carve out certain images, mythologies, analogies and discursive narratives that speak to the ideological/pedagogical effects of Time-as-Arrow. That is, here we are interested in the structural and discursive effects of the privileged tropisms of telling Time in education, rather than phenomenological experiences of students and teachers in their many diverse ways of being and doing under the constraints of hegemonic notions of Time and temporality in institutional education.

> So first and most generally, a psychological theory is about phenomena that exist in the world; there are psychological processes and patterns of behavior which the researcher may seek to describe and explain. There may be enormous difficulties in the way of providing secure explanations of psychological phenomena, but a presupposition of scientific psychology is that there is a nature of things psychological about which increasingly secure theories may be established. So Piaget's claim that 'Psychology is a natural science' is a fundamental premise to the program of scientific psychology. There is, however, no such thing as a natural educational process out there that we should be trying to find, describe, and explain. An educational process exists only as we bring it into existence. The main problem for the educator, then, is not to describe the nature of the process but to prescribe what ought to be done to create an ideal or good process. (Egan [1983] 2012: 3)

As scientific psychology has become the science with which education continues to justify its pedagogical interventions, it is important to discuss the core temporal tenets informing developmental psychology. We follow Kieran Egan's observations that the two constraints on educational processes resulting from grounding its interventions in scientific psychology, are linked to particular normative timelines organized by anachronism; namely, the adherence to linear processes, and the flawed idea that a child's mind is primitive and can thus be *known* through scientific research.

In discussing Herbert Spencer's flawed evolutionary theories that 'profoundly shape current practice' (Egan 2002: 34), alongside Piaget's developmental stages, Egan suggests that Spencer 'followed the mid-nineteenth-century conviction that the human race went through – recapitulated – all of the stages of development of our species, from a simple-celled creature, through gilled fishlike ancestors, and so on, to the present' (Egan 2002: 27). This is the recapitulation hypothesis proposed in Haeckel's *The Evolution of Man* study, written in 1879. The analogic coupling of cultural processes and individual development cemented the existent logic of bifurcation of nature and culture in his immensely influential formula: ontogeny recapitulates phylogeny. When the line is your only tool, first metaphors and then analogies start to line up.

This formula was adopted by scientific racism, equating people of colour with primitiveness and immaturity, 'the same developmental place that the White child held as individual. The child/savage analogy had appeared generations earlier, in the work of Autenrieth and Chambers, as well as Heinrich Kaan's *Sexual Pathology* (1844)[13], which compared "primitive" sexuality to infantile sexuality' (Rohy 2009: 4). Egan provides examples of influential educational thinkers who subscribed to recapitulationist discourses and scientific racism; for example, G. Stanley Hall and John Dewey. Dewey wrote that there 'is a sort of natural recurrence of the child mind to the typical activities of primitive people' (Gould 1977: 154, as cited in Egan (2002: 27)). And James Sully, the British leader of the child study movement, reportedly said (in 1895) that '[a]s we all know, the lowest races of mankind stand in close proximity to the animal world. The same is true for infants of the civilized races' (Sully 1895: 395, as cited in Egan (2002: 91)).

To the 'child/primitive/local' equation as a certain measure of Time-as-Arrow in education, we here add what American historian and queer scholar Valerie Rohy (2009) calls 'race/sexuality analogy', informing 'straight time':

> Straight time is not simply heterosexual time, but it has, in tandem with the cult of reproductive futurism, served systematically to devalue queer subjects. Nor is it always white time, but its notions of linear progress crucially inform racist discourses. The 'obviousness' of straight time masks its contingency: every child knows that the clock runs steadily in one direction. In literature, however, the artificial temporality of narrative form alerts us to the fictional dimension of chronology as such: after all time is a trope and anachronism a figure. (xiv)

What is interesting here for us, is, as Rohy goes on to show, how 'anachronism' (she uses the term to designate various temporal anomalies, such as regression, backwardness, or prematurity) 'has a contradictory ontology, structured by *the prohibition of the impossible*: it cannot exist, but it must also be prevented, punished, or expelled' (Rohy 2009; *emphasis in the original*). As Rohy shows, the 'gradual growth' in the recapitulation formula could never be 'continuous, for the savage could never become the "civilized man": instead, he would remain a victim of arrested development, historically stunted and doomed to trail behind the white standard' (Rohy 2009: 4).

This paradox, according to Rohy, speaks both to (a) a promotion of straight, progressive time as the best possible and the only 'real temporality'; and (b) a 'pervasive conflation of scientific and rhetorical time that serves to naturalize the latter's constellation of ideological forces' (Rohy 2009: xiv–xv). As so much of current educational thinking is grounded historically in structures founded on scientific racist perspectives promoted as biological facts – facts that were conditioned on and retroactively condition the different historical and developmental Time-as-Arrow for White Europeans and people of colour – the effects of these anachronistic temporal structures continue to perpetuate practices of racialization in contemporary educational research and practice.

> The sights we see and the sounds we hear now have none of the quality of the past; nor have we any share in the serenity of the person who, six months ago, stood precisely where we stand now. His is the happiness of death; ours is the insecurity of life. He has no future; the future is even now invading our peace. It is only when we look at the past and take from it the element of uncertainty that we can enjoy perfect peace. (Woolf 1930)

Here we are interested in how colonial and scientific discourses of Time produce and retroactively inform a certain equation of value between the child, the savage and the sexually perverse. This equation produces, explains, and reproduces the 'unknown in terms of the known, the unfamiliar in terms of the familiar' (Rohy 2009: 6). These metonymic narrative sequences condition the value of primary and secondary terms, paradigmatic and syntagmatic relationships of signification. 'Although both homosexuality and primitivism represent developmental origins, the primitive is the primary term of primacy, while homosexuality is only secondarily primary, belatedly posited as anterior' (Rohy 2009). In the recapitulation equation of value, primary process often manifests itself in a paradigmatic relationship of time to the masculine and of space to the feminine, based on their implied similarity (time and masculinity as primary, active agents and as movement/becoming; feminine, space, racialized and gay as secondary, passive/being and receptive envelopes).

What is interesting for us, is how these paradigmatic relationships inform and become informed by Time, and as such provide the support for metonymic and metaphoric relations which then introduce into theoretical texts specific ideological meanings because the play of linguistic difference almost always gives way to, as Silverman (1984) puts it, 'the dynamic[s] of desire' (108). This means that certain terms are privileged over others (typically Time is privileged over Space and Place) and signifying positions become somewhat fixed. But because child/race/sexuality relies on a 'certain temporal inversion, for it creates the similarities it purports to observe', wherein in the 'black/gay temporal analogy' from the standpoint of recapitulation theory, the 'first term of the analogy is retroactively defined by the second: following nineteenth-century sexology, blackness must to some degree signify in relation to queerness' (Rohy 2009: 7) and in education, to the figure of child (with her primitive mind and polymorphous sexuality/immorality). In education, all students (differently so depending on their positionality), not only children in early education, continue to figure as innocent 'agents' in need of professionally guided development (correction, growth and guidance).

In terms of processes of signification, students figure as tropes on the local, place-based scale and thus place is the privileged site of research and pedagogical intervention, over and above Time. The most durable metonymic (based on similarity) temporal composition between childhood, race and sexuality is that produced by the equation of value itself, 'which is to say by their shared (though by no means identical) marginalization', the equation of value between childhood, race and sexuality 'represents as metaphorically essential what is in fact a contingent, metonymic relation' (Rohy 2009: 7) Any term that facilitates the value of another within the same system is paradigmatically related to it. In order for one term to be of such assistance to another (child/black/gay), it must have points of divergence and points of coincidence. As Kaja Silverman (2009) suggests, 'the choice of one term does not imply the repression or censorship of those which are paradigmatically connected to it' (106). Quite the opposite, 'since their association with the chosen term defines it, they are all present in their absence', or in other words 'present through their *difference*' (ibid; emphasis in the original). Different racially and sexually informed biopolitical *tropisms* of Time, therefore, are present at just those points in educational theory, research and practice, where Time seems to be most absent (i.e. universal theories of cognitive and moral development).

Just like literary and cinematic texts, educational theory is a product of diverse interactions between the primary and the secondary signifying processes, and is rich in metaphoric and metonymic temporal configurations. So too is this book. There is a certain performative desire at play in our excavating the 'anachronistic' equation of value between child/savage/queer. With the persistence of discursive value placed on historicism in academic research and writing, falling into the trap of 'ahistoricism' and 'anachronism', in other words, of reading/projecting the modern and contemporary educational concepts *back* in time in our writing, would commit the same *fallacy of misplaced temporality* in the progressive scale of zooming either in or out of History. 'Hailed as the universal defence against universalism, historicism promises respect for difference, particularity, and pluralism where the ahistorical would impose tyrannical conformity' (Rohy 2009: 126). But these critiques precisely reveal their commitment to *proper chronology*. 'In the twenty-first century, we are told, the history of our time is not anachronistic but properly sequential. The discontinuous history held up against progressivism has become a mark of progress, relegating "transhistorical" thinking, like primitive belief – or like literary close reading – to the pages of the history whose lessons it has failed to learn' (Rohy paraphrasing Louise Fradenburg and Carla Freccero, in Rohy 2009: 127).

> And let the Creole Caribbean talk to the world which is itself creolizing. It has brought its multiplicities together into a surprisingly convergent diversity. But without any kind of uniformity. Let's consecrate that among us. This is not a Call, nor a manifesto or a political programme. The Call would be, for whoever makes it, the sign of a pre-eminence that has no place here. The manifesto would presuppose putting oneself forward. The political programme would not be suitable or convincing. This is a cry, quite simply a cry. Of a realizable Utopia. If the cry is taken up by some or by all, it becomes speech. A common song. The cry and the speech work together to lift up the possibilities, and also what we have always believed to be the impossibilities, of our countries. (Glissant [1997] 2020: 144–5)

Time is the cognitive tool with which we think about Time; thus thinking with and through Time presents itself as a difficult task. Educational theory depends upon a medium elaborated for the suppression of affect and the articulation of difference – that is, language. In using this medium, any theoretical text is obliged to stick at least to some degree to its paradigmatic and syntagmatic rules. This 'rhetoric has no outside: it interpellated everyone as a guilty subject of temporal self-governance and measures all against a standard none can meet' (Rohy 2009: 129). Some theoretical texts deliberately break those rules (for example, *When the Moon Waxes Red*, by Trinh T. Minh-ha (1991)). And such a violation (of proper temporal desire) has the paradoxical effect of evoking the rules themselves, gathering/inviting a profoundly radical impact on the reader.

Similarly, in *Getting Medieval*, American English professor Carolyn Dinshaw (1999) suggests ways of reading that 'demonstrate the simultaneous copresence of different chronologies', and imagines 'tactile, erotic affective connections across time as the bases of a new historiography, reclaiming transhistorical reading as a "queer historical impulse" distinct from simple identification with the past' (Rohy 2009: 131).

> A sublime and deadly conception, which the cultures of Europe and the West have transported around the world, of identity as the single root, excluding the Other. The single root implants itself in a land that becomes a territory. A notion that has now become 'real', in all composite cultures, of identity as rhizome, going to meet other roots. And that is how the territory once again becomes a land. (Glissant [1997] 2020: 120–1)

Temporal desire is deeply embedded in particular styles of reading and writing, enclosed by a canon of literary, philosophical and scientific texts and images that privilege the classical (heroic) narrative arc of growth, change and overcoming. In the field of education, this story is a scientifically 'naturalized' fiction grounded in the progressive (i.e. colonial, patriarchal and racist) narrative of telling Time-as-Arrow. How then do we provoke students to imagine other densities and dimensions of existence, outside the (dis)comfort of this very particular elevated, phallic, rootbound, extractive, unidirectional and finite spatio-temporal point of view?

:

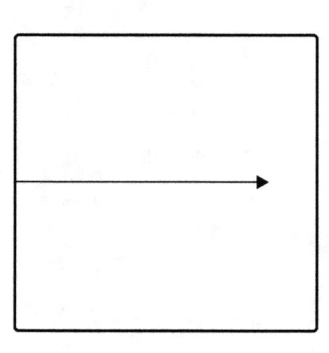

Lies 2: Time is a straight line.

(Jeanette Winterson)[1]

2

Revelation

Diverting Time-as-Deferral with Édouard Glissant and Sara Ahmed

revelation (n.)[2]

c. 1300, *revelacioun*, 'disclosure of information or knowledge to man by a divine or supernatural agency', from Old French *revelacion* and directly from Latin *revelationem* (nominative *revelation*), noun action from past-participle stem of *revelare* 'unveil, uncover, lay bare' (see **reveal**).

The general meaning 'disclosure of facts to those previously unaware of them' is attested from late 14c.; meaning 'striking disclosure' is from 1862. As the name of the last book of the New Testament (*Revelation of St. John*), it is attested from late 14c. (see **apocalypse**); as simply **Revelations**, it is recorded by 1690s.

The cubist painters of the early twentieth century were revolutionary for the way that they literally decomposed, multiplied and reassembled the single point of view that had dominated representational painting for five centuries. As the image in Figure 2.1 shows, in the geometry (a way of conceiving space) of perspective painting, a sense of depth is created by establishing a horizon line along with a 'vanishing' point, which is the point where lines that are perpendicular to the horizon line meet. Since parallel lines are lines that, by definition, do not meet, the vanishing point is taken to be infinitely far away, but represented on the canvas as an actual point. We have come to see the 8×8 grid, which might be a checkerboard or the tiled floor of a kitchen or a church, as being 'in perspective'. Shapes that would be squares in the three-dimensional world become trapezoids in a perspective drawing.

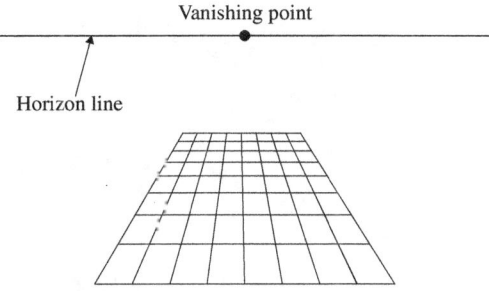

Figure 2.1 The geometry of perspective painting.

It is also possible to have 2-point and 3-point perspectives, which can be used to represent the depths of two and three dimensions, respectively. In each case, the point functions to create a sense of depth through a singular point of view: that of the human eye.

Over the past 500+ years, we have become proficient at reading perspective paintings, knowing that, despite appearance, we are looking at a square grid of squares. In a sense, the idea was so good that it formed the end of the theory of perspective, much like optimal distribution of energy in classical thermodynamics and optimal design in Darwinism were the ends of those theories (DeLanda 2000). Like the advances in biology and physics that followed – advances based on non-linear bifurcations – art, too, moved beyond the optimal or fittest representation. We would not see as 'real', or 'actual', a painting of the cubist painter Juan Gris, in which the checkered tablecloth seems more like a collage of different pieces of material rather than a proper representation of a bistro table (see Figure 2.2). The cubists refuse the single point of view and single directionality, instead inviting disorientation; they refuse the delimitation of representation to the three dimensions of space, choosing instead to fold it. They refuse the unified spatio-temporal point of view by disturbing the predetermined looking apparatus in which the 'narrative' unification of time and space in the given piece of art reinscribes the artist-viewer relationship as the producers/consumers of meaning. Gris' bistro table might be a composite view of the waiter and the customer; it might be the distribution across time, as the elements on the table are moved.

Figure 2.2 Juan Gris, *Nature morte à la nappe à carreaux (Still Life with Checkered Tablecloth)*, 1915 (public domain).

Origin Myths and Their Revelatory Logic

The vanishing point, developed by European artists and mathematicians, belongs to a geometry that grounds the perceiver as the revelatory agent. This maps onto time as revelatory, paralleling the Judeo-Christian origin myth. Such a myth belongs to what Martinique-born poet and philosopher Édouard Glissant ([1997] 2020) calls atavistic cultures, which are ones that have 'armed themselves with a corpus of mythical narratives aiming to reassure them as to the legitimacy of their relations with the land that they occupy. These mythical narratives usually take the form of a Creation of the world, of a Genesis' (119–20). Time is deployed unabashedly by the setting of a beginning, of a starting point, of Time = 0. This forecloses the possibility of a before, securing the myth's comforting narrative.

> Among the myths that have led the way towards the consciousness of History, the foundational myths have had as their role to consecrate the presence of a community on its land, by attaching this presence to a Genesis, without any discontinuity and by legitimate filiation. This is what gives them their

atavistic character. The foundational myth provides obscure reassurance as to the unbroken continuity of this filiation, based on a Genesis, and from then on authorizes the community in question to consider this land where it lives, which has now become a territory, as *absolutely* its own. (Glissant ([1997] 2020): 120)

Glissant contrasts atavistic cultures with composite ones, which 'do not consider the founding myth of a Genesis' (Glissant ([1997] 2020): 119). Composite cultures are a meeting of numerous cultures that may at times hybridize or integrate, interfere or clash. Composite cultures do not have a single point of view – like Gris' painting, they are a composition of narratives. Glissant's term for this, 'creolisation', is the breaking down of *the* myth of origin. The revelations in composite cultures are neither final, singular nor predictable.

Although creolization is occurring in many countries – such as Canada, with its 'multicultural' composition – Glissant points out that atavistic tendencies persist in composite cultures, and that they seek to 'lay claim to a permanence, an honorability of time, which would seem to be necessary to any culture in order for it to be sure of itself and to have the boldness and the energy to express itself' (Glissant ([1997] 2020): 120). For us, what is important is that atavistic and composite cultures proceed by different images of time: the former staying *on* time, honouring its mythic direction; the other creolizing time, multiplying its points of view.

The origin story of Canada, as a fur-trading colony, has produced what the Indigenous Canadian educator Dwayne Donald (2009) calls a *fort logic*. Forts are trading posts that have been recreated in many towns across the country to celebrate and perpetuate this story about Canada's identity. Fort logic is a colonial frontier spatial imaginary that places the settlers on the inside (of the four walls) and the Indigenous peoples on the outside. It functions through a temporality in which those outside can and should be brought inside (see Figure 2.3). Donald argues that new stories are needed – new images that do not erect walls and dictate paths to revelatory incorporation. However, like perspective painting, readings of the world and Time in terms of inside/outside are deeply entrenched, powerful formatters of socio cultural narratives and experience.

If the curriculum is seen as the walls of the fort, then Donald's (2009) proposal of *Indigenous Métissage*, a kind of land- and place-based creolization, reframes their rigidity, opacity, permanence and self-containment. He describes the land- and place-based understanding of rocks – which are considered animate entities

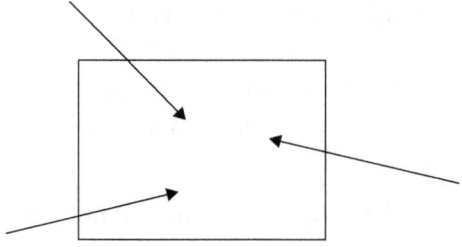

Figure 2.3 Fort logic.

by Indigenous peoples, possessing spiritual power – showing the tensions such meaning has with settler ones. As an image, his teaching transforms the hierarchy and the directionality of fort logic by imagining a fence rather than four walls – but a hopeful fence that is porous and bi-directional, allowing two points of view to sit side-by-side. *Getting inside* or *staying outside* become *going across*, or *going back-and-forth* (see Figure 2.4).

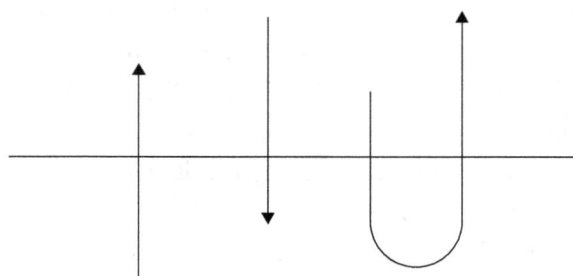

Figure 2.4 Indigenous Métissage.

These images may seem simplistic, but since they encode all our assumptions about time and space, they are actually quite powerful. They may resist atavistic tendencies; they may take *the fact of creolisation* somewhere new, to a place/space/time that does not yearn for origins, for promissory notes that pledge only to reveal the already-established truth. This could also be the circle logic that American scientist and Indigenous environmentalist scholar Robin Wall Kimmerer (2021: 114) writes about, a logic that refuses the hierarchy of Western 'pyramid' thinking, which puts man on top and 'dismembers' him from his relations, his responsibilities. While the circle dissolves hierarchy, it can often function as a spatial imaginary of inclusion/exclusion. That is why we like the image of the three-dimensional band shown in Figure 2.5, which

Figure 2.5 A one-sided band.

no longer even has a fence. Put your finger on the rightward flat part, trace it up and behind and around all the way until you return to where you started, but on the opposite 'side' – and then trace it around a second time to return to precisely where you started. This band only has one side, not two. *Beside* and *back-and-forth* now become *along with*. There is no origin – or rather, *any origin will do*.

This may be important for *cultivating the composite*, which is another way to talk about decolonizing, but without framing the work in terms of colonial fort logic. It precludes even a brief consideration of either/or exclusive disjunctions, like being 'on one side of the fence or another' – the Western way or the other – the kind of thinking that says: '[e]ither we have entered the Anthropocene and it is game over for humans, who should begin to come to terms with extinction of themselves and others, or the advent of the Anthropocene finally offers humans the chance for revolution, social justice, and an even better planet' (Colebrook 2016: 196).

Clearly, we don't want to repeat the capitalist, euro-centric, theological humanism of the past, the one that brought us to fort logic. But, as Australian philosopher Claire Colebrook argues, isn't there a messianism at play in the critique of the past, in the critique of teleological posture in which there is a fixed point towards which we are to move, because it represents 'a hope for a future that is radically other than the present, may emerge from the present but must also gesture infinitely, and absolutely, beyond any of its actualized figures or inherited modes' (Colebrook 2016: 197)? This includes the revelatory toppling of fort logic. Any messianism takes time into its own hands, seeing the revolution as sprouting from the now (and therefore, merely displacing Time = 0), inflected by the past, and moving into a (hopefully) open future that offers more than a repetition of the past. In this sense, our predictions and warnings and hopes and dreams are human claims on time, and these claims will inevitably lead to exclusive disjunctions and fort logic.

Perhaps cultivating the composite requires placing the reality of time outside human experience, so that any human experience of time is only ever a partial glimpse of a whole that is non-subjective and inhuman and can never be reduced to human narratives. But this sets up another exclusive disjunction in which time is *either* a function of human experience – rigidly linear in terms of past, present and future – *or* time is non-linear, open to multiple human and non human points of view. What if time is both, asks Colebrook, in a cultivating the composite move, and what if we operate through an inclusive disjunction that does not pit one state over the other? This is not about thinking that it *can be* one thing or the other, like Science being either Western or Indigenous, since such a stance offers 'the subject the somewhat good conscience of compromise' (Colebrook 2016: 201). Consider, for example, the 'on the one hand . . . on the other . . . ' reasoning offered here, in classic compromise style (from Alberta Education's 'Inspiring Education' project):

> Our educational system must both provide an inclusive environment where each student belongs, and equip them with the attitudes, skills, knowledge, and competencies that they need to be successful in tomorrow's economy . . . The continued development of a highly skilled, knowledgeable, innovative and productive workforce is critical to ensuring that Alberta sustains its competitive advantage in a global economy, allowing the province to attract investment, and high value-added industries. (Donald 2019: 111–2)

Instead, the inclusive disjunction would intensify the incompossible . . . affirming that students will be prepared to participate in the global economy *and* cease to have anything to belong to at all. In other words, it is about accepting that the future is something other than ultimately subjective – something other than what can be seen from any particular point of view; that the future is to be-made rather than to be-done or destined (in a revelatory key), and might then also be unmade as well; and that the future is choosing us rather than happening to us. Colebrook thus invites us to think of the possibility of a future alongside the possibility of no future, as an inclusive disjunction.

> If humanity affirms itself it does so – eternally – not as that which exists for all time, but as that which comes into being and passes away, and does so with the joyous sense that 'all time' is composed of nothing more than becomings. One affirms survival *and* extinction, technology *and* its annihilation, humanity *and* its non-being. (Colebrook 2016: 206)

Adopting an inclusive disjunction may strike many as dangerous play. In a world of composite possibilities, not all commensurable to each other, doesn't an uncomfortable relativity set in, one that precludes determinations of good, bad or better? As Canadian educational philosopher Kieran Egan (2002) writes, contemporary schooling in many Western countries already attempts to juggle an incommensurable set of goals for education: preparing children to be future citizens; perpetuating historical and cultural achievements; enabling children to reach their potential as humans. Egan argues that if education could choose only one of these goals, many of its problems and contradictions would disappear. We agree that schooling is troubled by the fact of trying to achieve these multiple goals but see atavistic tendencies in the proposal of returning to a single goal. Indeed, we could argue, with Glissant, that the multiple goals are a reflection of composite culture, and that the atavistic tendencies persist in the collapsing of goals into one mode of time. In other words, time isn't actually being multiplied, but intensified as time-as-revelation when each and every one of the goals speaks to a particular revelation of its own. Multiplying resists the collapsing of scales, of the psychological and the social and the political and the economic.

This collapsing can be seen nowhere better than in the mathematics classroom where approximately 240 lifetimes per day are devoted to doing algebra (Wolfram 2020: 71), a skill that computers now do so effectively that they are used in almost all workplace situations. It is therefore not the case that learning algebra can be described as being useful to producing skilled workers. Learning algebra could, however, be legitimized as a means of celebrating cultural achievements, or preserving the archive. If algebra was, in the past, useful to certain scientists, the extent of its usefulness has been hopelessly diffused in such a way that we no longer even know to whom it is no longer useful. As Australian–British feminist and queer scholar Sara Ahmed writes; 'To measure usefulness is thus to universalize use: what is useful to him becomes what is absolutely useful. The universalizing of use is how a "to" in "useful to" is redirected and erased' (2019: 134).

We imagine the mathematics teacher saying to her students: 'What I am about to teach you, and what I have to teach you in order for you to continue your schooling, will be of no use to you in the future. Algebra is important because it once was very useful for solving problems, particularly in engineering and computing, in addition to physics and mathematics.' This would be taking one of the purposes of schooling and offering it as an abstraction. Abstraction in this mode of nondeference interrupts Time-as-Deferral in the sense that there is no future for this idea – that the value of the use is in the reuse, a kind of queering of use, according to Ahmed. Teachers working within a historical approach – examining with students the people and contexts and values involved in the development of algebra – are also re-using, as well as changing the 'to' to which use is directed. Such a pedagogy – mindful of temporal apparatuses at play in teaching and learning – differentiates scales of knowledge production, of human and non human history, of the quotidian, of civilization, rather than collapsing these multiple scales, which allows for retroactive projection and mathematical appropriation of use. But, most importantly, it opens space for abstractions as temporal connections. Abstractions matter not in the sense of generalizations that apply across historical and cultural contexts, but as floating hypotheses not determined by experience: potentially dangerous *and* productive.

:

The School Bell: Arrows, Journeys, Stage

Perspective painting provides an origin (the human eye) and a destination (the vanishing point). Mathematically, the destination is infinitely far away. In the Judeo-Christian myth, the destination is death – still far away, at least conceptually if not geographically. The arc of life (from birth to death) is temporalized into the (hero's) journey, a line with two endpoints. Its logic runs as follows: keep following the line and you'll get there. There, off on its own, lies the ticket to heaven, oneness with the universe, the dream job. It is crucial, in fact, that *there* is not like *here*, that it is laid bare only after effort, after sacrifice, after doing or being. This is particularly true in Protestant religions, in which reward occurs after death. But it is also the logic of suicide bombers, who are told they will be rewarded in the after-life. When we consider an arrow on the line with two endpoints, it is also crucial that there be a continuous path from here to there. But following the path requires an enormous leap of faith. Will your redemption happen on Earth, or in heaven? Will handing in all of the homework, learning all that algebra, really land you the job? Will having a biological child secure your immortality?

The leap of faith is present for almost everyone. Just think: there is really no way to be sure that the sun will rise again tomorrow. Any one of a number of things could change, things that weren't part of the physicist's models: a hand covering up the sun; an eclipse by a new, giant moon swooping in from a distant galaxy. Now that it looks like the planet will change forever, that so many of the things that we've expected will no longer occur, the science fictions of the past have multiplied. Predictability is like continuity: it is a comforting bit of mathematical magic that smooths over gaps and unknowns.

In biblical time, revelation was in the hands of the divine. Now, it is (also) in the hands of other supernatural forces, like luck.

> *How would it feel to be smuggled back out of the future in order to subvert its antecedent conditions? To be a cyberguerrilla, hidden in human camouflage so advanced that even one's software was the part of the disguise? Exactly like this?*
>
> (Nick Land)[3]

Life has changed into a timeless succession of shocks, interspaced with empty, paralysed intervals. But nothing, perhaps, is more ominous for the future than the fact that, quite literally, these things will soon be past thinking on, for each trauma of the returning combatants, each shock not inwardly absorbed, is a ferment of future destruction. Karl Kraus was right to call his play The Last Days of Mankind. What is being enacted now ought to bear the title: 'After Doomsday'. (Adorno [1951] 1974: 54)

When we think of the time of schooling, the first thing that comes to mind is probably the bell that rings to indicate the beginning or end of the school day or of class. The beginning and the end mark the boundaries of a time period inside of which learning is meant to take place. Once we have a beginning and an end, a connecting line imposes itself; and once we have a line, it is with little effort that we can populate it with new points, like the waystations of a journey. Time becomes a sequence of intervals. Time-as-Deferral is also how we conceptualize the school year and, indeed, the whole K-12 stretch of mandatory education. The twelve-year interval is just one of the intervals in one's life (during which we start as children and journey into adulthood), marked off by milestones – none of which provide anything more than the promise to continue on the path (at the risk of falling off). This temporal territory seems to be as imperative as the tick-tock of a clock. Made a matter of necessity, the more or less universal agreement on the time of schooling seems to exist independently of events that occur in anyone's particular time of schooling. The time of schooling is territorialized and made absolute with regard to events that take place within.

Exhibit 2A: A Conversation about Bells

Petra and Nathalie: First, please tell us a bit about your school, Pinetree?

Leo Yamanaka-Leclerc: Pinetree is a secondary school for grades nine through twelve. Much of the administration's academic focus is on mathematics, science, technology, and engineering (i.e., the 'STEM' subjects), and the students are thought to be highly 'academic' in disposition (that term there itself being quite fraught).

Petra and Nathalie: So, at Pinetree, a decision was made at some point (before your arrival) to remove the school bell-schedule. Can you think of some reasons for this decision? What assumptions about time do you think informed this decision?

Leo Yamanaka-Leclerc: Perhaps it was believed that students would not require the audible signal of the school-wide bell to indicate schedule changes – that there would be enough uniformity and 'discipline' (another fraught term) within the student body to uphold the school's rigid schedule regardless. One would think that a lack of bells would lessen temporal constraints; however, in assuming that students would automatically follow rules of schedule and change without the bell system, there remains a conceptualization of time as somewhat inflexible and institutionalized. There is a further assumption that students will have been socialized from a young age into conforming to rules of educational time.

Petra and Nathalie: Why focus exclusively on bell-schedule and not (also) on some of the other institutional practices of discipline?

Leo Yamanaka-Leclerc: We felt that the phenomenon of the bell-less scheduling system was a fascinating case study into examining the changing landscape of the public education system. Though not unique to Pinetree Secondary, this system is certainly contemporary and somewhat experimental. In our time at Pinetree so far, we have found that this system continues to remain a point of contention for both the student body, and staff and administration.

> Petra and Nathalie: Now that a new school routine has been established without the bell-schedule, have new routines been introduced?
>
> Leo Yamanaka-Leclerc: No obvious new routines have been announced.
>
> Petra and Nathalie: Would you say that removing the bell-schedule has had both more noticeable and some less visible effects on the school culture? On individual students? Teachers? How?
>
> Leo Yamanaka-Leclerc: The bell-less scheduling system remains contentious for both students and teachers. Administration has made it clear that they would prefer that teachers begin and end classes, inviting and dismissing students, according to the exact prescribed minutes of the school schedule – despite the lack of bells to clearly demarcate chunks of time. Nevertheless, students continue to generally enter and leave classrooms at their own discretion. As another example of this modest independence, teachers allow students to leave the classroom at any point they wish to use the bathroom – without the need for direct permission.
>
> Petra and Nathalie: Is there something about the population of the school (teachers and students) that helps make this bell-less system work?
>
> Leo Yamanaka-Leclerc: As we previously noted, Pinetree Secondary generally has a reputation of being 'academically' oriented, with a large international student body and a clear focus on the STEM subjects and preparation for postsecondary education. As such, we stipulate that the administration assumes students will be able to independently follow the rules of time. Since Pinetree Secondary serves adolescents from grades nine through twelve, students have spent many years integrated within a public or private education system and thus enter the school with a preestablished understanding of educational time.
>
> Petra and Nathalie: How does allowing for some freedom from school's temporal constraints inform the long-term mission of schooling at Pinetree? In other words, does allowing students to freely come in and out of classes have significant effects on how schools might perceive student's individual freedoms from discipline, accountability and responsibility?
>
> Leo Yamanaka-Leclerc: The bell-less scheduling system is one major tool through which Pinetree Secondary strives to provide its students with greater independence and autonomy in body and mind. There remains, however, some sense of temporal rigidity in that administration and staff still expect students to enter and leave classes 'on time'.
>
> (Leo Yamanaka-Leclerc, personal correspondence, December 2021)

Time-as-Deferral, with its starting and ending points, and a continuous straight path joining them, gets transparently mapped onto conceptions of learning. The student starts with knowing nothing and ends up knowing something, and the straight path in between is development – literally, the unwrapping (develop/envelop) of that which was foretold. And from the metaphor of the line, many powerful concepts are inherited. You can't go back in time. You can't hop in a discrete step to a location further down the line. You can develop but not 'revelop'. Wandering off the line messes with the one-dimensional progress, and it may not even be possible. Finally, there is no learning if there is no arrival at the end point. The line is a path, a path so well-worn that nobody imagines walking any other way – it's how you get there; it's straight; it's narrow.

> Wayfaring, I believe, is the most fundamental mode by which living beings, both human and non-human, inhabit the earth. By habitation I do not mean taking one's place in a world that has been prepared in advance for the populations that arrive to reside there. The inhabitant is rather one who participates from within in the very process of the world's continual coming into being and who, in laying a trail of life, contributes to its weave and texture. These lines are typically winding and irregular, yet comprehensively entangled into a close-knit tissue. [. . .] From time to time in the course of history, however, imperial powers have sought to occupy the inhabited world, throwing a network of connections across what appears, in their eyes, to be not a tissue of trails but a blank surface. These connections are lines of occupation. They facilitate the outward passage of personnel and equipment to sites of settlement and extraction, and the return of the riches drawn therefrom. Unlike paths formed through the practices of wayfaring, such lines are surveyed and built in advance of the traffic that comes to pass up and down them. They are typically straight and regular, and intersect only at nodal points of power. (Ingold 2007: 81)

In her book *What's the Use?*, Sarah Ahmed (2019) shows how this path is not just used and well-worn, but also how it becomes useful as a way of herding, steering and avoiding deviations. One could argue that its primary use, in mythic terms, is to defer. School is used to defer: 'You will need this later.' School prepares children for a life of deferring (later, you will get a job; later, you will get a promotion; later, you will get to retire). And, as Ahmed writes, it does so by repeating the double technique of Thorndike's behaviourism: 'the law of exercise and the law of effect' (Ahmed 2019: 120). Strengthen the line by repeated use. Encourage sticking to the line by providing rewards. In this way, '[p]ositive affect becomes a pedagogical tool: the teacher aims for the children to associate what they want the children to do with a happier outcome' (Ahmed 2019: 120). This is how happiness narrows the path. All this is made possible by the image of Time-as-Absolute; as a given interval – as Plato and Newton both saw it – the container in which schooling occurs, giving form to any event or thing. In a relational or relative view of time, as suggested by Aristotle and Leibniz, among others, there would be no container; no requirement to wait until Grade 12. Learning would not happen over a prescribed time; rather, it would *make* time.

> Curriculum, from the learner's standpoint, ordinarily represents little more than an arrangement of subjects, a structure of socially prescribed knowledge, or a complex system of meanings which may or may not fall within his grasp. Rarely does it signify possibility for him as an existing person, mainly concerned with making sense of his own life-world. Rarely does it promise occasions for ordering the materials of that world, for imposing 'configurations' by means of experiences and perspectives made available for personally conducted cognitive action. Sartre says that 'knowing is a moment of praxis', opening into 'what has not yet been'. Preoccupied with priorities, purposes, programs of 'intended learning' and intended (or unintended) manipulation, we pay too little attention to the individual in quest of his own future, bent on surpassing what is merely 'given', on breaking through the everyday. We are still too prone to dichotomize: to think of 'discipline', or 'public traditions' or 'accumulated wisdom' or 'common culture' (individualization despite) as objectively existent, external to the knower – there to be discovered, mastered, learned. (Greene 1971)

Structured according to ages and stages of Piagetian cognitive development, moving ever higher from concrete to the more abstract conceptual learning, upholding the directional movement of knowledge reproduction from past to future on a progressive interpretation of history and scientific-technological advancements, Western schooling reinforces (via everyday pedagogical practice and knowledge reproduction) a particular notion of scientific Time as a linear continuum. Along this continuum, there is an accumulation of new ways of thinking, of reasoning, while previous ways are left behind, belonging as they do to *another* time. The evolution of the child mirroring that of the human, along a temporal axis of progress. Indeed, in a pre-Darwinian time, before Time became associated with a melioristic striving towards the fittest, the weight of the macroscopic line of human evolution might have allowed the line of human lifetime – and especially that of schooling – to curl up or fray.

> ***progress (n.)***[4]
>
> early 15,. *progresse*, a 'going on, action of walking forward', from Old French *progres* and directly from Latin *progressus* 'a going forward, and advance', . . . from *pro* 'forward' + *gradi* 'to step, walk'.

But there is no turning back. And yet – like American writer and Black studies scholar Saidiya Hartman's (2008) critical fabulation, which grows out of attending to what is missing from the archive – this book hopes to formulate 'presence' in empty quotidian spaces, employ omissions, trace patterns and consider the temporal structures that generate absences. What might these absences be? Like in this book, they may be the lack of a conclusion, or of conclusive meanings more generally, or of concrete solutions! All of these can be used for certain ends, used to summarize, replace, simplify and compress. We see this absence as creating potential, of leading to new and multiple uses (including strange and rebellious ones). Readers may be frustrated by the work required – especially teachers and students who have been taught to expect conclusions and solutions, and who even think they have a right to them. Providing the conclusion is closing down the abstraction, long before it has been adequately cared for, in the words of British mathematician and philosopher Alfred North Whitehead ([1929] 1978). To care for an abstraction is to make sure you haven't extended it too far, forgotten the contingencies on which it depends, applied it flippantly or used it to foreclose thinking. If we refuse to provide prescriptive notions of how creolization and fabulation might work, be used or applied, it is not because we are trying to be esoteric, or use the power of theory to exclude. On the contrary, this book is steeped in our own experiences of being in education, as students, teachers, teacher educators, researchers, parents and citizens. We have experienced the tensions of working with large groups of diverse children, with teachers anxious about assessment and classroom management, with parents trying to find out where their children rank, with colleagues exasperated by ongoing colonialism, capitalism and individualism. While we explore how Time in the key of Revelation matters to these contexts, we could hardly aim to be more relevant.

:

Differing Deferral and (dis)(ab)use

What if, to move forward, you had to look back?

> In Aymara, a tongue spoken by about 2 million indigenous people of the same name in the Andean highlands of Bolivia, Peru, and Chile, the word 'nayra' can refer both to objects that are physically in front of the speaker and to events in the past. '"Nayra mara", for example, means "last year"', explains Rafael Núñez, a cognitive scientist at the University of California (UC), San Diego. 'Qhipa mara', on the other hand, indicates 'next year'. 'Qhipa' means back or behind and is incorporated into other future-oriented expressions such as 'qhipüru' (a future day) and 'akata qhiparu' (from now on). This concept of time extends to gestures as well as words. Speakers point backward or wave over their shoulders when talking about a future event and extend their hands and arms forward to indicate a past event – reaching farther out for events that happened long ago. (Miller 2006)

The past is in front because it is what you have already seen.

This idea of progress is already rampant in the Enlightenment, also known as the 'age of reason', when human beings triumphed over the blindness of ignorance. Diderot. Newton. Locke. Kant. The scientific work of Newton, for example, whose laws revealed how nature really works – how there can be a concept of nature that obtains to everywhere on Earth, even places where humans have never been. For Jean-Jacques Rousseau, the 18th century French philosopher – whose image of the development of man went in three stages, from the pre-social animal functioning according to the laws of nature, to the socialized, linguistic human, to the human corrupted through enculturation,

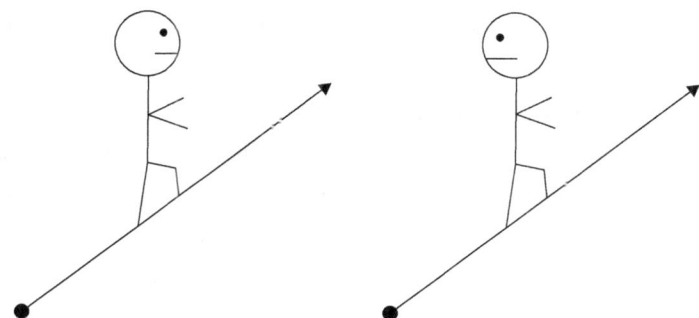

Figure 2.6 Past in front, future behind.

unable to control or manage his deceitful, jealous ways – it was the paternal law of the social contract that would guide the moral conscious of the errant human and return man to his true, pristine nature. By following this law, one could become a citizen and achieve judicial equality.

For Rousseau, then, in turning his attention to education, it became clear that the ultimate goal – the endpoint of education – was to produce humans uncorrupted by culture, and therefore true to their natural state. The means of education became obvious: to allow the child to freely develop without imposing any secondary, artificial culture. Three psychological laws ensued: respect the march of natural mental evolution; do not control the activities of the child by imposing premature or theoretical forms of reasoning; and, since the most natural activities are those which satisfy the child's interests, motivate the child to learn. Education is about revealing one's true self. This involves finding the origin, and placing yourself on the origin so that you can move forward *in the right way* and *towards the right goal*. Time provides the one-dimensional measure of progress.

> Indigenous worldview is predicated on an intimate connection to place and all the ecosystem implications of that. How the ecosystem is connected to the knowledge system – and so this very place-based understanding. And so he [Vine Deloria Jr.] said, Western worldview is preoccupied with notions of time and development. So there's a zero year and everything from that time gets bigger, better, stronger, faster, smarter. So it's preoccupied with capital P progress, which runs in direct conflict with a place-based worldview. This is at the heart of the relational psychosis. (Donald 2020b)

The one-dimensional line of progress is the myth that creates not only the origin, but also its counterpoint: the destination or death. As Russian philosopher Mikhail Bakhtin shows, this myth pervades Western literature. Indeed, his 'adventure time' novels – one of the four chronotypes Bakhtin identifies – loosely follow this script: boy and girl meet and fall in love; they experience many ordeals that keep them apart; they are finally reunited. The starting and ending points are fixed as temporally distinct extremes, but they themselves are arbitrary. All the action happens in the time between these two points, but the amount of time matters little. In other words, the action lies outside of the biographical, historical or quotidian time. The characters do not change; there is no duration or cyclicity in the days and years; and no trace of time having passed. Like beads on a string, '[t]he adventures themselves are strung together in an extratemporal and in effect infinite series: this series can be extended as long as one likes; in itself it has no necessary internal limits' (Bakhtin [1981] 2008: 94). There is no human initiative; instead, it is fate that controls the plot, which is concerned with meetings and partings, losses and acquisitions, searches and discoveries, recognitions and misrecognitions.

Space and time are only tied together at the moments of meetings, when they become inseparable. Otherwise, space is not concrete or specific (not *this* village or *that* forest), since it is the absolute power of change that prevails. We could also say that space – like the classroom – gets *used* as a convenient site for development, but plays no actual role in directing the progress of cognition– as Ahmed (2019) writes, it is not *used for*.

In Bakhtin's second chronotype, we find the adventure novel of real-world experience. In this chronotype, time matters. Revelation occurs through the actual travelling of the hero in time, his metamorphosis. In order to account for the metamorphosis, time is broken into isolated and self-sufficient intervals that define critical turning points. In the cognitive development landscape, those critical points might be when the child moves stages, from the sensorimotor to the pre-operational, or from the pre-operational to the concrete operational. While the hero's fate depends on major moments that are unusual or exceptional, the child's fate depends on their age, and therefore has less to do with them as individuals than with the somewhat arbitrary chunking of Time (0–2 years old, then 2–7, etc.), which produces critical turning points (of 2 or 7). The behaviours of a small group of children are used to produce categories of ages, that are in turn used to establish benchmarks. The *exceptional* of fiction becomes the usual or the *expected* cognitive development. Learning doesn't happen in time, but at certain times (though not all the time). In any case, the protagonist/child is formed outside everyday life. They observe their lives but do not participate in it, since only extraordinary events shape them.

Exhibit 2B: How Children Understand Time

When researchers in education try to understand how children develop their sense of time, what is in question is the degree of correspondence between the Newtonian scientific explanation of time and children's epistemological beliefs. For example, in the recent study on pre-schooler's understanding of the abstract concept of time (Güneş & Şahin 2020: 307) the researchers asked children to draw time machines and then asked them questions about their understanding of time. They graded the answers such that the more the notion of time corresponded with the particular techno-scientific image of time as a continuum, the higher the points awarded. Asking the children 'Do you think we can stop time? How?' they graded the answers as 'realistic and scientific' with three points as follows (all quotations Güneş & Şahin 2020: 307):

Child 2, Child 13: 'Stopping time only happens in movies' (Three points).
Child 15, Child 20: 'Stopping time only happens in cartoons' (Three points).
Child 17, Child 28: 'Stopping time only happens in tales' (Three points).
Child 11: 'Time doesn't stop because it constantly passes; I don't think we can go back or forward in time' (Three points).

Those who gave what the researchers deemed 'the children's science fiction/imagination-based responses' were also given three points:

Child 1, Child 29: 'I think we can stop time if we press the 'stop time' button on the time machine' (Three points).
Child 4, Child 12, Child 23 and Child 30: 'I think if we pulled the plug of the time machine, then our time machine would stop, and time would stop' (Three points).

The explanation for why the children's imaginative responses were also given three points is that 'the children's imagination related to time machines can be evaluated as the relationship they established between time and technology'.

The eleven children who received two points instead of three, 'gave answers that were not based on science or imagination':

Child 7, Child 21: 'We need to remove the batteries of clocks' (Two points).
Child 24: 'Sometimes clocks stop and don't work; I think it is when time stops' (Two points).

The authors make several undeclared assumptions about time in their data analysis as well as in the posing of the problem of children's understanding of the concept of time. In particular, what we are interested in is that they take the techno-imaginative-scientific notion of time as continuous, with action and movement on a temporal line (something that can therefore stop), to be the condition for evaluating the epistemological validity and the level of abstract cognition in children. Had they taken the quantum, geological,

> Leibnizian, or any one of the various Indigenous theories of time to be the condition for posing and evaluating children's understanding of time, their 'data' interpretation would significantly change. In addition, they assumed a certain reality or actuality of time as outside of the tick-tock of the clock, and so assessed the children's answers that assumed no such *imagined* reality outside the *technological* object representing such conventional time, namely the clock, to not be 'based on science or imagination' (Güneş & Şahin 2020: 307).

Bahktin's adventure chronotypes of fiction are the learning chronotypes of schooling, both deferring to time – and more, using time as the singular narrative arc.

defer (v.1)[5]

'to delay, put off, postpone', late 14c., *differren*, *deferren*, from Old French *diferer* (14c.) and directly from Latin *differre* 'carry apart, scatter, disperse'; also 'be different, differ'; also 'defer, put off, postpone', from assimilated form of *dis-* 'away from' (see **dis-**) + *ferre* 'to bear, carry', from PIE root ***bher-** (1) 'to carry'.

If instead, we *differed* to time – scattering it, fraying its singularity – what would we see, and where and when would we look?

> *We've heard it, we've all heard about all the sticks and spears and swords, the things to bash and poke and hit with, the long, hard things, but we have not heard about the thing to put things in, the container for the thing contained.*
> (Ursula Le Guin)[6]

As American speculative fiction writer Ursula Le Guin ([1986] 2019) recounts, the invention of the vessel, of the container into which one can place seeds, roots, sprouts, shoots, leaves, nuts, berries, fruits and grains – the primary diet of prehistoric times – in order to avoid having to go gathering the next day, exploded time and space. Instead of focusing on the here-and-now, the movement of the hand from the bush or the river to the mouth, the vessel allowed our ancestors to satisfy their hunger when and where they wanted. The future becomes something, a time when one might be hungry, a hypothetical time that is independent of a particular place. Space is distilled from the distributed rivers and forests into a singular location. The future and the past are created at the same time, around the planning for sustenance and the satiating of it. Time contracts – fewer hours spent gathering, more for hunting large prey; more perhaps for storying. And the stories that come to be worth telling – about hunting large, dangerous mammoths – are the stories of heroic undertaking, about the conquest of animals, the earth, space, aliens, etc.

There is the drama of the narrative arc that ends tragically, in apocalypses, holocausts and planetary devastation. But if we avoid 'the linear, progressive, Time's-(killing)-arrow mode' (Le Guin ([1986] 2019)) of technology as a weapon of domination, and instead embrace the carrier bag theory, then alternatives to the Promethean or apocalyptic stories can be made. The stories that we might tell would involve 'a way of trying to describe what is in fact going on, what people actually do and feel, how people relate to everything else in this vast stack, this belly of the universe, this womb of things to be and tomb of things that were' (Le Guin ([1986] 2019)). This might be curriculum as science fiction. It would have room enough for arrows, but also for gathering seeds of knowledge and sowing them, dispersing them too and joking and caring and making time. Making time, like American feminist philosopher of science Donna Haraway's (2016) making kin, requires looking beyond predictive, one-dimensional lines of progress, lines of filiation and most of all, deferring differently. It requires cyclic, ecological kinship (with chimpanzees, rabbits, trees) of a biogeochemical order: 'Every molecule that is in me has its origins in another body' (Kimmerer, 2021: 114).

> To disengage filiation
> That absolute of legitimacies, to divert
> The supposed time-world from its line,
> Is to gush forth in chaos at last
> In the multiplicities of time
> Which all mean that anyone can envisage it
> Or stare it down
> Without faltering.
>
> (Glissant [1997] 2020: 139)

In the ever-moving-forward ideas of development, of arrows joined end to end, we are enchanted by monumental, spectacular narratives. But if some of those arrows take off in a different direction, stack on top of the previous one, bend slightly, contract to a point, then the newly spatialized temporalities can cause disruptions, create new relations between past and present, change speeds, pause (but not postpone indefinitely). Repeating the same paragraph of a book read aloud in the classroom (maybe once inside and the other time outside, to explore the different space-time meanings); taking one sentence and exploring the omissions and thus what was not said, or taking it out of its narrative flow so that it becomes a static image; changing the rhythm of counting; spending all year on triangles; delaying the introduction of fractions so long that it becomes a point of pride; dwelling, in math class, on what it must have felt like to have discovered numbers that are not commensurable and to have been put to sea in a barrel for it.

Why might this seem impossible? What is it about our devotion to time – to getting *there*, to moving ahead – that is so compelling? If we loosened our thinking about time as being given and static, we might, as British geographer Doreen Massey suggests, reconceive it as 'the product of interrelations' of multiple trajectories, as 'the dimension of a multiplicity of durations', and as an open system 'always under construction' (Massey 2005: 55). This can happen in literature, particularly in contemporary novels concerned with memory and subjectivity, as in W.G. Sebald's fiction. The following is a description of just one of his sentences from *Austerlitz* (2001), a book about the holocaust. We invite you to consider what is evoked if you replace 'narrator' with 'teacher':

> In general, Sebald's sentences tend to create a space that allows for the coexistence and interaction of voices that belong to different spaces and times, of histories of objects and people different from those of the narrator in the here and now, but at the same time related to him and crucial to understanding his situation (and his responsibility) in the present. The sentences serve as a space for the meeting up of multiple stories. This is not to say that the space of the sentence is barrierless. After all, it is the narrator (regarded by many as a fictional version of the author) who makes the decision to select and incorporate the words of others and place them along his own. But he moves to the side, so to speak, and allows them to share the same space. (García-Moreno 2013: 361)

It might also seem impossible because what Massey is asking for would require not just meeting children where they are at, personalizing their learning, making sure we are in the right ZPD, connecting to their interests and so on. It would require letting the trauma and anger and resistance in; not deferring it in the hopes of a happy future. When a door closes along the path, we speak of providing scaffolds and tools, alternative routes and modified paths. What we don't do is consider changing the contract with Time.

This contract with Time was perhaps more visible in the monitorial schools of the early nineteenth century, set up in Britain but spread across countries such as Australia, the United States and India. These schools, as Ahmed writes, were used to produce useful citizens. In contrast to the schools for the elite (in which 'un-useful' knowledge was taught!), the monitorial schools prepared the working class to work, to labour. Teaching useful knowledge to people can in turn make them useful. With this single purpose in mind, singular pedagogies ensued. Indeed, the main *dispositif* or method, was 'that the best students would teach the other students, thus freeing time of the master' (Ahmed 2019: 116). By delegating instruction to others, the master was free to regulate and control. The monitorial schools not only produced a useful class but also did so in an efficient and cheap way. It was efficient not only in terms of time saved but also in the simultaneous explosion of master/slave relations that preclude the formation of any resistance. Everyone but the last boy is a master, while also being mastered into a life of obedience.

Ahmed evokes these monitorial schools as a way of showing how use became a technique, one to produce a working, servant, colonized class (that was, furthermore, made to be 'happy to serve'). We draw on her description to highlight the singularity of the purpose of these schools and the ensuing clarity with which deferral operates through time-as-revelation. As Ahmed writes, '[h]appiness is used as a technique to narrow the route' (Ahmed 2019: 121). Students are rewarded for obeying, for spelling the word correctly, and then that reward becomes the impetus towards future obeying. Happiness is a double bind that operates as something that is useful *and* something fundamentally tied up with the idea of growth and progress. Everything else gets subordinated to the deferred goal of achieved growth. What gets revealed in time is the deferral. It is perhaps not deferral in and of itself that subordinates education to time, but deferral to the future. This very fact provides some initial strategies for differing deferral. We could, for example, defer to the past, defer to the present or even defer to a future without us.

It may be that teachers do this already. The increasingly popular practice of mindfulness can be seen as a deferral to the present. In an elementary school where we have done research, classes are interrupted twice a day. A student's voice is heard over the PA system inviting everyone to close their eyes, engage in deep breathing and reflect on a prompt offered by the student. But it is hard not to notice the atavistic tendencies underlying the twice-daily, time-stamped moments of mindfulness, in which only certain moments count as present and where presence must be manufactured in timed collective participation.

The origin myths of atavistic cultures sneak their way into composite ones and, as they do, they formulate a powerful dialectic of origin/death. This gives meaning to the atavistic cultures, as the myth of origin conditions death, and death gives retroactive support to that very same myth. Composite cultures do not have this dialectic. However, composite cultures can also have meanings; they are not just flux. They are, as Glissant would have it, archipelagic. Or, borrowing from French philosopher Michel Serres, who mixes a brew for another dialectic (fixed/fluid), composite cultures are

> more of a scattering of islets in archipelagos on the noisy poorly-known disorder of the sea, peaks whose edges are slashed and battered by the surf and are in perpetual transformation, erosion, ruptures and encroachments; with the emergence of sporadic rationalities whose links with each other are neither easy nor obvious. (Serres 1980: 23–24; our translation)

While Serres engages in mixing, Glissant in creolizing and Hartman in fabulating, what we see is a turn to magic. Ahmed might call it queering and in her meditation on queering use, she means attending to what might be useless, changing for whom something might be useful, widening the use to beyond the beaten path, re-using; she means 'to shatter what has provided a container' (Ahmed 2019: 209). If this all relates to magic, it's because queering is about releasing the potential of the objects and ideas laden down by proper or common use. This may not be the magic of picture books (so often confined to a 'childish' imagination), but it may well belong to the domain of religion. We recognize that secular schooling has been a formidable achievement of Western countries, but in erecting a mind spirit binary, it cast away both its 'promising and destructive monsters' (Haraway, 1991: 190). It may very well be that we cannot get very far in changing the contract with Time without plugging into magic.

We are not necessarily talking about a Harry Potter education of casting spells. The magical universe, for French philosopher Gilbert Simondon ([1958] 2017)[7], is that which precedes the segregation of subject and object; it is the 'reticulation of the world into privileged places and privileged moments' (178). By this he means the promontory by the sea, the crater in the desert, the darkest part of the woods, the moment of sunrise, the night of the full moon – places and times and things that have power, where the distinction between reality and human reality is at its most fleeting. While Simondon sees magical thought as the simplest and most concrete, that doesn't mean it is a phase that passes in childhood; on the contrary, he imagines 'high, noble, and sacred forms of thought' (Simondon [1958] 2017: 179). Rather than being motivated by conquest or competition, magical thought seeks human-world friendship. From the mixture, or the soup, of magical thought, it is through technicity and religion that figure separates from ground, human from nature. Both technicity and religion are ways of cleaving the living from its milieu. Once detached, technics and religion can become 'mobile, fragmentable, displaceable and directly manipulative because they are not bound to the world' (Simondon [1958] 2017: 182). The promontory becomes merely observable and describable, then useable and even copyable to other locations.

However, if technical and religious thought are the heirs of magic, then magic can occur through their coupling. (Not by marking special places or times just *because* they are special (Hallowe'en, solstice, etc.), though, since this prolongs the split by instrumentalizing these moments, which maintains a figure/ground separation.) As Simondon writes, this would involve extracting from every instance that which is pleasurable in order to compose a happy life; it is to 'proceed in an inductive manner, by trying to replace the unity of life's duration and the unity of human aspiration with a plurality of instances and with the homogeneity of all successive desires' (Simondon [1958] 2017: 189). We return here to Ahmed's path, which, without magic, is a path made by hopping from instance to instance, with no figure/ground unity. Magic though would then be a non-use, un-use, diff-use, pre-use. It is the retreat from use;

the plugging of figure into ground that recovers and discovers the stunning and extraordinary fact of the world.

The school curriculum, which devotes itself to technicity, is all about figure. This is intensified by assignments in which students are asked to write their autobiographies or draw an image of their communities – activities which rely on a figure/ground split that wrenches the subject from its milieu in order to be able to look upon the subject, its history, its location and its experiences. Perhaps an assignment where students write about their birth might elicit magic – the very idea of a beginning having a force and power that exceeds explanation. Or a visit to a building scarred by lightning, where they might encounter their own electrical capacity for magic. Or contemplating the idea of deep-time (or geologic time), which can really only be sensed, perhaps by touching the striations of rocks, or through poetry (as Stephen Jay Gould does when he writes about the 'stroke of a nail file' on the spot between the King's nose and the tip of his outstretched hand that corresponds to his middle finger, that would 'erase human history' (1987: 3)). Of course, touch and metaphor are rarely taken as proper forms of thinking in Science, perhaps because of their collusion with magic. This is why the French philosopher of mathematics, Gilles Châtelet (1987), implores teachers to insist on the magic of mathematical ideas such as the derivative or the point at infinity. If we say that they are merely *like* processes we can understand, then we refuse the abstract – that is, we refuse the magic. When Armenian mathematics education researcher Dick Tahta (1980: 7) writes that 'the geometry that can be told is not geometry', he's talking about magic.

These propositions have a family resemblance to the recent place- and land-based learning being pursued in many schools across North America, influenced by Indigenous epistemologies and ontologies. That these traditions plug into magic is incontestable. When they speak of being in places where they encounter ancestral time, locations that superpose temporalities, they are mobilizing the abstract, the magic, as well. Indigenizing the curriculum will require ceding to this magic; we are not sure if current policy-makers have fully embraced this.

The cubist paintings were provocative in the way they brewed up the singular point of view. They toyed with representational assumptions, particularly around space. We are also toying with representational assumptions related to time. Disrupting certain stories about dominant ways of thinking time, which operates through deferral. In differing deferral, we reuse time, diffuse it and refuse it too. We offer magnets that can be moved around to break down the directionality of time from a given point 0. To offer a closing abstraction: if we think with vector fields, then time is less about arrows all going into the same direction, and more about cultivating a composite (see Figure 2.7).

Figure 2.7 Two contrasting representations of time as a vector field.

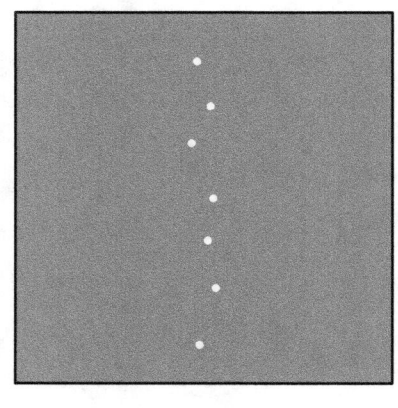

Lies 4: We can only be in one place at one time.

(Jeanette Winterson)[1]

3

Rupture

Discretizing Time with Denise Ferreira da Silva and Luce Irigaray

> *rupture (n.)*²
> late 14c., in medicine, . . . from Latin *ruptura* 'the breaking (of a vein), fracture (of an arm or leg)', 'from past participle stem of *rumpere* 'to break', (from PIE root **runp-* 'to break'; see **corrupt** (adj.)).
> Specifically as 'abdominal hernia' from early 15c.

I know that people want to read certain things. One has unbearable reading experiences, right? I remember reading my favorite text of Robert Musil's, a short novella called *The Perfect Thing of Love*. It's forty pages, but it's extremely dense. It's a nightmare to read, actually – I start with this reverence, every time, and then slowly it becomes unbearable. I've read it a couple of times, but I've also failed to finish it multiple times. For somebody who I know is a wise person from whom I have something to learn, I'm willing to read an unbearable text. But we don't live in a literary context, a literary culture, where unbearable reading, or reading that one has to struggle through, is tolerated. Have you read this book by Thomas Bernhard, *Extinction*? (Arudpragasam in Braneck (2021))

While writing this book, we are teaching ethics and a class coded 'Education, Knowledge, and Curriculum' to pre-service teachers. In order to make time become perceptible in our class, we focus on deep reading (what students repeatedly express as difficult, unbearable reading); on film content that makes speed, pace and time stand out (see Exhibit B); and by recording as podcasts their many communal discussions of reading materials, which we then listened to and engaged with in class.

We begin our classes by looking at how Western epistemology (grounded in reason, science, bifurcation of nature and culture) and its grammar of thought (Subject-predicate logic) are conditioned on a very particular colonial regime of Time and Space. The aim is to show the pre-service teachers what undoing colonizing pedagogies entails, meaning, that as teachers, they cannot stop at picking and choosing Black and Indigenous literature and/or rituals, queer and feminist films and celebrating festivities from various different cultures, without accounting for how Time and Space are the privileged and Unthought sites where colonial epistemologies reproduce themselves. For example, here in Canada's British Columbia, the new curriculum would look much different if the conceptual starting point was Place, as theorized by many Indigenous scholars[3], instead of the now-implemented triad 'know-understand-do'. *Celebrating* (looking at) difference in One-ness benefits and corresponds with

Figure 3.1 Detail of *Father Time* in the *Rotunda Clock* (1896), by sculptor John Flanagan (1865–1952). Photographed in 2007 by Carol Highsmith (1946–), who explicitly submitted the photograph in the public domain. Library of Congress, Prints & Photographs Division, LC-DIG-highsm-02121.

the 'multicultural' and neoliberal juridico-economic system that demands integration according to a logic where Us-All implies Sameness, while *respecting* (looking with, alongside, from) the Other in their Difference/Pluriness juridico-economically, ruptures, disobeys the logic of all-encompassing One-ness.

According to the Online Etymology Dictionary,[4]

> [The] abstract sense of 'time as an indefinite continuous duration' is recorded from late 14c. Personified at least since 1509 as an aged bald man (but with a forelock) carrying a scythe and an hour-glass. In English, a single word encompasses time as 'extent' and 'point' (French *temps/fois*, German *zeit/mal*) as well as 'hour' (as in 'what time is it?' compare French *heure*, German *Uhr*). Extended senses such as 'occasion,' 'the right time,' 'leisure,' or *times* (v.) 'multiplied by' developed in Old and Middle English, probably as a natural outgrowth of such phrases as 'He commends her a hundred times to God' (Old French *La comande a Deu cent foiz*).

Some measurements of time in ancient Tamil history (*Tamil Units* (2011); *our emphasis*):

- 1 kuzhi(kuRRuzhi) = 6.66 millisecond – the time taken by the Pleiades stars (aRumin) to *glitter* once.
- 12(base 8) or 10 kuzhigaL = 1 miy = 66.6666 millisecond – the time taken by the young human eyes to *flap* once.
- 2 kaNNimaigaL = 1 kainodi = 0.125 second.
- 2 kainodi = 1 maatthirai = 0.25 second.
- 6(base 8) or 6 miygaL = 1 siRRuzhi(nodi) = 0.40 second – the time taken for a bubble (created by blowing air through a bamboo tube into a vessel 1 saaN high, full of water) to *travel* a distance of one saaN.
- 2 maatthiraigaL = 1 kuru = 0.50 second.
- 2(base 8) or 2 nodigaL = 1 vinaadi = 0.80 second – the time for the adult human heart to *beat* once.

These measures of time, like in many people before the time of Newton, were situated and subjective – in the words of Italian physicist and philosopher Carlo Rovelli (2018), 'no one had thought that a time independent of things could exist' (61). Much like with the standardization of length units, such as the metre, the very idea of a standard unit of time took centuries to sink in. Like a crack in the cement that fractures ever so slowly, before becoming a deep jagged cut, time was eventually ruptured into two nation states – the standard, objective, extensive time of train schedules and clock-makers, tick-tocking metronomically, and the personal, intensive, heterogeneous time of human experience, made famous in Western literature by Proust and the memory of his madeleines. These two times were incommensurable. If that rupture was not enough, Einstein's intervention fell like an obelisk on the cement, fracturing it further, into a dissolution of the very notion of time.

The notion that time is relative, that it speeds as you travel up from the earth's surface, that your clock will tick less languorously – this might accommodate a new place-based understanding of time.

> If things fall, it is due to this slowing down of time. Where time passes uniformly, in interplanetary space, things do not fall. They float, without falling. Here on the surface of our planet, on the other hand, the movement of things inclines naturally toward where time passes more slowly, as when we run down the beach into the sea and the resistance of the water on our legs makes us fall headfirst into the waves. Things fall downward because, down there, time is slowed by the Earth. (Rovelli 2018: 12)

There's more. The time of physicists also speeds up the faster you go – travel the speed of light or oscillate frantically, and you will get older quicker. If that doesn't sound too concerning, then you haven't yet understood the consequences: there is no universal *now*. Clocks have been useful to us because they enable a coordination of time – that all students show up to class *at the same time*. Standard time enables the actualization of a sense of presence; we all show up on Zoom, from different corners of the world, at the same *now*. However, modern physics asserts that 'there is no such thing as "the same moment" definable in the universe. The "present of the universe" is meaningless' (Rovelli 2018: 41). In this sense, there is no universal arrow of time where we can all claim to be at the same spot – there are only local bubbles of newness. It is reasoning we are accustomed to. Locally, in our bubble, the earth is flat. It is only as we change the scale, zoom out, travel intercontinentally, that we must adjust to its sphericity. With time, it might be more disconcerting. When you are in the classroom looking at students, you are actually seeing them in the past – by the time light travels to you (yes, only a few nanoseconds), they have already moved on to their new selves. This means that we are a multi-clocked universe; everything in it that moves has its own clock, its own preferred time.

Here the process philosophers were onto something, in that it makes less sense to speak of objects than of events (objects moving).

It gets weirder. In the physical laws of the universe – which describe gravity, light, black holes, motion and so on – the variable time (t) does not appear. These laws do not distinguish the past from the future. It is only when heat is involved, in the law of thermodynamics, that time matters. Another way of saying this is that every situation that distinguishes past from future somehow involves heat. If a pendulum swings back and forth indefinitely, we cannot tell past from future. If it slows down, however, because of friction, then the arrow of time is back, and heat has been generated through the disordered motion of molecules.

> It's a conclusion that leaves us flabbergasted: is it really possible that a perception so vivid, basic, existential – my perception of the passage of time – depends on the fact that I cannot apprehend the world in all of its minute detail? On a kind of distortion that's produced by myopia? Is it true that, if I could see exactly and take into consideration the actual dance of millions of molecules, then the future would be 'just like' the past? (Rovelli 2018: 31)

Of course, we cannot go back to the past and hand our homework in on time or change the fact of wars, deaths, marriages or births. We are ourselves ongoing events of our past memories and future expectations. Our brains are not structured like the laws of physics – they function on multiple time scales, bubbling away in Tamil time *and* quantum time.

> Temporality is profoundly linked to blurring. The blurring is due to the fact that we are ignorant of the microscopic details of the world. The time of physics is, ultimately, the expression of our ignorance of the world. Time is ignorance. (Rovelli 2018: 123)

Some measures of time in the early twenty-first century:
- 1 second = 9,192,631,770 oscillations of a caesium atom.

Exhibit 3A: The Grizzlies, and Biidaaban (The Dawn Comes)

The Grizzlies (2018) is a feature-length, feel-good movie, produced and directed by Miranda de Pensier. It depicts a white male teacher named Russ, who finds himself in a teaching position in a small community in Nunavut. We follow his story of development as a teacher from the moment of his arrival, through various professional and personal setbacks and existential crisis until he arises at the end as someone who has changed due to the influence of his students and the community. The film opens with a (porno)graphic viewing of a young boy committing suicide. The changes Russ makes in the lives of Indigenous students are, we are to believe, profound, as his introduction of Lacrosse (sport initially created by Indigenous peoples) to the students significantly lowers youth suicide rates.

This is no doubt a heroic story with a heavy dose of 'white saviour complex' and 'white fragility'. Time extends linearly from his arrival up until the last Lacrosse match in Toronto. It is punctuated by points of heroic growth, wherein all others (students, animals, community) function as prompts in the efficiently causal protagonist temporality, proceeding through the classic narrative arch. We are invited as viewers, to align our viewing pleasure and desire (our point of view) with Russ's desire to 'save' his students from death, depression and desolation. The story is based on true events, and the film ends with portraits of the real students, now grown up and more or less successfully leading their adult lives.

Biidaaban (The Dawn Comes) (2017) is a Canadian animated short film, directed by Michif Indigenous filmmaker Amanda Strong and based on the stories and poems ('Caribou Ghosts and Untold Stories', 'Plight', 'The Gift is in the Making') by acclaimed Indigenous writer/musician Leanne Betasamosake Simpson. It was released in 2018. Filmed in a stop-motion technique, we follow an Indigenous youth named Biidaaban, a young Anishinaabe gender non-binary person who, while living in their present time and space, can see through multiple dimensions. Biidaaban is accompanied by a 10,000-years-old friend Sabe (Sasquatch, a shape-shifter, who is also texting), Ghost Caribou, Ghost Wolf and other ancestors. Biidaaban sets out to harvest sap from Sugar Maples in urban Ontario neighbourhoods, to reclaim this ceremony. These neighbourhoods (primarily inhabited and occupied by non-Anishinaabe settler people) are being developed on lands that have been used and stewarded by the Anishinaabeg, the four-legged and winged creatures since time immemorial. Biidaaban sets out in the thick of the night to harvest sap to create a syrup, like their Indigenous ancestors did for generations, from old-growth trees now growing on private property. They must overcome their fear of getting caught 'trespassing' while harvesting.

In this short stop-motion animation, Amanda Strong chose not to film in live action: 'Live action could never have created these personas or these worlds.

So yes, it's insane, but there's just something very magical about it, and I think anybody who does work in stop motion would agree that that's why they do it.'[5] Instead, with stop motion, we see time will freeze, crinkle, flap, beat, glitter and warp. As viewers, we are disoriented; we see the past in the underpass, superimposed, but we remain anchored in the present. Biidaabaan can see traces of past times, peoples, creatures and land. These images reverberate time underpassing; we see the past is unwavering in the present, an underground force always as virtual potentiality to be different, to 'transubstantiate' the present.

Contrasting the two films in class, we discuss how far it is possible to decolonize pedagogies, epistemologies and axiologies, if we do not account for how Time informs, structures and categorizes the process of knowing and being in the world. Students watch *Biidaaban* and want/need to understand; they grasp for meaning and comfort.

So, we push deeper.

Are we outsiders (White *and* settler teachers) invited to understand the film, to interpret it? Or are we not obligated to sit with, sit with its ethical demand uncomfortably; welcoming disorientation in not having the cognitive tools to make it mean something to and for us?

Time is a cognitive apparatus with which we think. It is carried over in languages humans speak, stories we tell, knowledges we re-produce. Since Time is an apparatus we think-speak-read-write-imagine-desire-with, it proves difficult, if not outright tricky, to think it and write about it, let alone decolonize it – for that would require a complete refusal of Time as a Thing that can be Named, of *Kategoria*[6] *of Time* itself. The colonial, juridico-economic Kategoria of Time affords the Subject freedoms of emotional, cognitive and corporeal protection and support. It *is* the material, ethical and affective (re)productive comport/Limit to His Life. To the Other, like Biidaaban, Kategoria of Time offers no shelter, no safety or protection – only Death, always deferred.

:

What follows is an ~~interview~~ invitrum[7] with Brazilian feminist philosopher Denise Ferreira da Silva and French feminist philosopher Luce Irigaray, observed/actualized in 2014, 2019 and 2008 respectively, virtually reverberating sometime in the underpass between dusk and dawn of summer 2021. The moon shines hot and bright, punctuating the black smoke infusing our daughters' book 'Goodnight moon and goodnight air everywhere', the political, racist, misogynist and forest fires flooding across the earth, reverberating in 'I can't breathe!' . . . anaphorically.

she: You are among those (we can think of Hartman, Grosz, Wynter, Cixous, to name a few) thinkers whose feminist work is *systemically* engaged with the concepts and structures of Time and Space at the core of Western philosophy. Why is Time important to you, in your academic work? (Summer, 2021)

DFdS: In my project, similar to Wynter's, I ask the question of how 'to find ways of escaping dichotomies – such as interiority/exteriority, self-determination/affectability, temporality/spatiality, etc. – that have been so central to the delimiting of man's/the human's privilege'.[8] (12 April 2019)

she: Would you say that it is possible to de-bifurcate Time without privileging one scale (phenomenological, cosmic, quantum) over another, that is, without reading One in Terms of the Other through reading practices such as opposition, displacement, critique? (Summer, 2021)

DFdS: 'Of course, it is not a question of thinking without exteriority, but of thinking, as I try to do with "fractal thinking", about different scales simultaneously: cosmic, historic, organic and quantic. For instance, while time (sequentiality) becomes irrelevant at the cosmic register, space doesn't make sense at the quantic level because whatever happens at that level cannot be attributed to something that has extension'.[9] (12 April 2019)

she: Yes. In our other works, we also propose that this kind of simultaneous reading of different scales is a kind of stratigraphic reading, reading side-by-side, wherein contrasts rather than relations reign supreme. (23 July 2021)

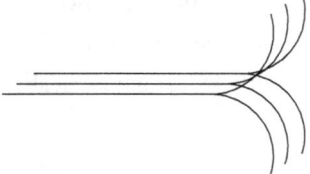

DFdS: '"Deep Implicancy" as "Radical Immanence" is for me a way of imaging the world without the idea of relations, which always presuppose that things are inherently separate or separable. What if thinking took a step back, found itself as a part of the whole mess of it all that is the plenum and became happy with providing momentary resolutions at each instance according to an intention mediated by the given context?'.[10] (12 April 2019)

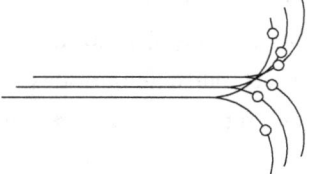

LI: In my work, I too focus on imagining the world without the idea of *relations as we know them*, relations that are conditioned on patriarchal familiarity and Sameness. This idea of relationality continues to function as the transcendental One, 'metaphysical' comp(f)ort to all life. And so 'Appealing to a relation still to be built, it demands that we be able to suspend the relational world that was ours – to open this world to the call of another world. Which does not mean to relinquish, to renounce our own world, but to bring it back to a possible becoming thanks to a relation for which I long but which will always escape the familiarity that I felt in a world closed only on, or by, my own subjectivity, whatever the relations taking part in it'.[11] (Sometime in 2008)

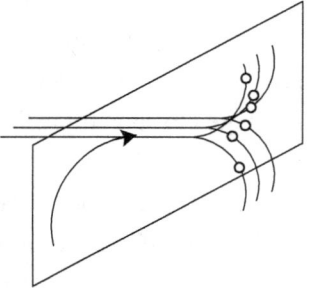

DFdS: So, this would then be 'A reminder to the speculative realists: wishing the subject out of existence by holding onto an independent object without attending to how one informs the other is not enough for announcing a whole new philosophical age'.[12] (February, 2017)

e

she: LI, in your work, you speak of space and place as onto-epistemological effects of Man assigning a fixed time and place for the Other to dwell in, in confinement, at His disposal. If for Hegel, there is only *Wirklichkeit*, the 'actual', or a *system* with no inside or outside, for Heidegger, of *Being and Time* – the outside is not 'the external' in opposition to eternal, it is external only in the sense of an opening, a kind of movement of time itself. We could say that like Heidegger, you argue that humans are not yet fully what they are, but need a future to become who they are. Yet against Heidegger, you perhaps argue that any such future, as a transcendental opening/movement of time is something that happens *within* the *system*. (24 July 2021)

LI: Yes, because the Subject (Man) has not yet gained 'autonomy, a capacity of being in oneself, a dwelling in oneself and returning to oneself not ordered by dependence on an already existing world, wrongly imagined as his own.' His dependence 'on the surrounding world in order to define his "here"'[13] and *now* comes, 'at least in part, from his dependence on the maternal world, a dependence of which he has *not yet* become aware, has *not yet* explored, nor whose impact on the constitution of his own horizon has he assessed'.[14] I would agree with DFdS that we need to attend to the idea of relationality, to how the Subject informs the Object, because Man depends on this idea of 'his own centering, as familiarity and proximity', which 'is, in fact, determined by a lack of differentiation with regard to the maternal world, which, historically, has been transformed into a gathering of "one(s)" or a collective neutral "one". This sort of "one" – as linguistics teaches us – amounts to an "I" to whom is added a "you", a "he", a "she", or a "they"; that is to say, that this "one", amounts to a "we" in which persons are barely differentiated. Here it is a question of masculine subject and a feminine world – in which participants are hardly separated, thus a "we" remaining at the stage of the "one".[15] There is no outside of this structure, because the opening, a sharing of a life, an 'elaboration of the world that *will be* built by the one and the other', this life/desire/immanence will have happened 'without ever belonging to the one or the other'.[16] In other words, in this future conditional tense, relating and sharing of a life (plant, human, nonhuman, viral) will not be reducible to the terms and conditions of its self-determined temporal/transcendental structure. (Sometime in 2008)

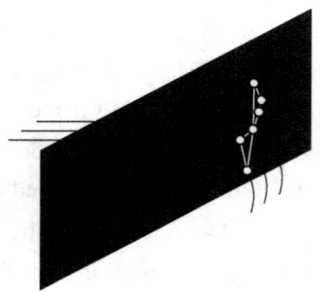

she: DFdS, you as well speak to this particular, what we call, Grammar of Thought (Subject-predicate propositional logic producing modern enclosures). We agree with you that *determinacy, separability* and *sequentiality* are *the* spatio-temporal thought processes that constitute this ethico-political syntax, imagined as His Own. In your feminist speculative thought experiment, what you call the *Equation of Value* designed to help move away from modern thought, you break away from Blackness as a category and propose that Blackness be understood as a method. (24 July 2021)

DFdS: Yes, this is because '[w]hen taken not as a category but as a referent of another mode of existing in the world, blackness returns The Thing at the limits of modern thought. Or, put differently, when deployed as method, blackness fractures the glassy walls of *universality* understood as *formal determination*. The violence inherent in the illusion of that value is both an effect and an actualization of self-determination, or autonomy'.[17] (February 2017)

So, look at an example of political relations. Because racial knowledge transubstantiates (shifts) political relations 'from the living to the formal register' or in other words, to the 'effects of efficient (scientific reason's) causality, its critical tools fail to register how the total (past, present and future) value expropriated is in the very structures (in blood and flesh) of global capital'. Total Value understood this way 'requires a suspension of the view that all there is is in Time and Space, as appropriated by the tools of universal (scientific) reason'.[18] (Summer 2014)

she: In his geographical story of the development of *geist* Hegel suggests that 'Since the original American nation has vanished – or as good as vanished – the effective population comes for the most part from Europe, and everything that happens in America has its origin there' (Hegel [1861] 1975: 165). By the geographical *there*, he means Europe as the most advanced stage of human development for which America, as an empty land, offers nothing but further resources. The resources he has in mind are not those of human intellect as 'the Americans, then, are like unenlightened children, living from one day to the next, and untouched by higher thoughts or aspirations' (Hegel [1861] 1975: 165), but those of Black slave labour in order to extract energy from plants and minerals because '[t]he weakness of their physique was one of the main reasons why the negroes were brought to America as a labour force; for the negroes are far more susceptible to European culture than the Indians' (Hegel [1861] 1975: 165). In his *The Philosophy of History*, Hegel also maintained that:

> Negroes are enslaved by Europeans and sold to America. Bad as this may be, their lot in their own lands is even worse, since there a slavery quite as absolute exists; for it is the essential principle of slavery, that man has not yet attained a consciousness of his freedom, and consequently sinks down to a mere Thing – an object of no value. (1956: 96)

If the Anthropocene is a story of geological time and the human impact on the deformation of the planet, it 'raises the problem of intersecting scales' (Grusin 2017: 1) of such historic and dialectic conceptions of a geopolitically *empty* 'New World', with the rendition of European subjects as enlightened, and the extractive labour of Black and Indigenous bodies as geologic objects. The British geographer Kathryn Yusoff (2018) thus suggests that:

> The inhuman, as both geologic property and mode of subjective relation in chattel slavery, rendered a coercive interpretation between human and inhuman categories, or what Spillers calls an 'alien intimacy' that predates the 'new' imagined subject of the Anthropocene. Rather, diaspora was a social sedimentation that names the violence of geology in its inception, not as an overlooked aspect of spatial and environmental relation that can be subsequently claimed as mastery over nature and geologic force, but as one that is more properly located in the grammar of geologic determinism established in genocide and the master-slave relation. This master-slave relation is initiated through the geologic praxis of extraction that required both slavery (first for mining) and its continuance as a mode of labour and psychic extraction of pleasure and sadism, which in turn codified Blackness in proximity to the qualities and properties of the inhuman. (57)

In your work, you want to rescue Hegel's Thing, or 'an object of no value' that he 'reads in blackness', in order to move it onto a different scale of reading, one that suggests a radical potential for undoing modern onto-epistemological categories by staying with violence. In your words, 'to find the gifts of the Thing' (Ferreira da Silva 2014a: 529). (Sometime in winter of 2022)

DFdS: 'By their nature, as effects of comparison – that is, measurement and classification – social categories pair *self-determined and affectable (outer-determined) subjects*. In doing so, however, those categories do not erase The Thing's promises. For categories hold violence in the subjects of affectability produced by the biopolitical and disciplinary apparatuses that deploy them – in the black other, the female other, the sexual other, in which other possibilities also hide'.[19] (Sometime in 2014)

she: While for you LI, in Western metaphysics, mother has been erased as a desiring Subject, and is thus founded on the erasure of 'maternal genealogy'[20], severing both the Symbolic and Mythic connection to maternal body, for you DFdS, in the extractive apparatus of 'Coloniality-Patriarchy-Slavery – that is, in accounts of domination, in bondage, marriage, and rape', the Thing (object, Other, commodity) offers promises before and beyond processes of signification/figuring of the 'sexual hosted by the female body'. This excess in the Thing, or the non-Sovereign sexual power, is non-reproductive (in contrast to the reproductive body/place of mother), virtual (as Plenum, free radicals), and refusing representation ' – without the letter and its signification, before writing yet not in speech – ' (Ferreira da Silva 2014a: 534). How can the sexual of female body/place, as excess expressed in the scream – rhythmic, sonic, force of desire before signification – 'open up to considerations of the Otherwise of excess, of the no-value of The Thing' (Ferreira da Silva 2014a: 534)? (Sometime in winter of 2022)

DFdS: 'More importantly, the scream, the expression/exposure without signification – that is, outside signification under the rule of pure reason and its tools (the pure intuitions and categories of the understanding) – makes one wonder. For there is always the possibility that in response to a touch, even one with maximum force, there is no way to state whether the scream refigures pleasure or pain. In that undecidable lies the in/distinction of violence/desire, the one that the body always signifies; and for that reason, modern philosophers have had to work hard to keep it at bay, to deny the body any determining ontological or epistemological role. Tamed, apprehended as a signifier of exteriority, the body in modern Western thought has consistently referred to other ways of existing as human beings, of that which exceeds and hence threatens the accounts of law and morality authorized by sovereign reason'.[21] (Sometime, 2014)

she: You want to decouple the equation of body and space ontology in the apparatus of the Thing? (Sometime in winter of 2022)

DFdS: 'Here I am attending to Moten's invitation to rescue the body from spatiality-exteriority, the signifying moment in which the modern philosophy has imprisoned it, but I do so by returning to the very figure, the colonial (native/slave) female, through which he locates the emergence of resisting black su(o)bject – as a referent of The Thing, with no value (not in knowledge, morality or exchange). The Thing resists as excess'.[22] (Sometime, 2014)

she: Can you give us an example of how to read the Thing, excess without modern categories of Time and Space, exteriority and interiority? (Sometime in winter of 2022)

DFdS: 'Free radicals, as referents of the excess that always already justifies (renders just) racial violence – are that other possibility, which The Thing, between the

I and its objects, others, and commodities, holds and hosts. How is one to recuperate excess? By focusing on the relationship exposed when The Thing is addressed as a mediator and not as a measure. The Thing is no-thing, Hegel tells us. It has no value. Like a virtual particle – without space-time – The Thing signifies the productive immediately/instantaneously registered relationships, violent and otherwise, that constitute our existence'.[23] (Sometime, 2014)

she: While you speak to the Thing as excess (instantaneous, with no value) that resists modern categories, through the figure of 'the colonial (native/slave) female' body, you also speak to a particular arrangement of Time and Space as modern categories sustaining (White) Subject's universality. Interesting for us in terms of Time and schooling, is the question of how do we educate for knowing and understanding without the violence of modern categories that sustain and reproduce this White universality? In contrast to LI's maternal genealogy and feminine dwelling, you speak about the Thing and Blackness's capacity to denounce the fallacy of this arrangement upon which the colonial Subject rests His self-determining authority. You say that Blackness 'lies at the turn of thought'. How can 'Blackness knowing and studying' announce 'the End of the World', and education, 'as we know it' (Ferreira da Silva 2014b: 83–4)? (Sometime in winter of 2022)

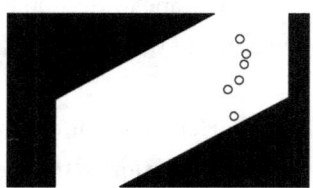

DFdS: I would say that Blackness 'invites a consideration of the possibility of knowing without modern categories' and this is '[b]ecause neither Space nor Time, our fundamental descriptors of the World, seem to be immediately retrievable from universal reason's rather limited stance before the World, Blackness's capacity to signify otherwise – beyond universality and its particular arrangement of Space and Time, but also away from transcendentality (self-determination)'.[24] (Sometime, 2014)

she: Like this text, your work focuses on how the Subject, the Thing that thinks itself, and the World (*res-extensa*), are effects of Thought, universal (scientific) reason's productive tools, but more importantly, how this Grammar of Thought is supported by and functions in 'an ontological context governed by Time' (Ferreira da Silva 2014b: 87). We might say that with your demand to think Blackness alongside Time, like LI's demand for more than one ontology, you push the quest to de-structure the principle of Sameness and Difference at the core of modern episteme radically further.

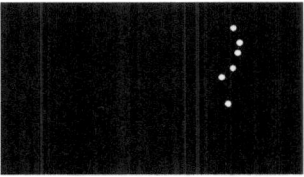

DFdS: 'To be sure, the hope is that the End of the World will emancipate the Thing from Categories (strategies of particularization) as well as from anything that resembles an attempt to give it an Essence (of the teleology of Spirit or the flow that is Duration), whether or not it is modeled after time. . . . The World of Categories, as I claimed above, is always already in Time, of Time. And Time, as one can verify reading Henri Bergson and Martin Heidegger, has managed to survive the critiques that disavow scientific reason's attempts to answer the question of the Being of Man, the Subject, the Human. For this reason, I find that the principle of Sameness and Difference in either its religious or biological formulation is an insufficient point of departure for the question of Blackness. For this reason, I am convinced that a radical departure, one that does not stop at the critique of the formal table of sameness and difference, is in need'.[25] (Sometime, 2014)

she: If you will allow us to paraphrase your thoughts and to think with your Black Feminist Poethics, we might need to break away from focusing on categorizations of Time as a critical praxis in the fields of Human and Social Sciences, Arts and Literature. Instead, you propose we begin from 'a consideration of the Temporalizing of Forms (as Categories)'. In this book, our intention is to begin to make visible how Time works through the Categories we operate within the field of schooling. For example, in discussing Time in the film *Biidaaban* with our pre-service teachers, we try to show them that the Sameness-Difference dialectic at the core of decolonial pedagogies can reproduce racial dialectic, if we do not examine how, as you say, 'Time works through our Categories', how it is inscribed in the onto-epistemological tools that sustain the Subject. As you show, the 'effects of time were not a concern' in the colonial project – 'Natural history's Table of Man deployed the principle of difference and sameness' – which 'coined the racial categories used to this day' (Ferreira da Silva 2014b: 88). In our chapter on time as remediation, we show how the triad child-savage-queer in education exposes an antithesis of progress, that is, 'arrested development' with 'the effect of its articulation as a category of the analytics of radiality' (Ferreira da Silva 2014b: 89). We contrast this Logic with the predominant educational focus on categorizations of Time, for example, pre-posed as a movement of development/change *within* Time (Piaget, Kohlberg); progressing steadily from earlier stages of cognitive and moral development to the more abstract. Why is claiming The Thing important in rupturing this Grammar of Thought? (27 July 2021)

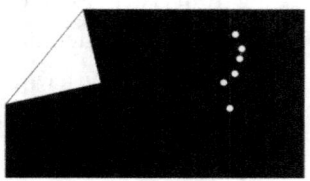

DFdS: 'With this move to claim The Thing – which here refers to Hegel's formulation of it, . . . I am proposing a radically immanent "metaphysical" point of departure inspired by the failures of quantum physics, which expose the fundamental indeterminacy of the reality beyond space-time, at the quantum level, that is the plenum'.[26] (February, 2017)

she: The production of child sociality in school is essentially temporal, in that a student's future self is desired, imagined and mobilized in and through their present positionality in relation to the other. This temporal distance (from the future self and the other) invites a consideration of time pedagogy as a teaching apparatus through which typical (as ideal, desired *for* types) power relations are maintained through deferral into the future conditional, always in time and supported by it. So then, to return to relationality, at the beginning of our conversation, in thinking with feminine dwelling, Blackness, *The Thing* and *plenum*, is it possible to suggest that distance (in contrast to proximity, familiarity) might, paradoxically, simultaneously express a suspension and an opening/movement of time inside the System? In 'On Touching', American feminist philosopher and physicist Karen Barad reiterates the primacy of proximity in the world touching itself:

> Theorizing, a form of experimenting, is about being in touch. What keeps theories alive and lively is being responsible and responsive to the world's patternings and murmurings. Doing theory requires being open to the world's aliveness, allowing oneself to be lured by curiosity, surprise, and wonder. Theories are not mere metaphysical pronouncements on the world from some presumed position of exteriority. Theories are living and breathing reconfigurings of the world. The world theorizes as well as experiments with itself. (Barad [2012] forthcoming: 1–2)

Such an exposition, we could say, is a Whiteheadian 'lure for feeling'; it evokes affect, mesmerizing images of the world's proximity in its 'patternings and murmurings', a 'living', 'breathing', 'aliveness'. It sets out premises and lays out conclusions, without much work being demanded on the part of the reader. What it does not do, is pose a functional limit, that is, it does not limit the questions and problems thus posed, and not otherwise. It takes a *view* of an assumed world's aliveness, but does not define spatio-temporal part-whole relations. That is, when the 'world's aliveness' is presupposed and the problems and questions of 'touching theorizing' not declared as parts for this particular quantum 'aliveness' only, without a functional limit, what is lured in advance is a certain affective and easy comfort in assuming that thought and the outside of thought are somehow always already proximate and embodied. The marked term in this topological exposition becomes that which is opposed or condemned in the name of such proximate, living, breathing, intra-connected whole, namely distance, detachment.

While Barad pursues the possibility of touch touching itself, LI, you are known for your interest in *self-affection*, embodied by the image of two-lips-touching. Self-affection is an inside–outside mucous operation that makes possible relations with the Other (including the self), and that requires a new 'space-time of the middle-passive voice' (Irigaray 2008: 128). Would the idea of Radical Immanence demand that we therefore *not* begin by assuming a spatio-temporal relation of necessary proximity, a relation that can always be reduced, subsumed, appropriated, negated by its terms, the One or the Other? (25 July 2021)

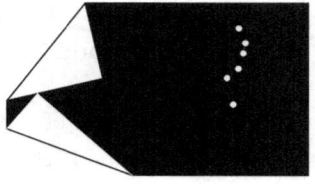

LI: *She laughs before she continues*: the self-affection, proximity if you will, that would not reduce a given relation to either of its terms, has not yet been invented. 'It is not only by that which surrounds us that we have to be touched. Or, at least, such an affect must be accompanied by self-affection, which puts it into perspective. Even if the world, the other or others can question this self-affection, they cannot, for all that, substitute themselves for it. Now it is this that our culture commonly suggests to us as an economy of affect, indeed, as an ethical model. Which makes intersubjectivity impossible, except as a co-belonging to the same world and not as a relating between subjects'.[27] (Sometime in 2008)

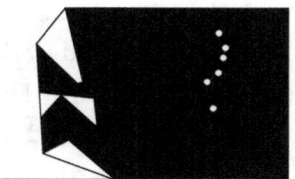

DFdS: 'Framed in such a humble position, pre-posed by (before and toward) Man, a Poetic engagement with humanity begins with affectability (relationality, contingency, immediacy), and can only announce the constitutive relation. Between the past and future, the old and new, asking the question of the World, toward the End of the Subject's apprehension of it, interrupts the desperate reaction-of the questioned before a line seemingly caught in a deadly knot. Born into a World it cannot claim as its own, the Subject participates in the eternal present; oscillating, vibrating, as if stuck: in/to the World, the life of the Subject becomes a here, a position, a context that all but ignores the story of change, of progress, or development'.[28] (Spring, 2014)

LI: Yes. Another way to think of relationality is through distance and proximity, Time and Space, which is, I think, what you are asking here. I would say that we need to begin with Space and place. 'The other stands in a space that I will never occupy. Through this, he or she eludes my relation to spatiality. What was familiar to me in the perception of space is disconcerted by the presence of the other. Unless I include this other within my world, which annuls them as other. Moreover, the other moves in space, and this prevents me from assigning to him, or her, a place where they would in some way be at my disposal... The fact that the other stands in a space inaccessible to me and that the other does not stay in place fixed by me, or at least for me, means that nearness here is also always remoteness. Even when sitting at my side or present in front of me, the other remains distant, strange to me – the other does not dwell in my word. The privilege of the same with respect to the other, the fact that most of the time the other is considered as an other-same or an other-of-the-same can be explained by the difficulty of calling into question the familiarity of the space in which I dwell'.[29] (Sometime in 2008)

The one and the other cannot be at the same place at the same time, but can be at the same place at different times, spaced out and timed in by *breath*, which is 'a vehicle both of proximity and of distancing, of fidelity and of destiny, of life and of cultivation... The near becomes one's own, through air. If breathing estranges me from the other, this gesture also signifies a sharing with the world that surrounds me and with the community that inhabits it. Food and even speech can be assimilated, partially become mine. It is not the same for air. I can breathe in my own way, but the air will never simply be mine'.[30] (Sometime in 2001)

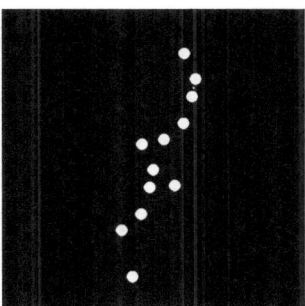

DFdS: 'Because without Desire, the object, the other, and the commodity dissolve; thus released from the grips of the Subjectum, the World is emancipated from universal reason, and other possible ways of knowing and doing can be contemplated without the charge of irrationality, mysticism, or idle fantasy'.[31] (Summer 2014)

she: And of familiarity of Time that offers Him support and protection? (25 July 2021)

LI: Well, '[i]f the other is situated in the same world as me, or if I can imagine the world where the other dwells, this other no longer upsets the familiarity that I experience towards my surrounding space. Then the *epoché* of the perception of space – but also of imagination – that the other imposes on me as other becomes groundless. Which suspends the transcendental dimension needed in the meeting with the other – including at the level of imagination. An imagination that remains silent, it is true, but which restores a virgin space, still devoid of familiarity, and even of orientation, other than an availability to the other as other. And moreover, to me, as a being beyond an undifferentiated but oriented world'.[32] (Sometime in 2008)

she: It is interesting, the phrase you use – '*epoché* of the perception of space' – could you say a bit more about the word *epoché* in this context of spatial perception? (25 July 2021)

LI: Yes. I draw here from the Greek etymology of the word *epokhe*, meaning '"stoppage, fixed point of time", from *epekhein* "to pause, take up a position", from *epi* "on" (see **epi-**) + *ekhein* "to hold"'.[33] The pause, or suspension of the *epoché* – fixed temporal hold, or position – that His perception of Space imposes on me as other, would give me freedom. 'One could speak here of a transcendental freedom, or of a freedom in relation to transcendence. This freedom is mine.' It is not 'sharable as such. At least not directly. It is even the renunciation of an immediate sharing that permits me to discover and safeguard it. In the space thus opened, or uncovered, the distance from the other cannot be overcome. I cannot bring the other close to me – the distance between us is insurmountable. I can get closer to the other, long for their transcendence, if this is safeguarded and kept, without being able to appropriate it'.[34] (Sometime in 2008)

She: What would this freedom from *epoché* look like? Is it possible to leave the Kategoria of Space and Time for the manifestation of otherness? (25 July 2021)

LI: Like DFdS's *The Thing*, or Leibniz's Plenum, I would suggest we 'enter another space in which the field of attraction and orientation no longer obeys a single focus ... which makes the field of attractions and orientations complex. Which also makes it irreducible if each one maintains one's desire as one's own with respect to a different desire'.³⁵ (Sometime in 2008)

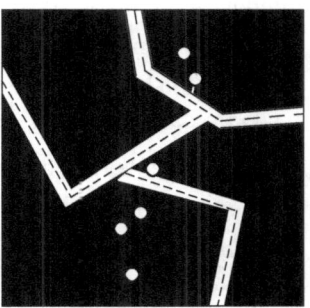

DFdS: 'Exposing time as it is inscribed in the onto-epistemological tools that sustain the Subject recalls its worldly-ness without the primacy of temporality. Born into the world, Édouard Glissant states, the Subjectum is immediately caught in constitutive relationships, which point to an "absolute elsewhere", another place which is not his-of Man's or of its late twentieth-century ethical rendering, the Human's. Time as a here violates the most basic truths of history and science, as imagined by the Western philosophical tradition exemplified by Kant and Hegel, for instance'.³⁶ (Summer, 2014). It is important to explain, that 'When a relationship is ascribed it generally takes its shape from identity or effectivity: events are related because they are of the same kind or in terms of cause and effect. On the other hand, concepts and categories describe what happens in a way that rehearses the workings of spatiality, descriptions of what happens in time. Indeed, spatiality is refigured when (a) what is simultaneous is comprehended in terms of variety or a modality; or (b) when what is successive consists in a stage in the progression, retrogression, or disappearance of a particular existent. What I am proposing, then, is that decolonization requires descriptions of events and existents that violate separability in both instances, without rehearsing the Hegelian Same.' (Summer, 2022).³⁷

she: Can you say more about Time as a here? How do we put an end to the World of Time?

DFdS: 'Temporality as a here, nevertheless, also resonates with the most basic assumption of modern knowledge, with the view introduced in modern philosophy by Kant that time is nothing else but a pure intuition, a tool of the senses, which allows the understanding – that region of the mind where knowing (as reflection) takes place to grasp as form that which occurs in the world, in the mind itself, in interiority. If the World has and has not changed; if it is always all at once, if it is no longer the playground of Time, interiority itself cannot but be located; it too becomes a here, a place; in space, a position from which the World might be engaged. That is, Time has no priority in the quest for the Being of that which is in the World. Further, as the privileged Subject of History and Knowledge (Heidegger's sole entity that asks the question of being) is a thing of time, of temporality. In sum, the Subject, the historical entity, the interior/temporal thing, becomes a place, located in space, nothing more than the name for a position in the World of Space and Time. Nevertheless, from without Time, as a Category assembled in the Stage of Science (exteriority/spatiality), Blackness releases the Subject into the World to put an end to the World of Time where the racial dialectic makes sense. Whatever manner one decides to go about accomplishing the task – releasing the Subject, Man, to the World, and from Time – it would have to begin with a fracturing of Hegel's and Marx's versions of dialectics itself, and its sequestering of Space in the unfolding of time'.[38] (Summer, 2014)

she: And just like you both, contra Hegel, Whitehead as well avoids confronting Thought directly, but instead confronts its grammar, the structure of its possibilities: 'Philosophy is the ascent to the generalities, with the view to understanding their possibilities of combination. The discovery of new generalities thus adds to the fruitfulness of those already known. It lifts into view new possibilities of combination' (Whitehead [1933] 1967: 235).

DFdS: 'Ending the grip of Time restores the World anew, from the position Blackness registers – that is, the halted temporality that preempts recognition and opens the World as Plenum, becomes a *Canvas Infinita*, where the Subject figures without Time, stuck in the endless play of expression, with the rest of us. Without Reflection (the distinguishing attribute of Kant's subject of knowledge) and Recognition (the final moment of Hegel's subject of morality), both the account of poesis that creates the World as the product of the Subject's Desire (that is, its auto-actualization) and the account of ethics that demands that the World become the fulfillment of this Desire (its actualization) become unwelcome. In the Plenum, Refraction, as everything mirrors everything else in the "Play of Expression", becomes the descriptor for Existence, as what exists becomes only and always a rendering of possibilities, which remain exposed in the horizon of Becoming'.[39] (Summer, 2014)

:

In the plenum, there are new temporalities, ones that do not obey the natural order of evolution, of progress, of moral development. When temporalizing becomes an abstract enterprise, we return to the universals of univocal time lines. In her 'Equation of Value', Ferreira da Silva (2017) offers a unique temporalizing that addresses the particularities of the value of black life. She argues that the question of why Black lives do not matter hides the question it answers. It relies on the equation of the universal and the formal by creating the category of Blackness, which figures the operation of efficient and formal causes in the production of an abstractly temporalized racial subject destined to be obliterated.

In the nineteenth century, the notions of racial and cultural differences are manufactured in knowledge procedures that produce physical and social configurations as effects and causes of mental differences. Man is the universal gauge, because he alone has determination, as per Kant. Determination is a task for the mind. Determinacy is at the core of modern thought. Knowing is reduced to determinacy, which involves the assignation of a value that refers to a universal. And the objects of knowledge are those which can be produced through measurement and classification. In other words, the very arsenal designed to determine and to ascertain the truth of human difference has already assumed Whiteness as the universal measure. It follows that there are a plethora of effects that are then ascribed to the cause of racial difference.

Here, the laws of arithmetic are used as abstract machines to 'explore [the] potential of blackness to unsettle ethics' (Ferreira da Silva 2017: 8). Ferreira da Silva shows Blackness's capacity to unravel modern time-as-arrow thought without reproducing the violence housed in Western concepts of knowledge. Setting life (whiteness) equal to 1 and not-life (Blackness) to 0, she computes. 0 added to or subtracted from itself is still 0. 0 multiplied by anything is still 0; multiplication reproduces itself. But division turns out to be a generative operation. Arithmetically speaking, it is impossible to divide by 0. Diving by 2 leaves half. Dividing anything by 1 leaves itself. Dividing by 1/2 leaves twice more. Dividing by 1/10 leaves 10 lots more. Dividing by a million leaves a huge amount. Dividing by 0, though, is undefined. Too much to count. Too much on which to operate. Excessive. Incompossable with the timeline, with the logic of evolution. In mathematics, the term used is 'undefined'. This is how Ferreira da Silva achieves the indeterminacy that refuses to contain Blackness, within the system. Blackness has the power to unsettle the ethical programme governed by determinacy, by exposing the violence that the juridical modalities refigure.

We like Alfred North Whitehead's mereotopological 'structure of possibilities' (rather than determinacy and necessity) in thinking with DFdS and LI. Both DFdS and LI expose the radical force of establishing different structural possibilities/departures, such as DFdS's immanent 'metaphysical' *The Thing, plenum* and LI's *field of attractions*. These *guides for imagination* beyond Space-time (as a particular colonial and patriarchal Grammar of Thought conditioned on the Category of Blackness) enable us to think relationality through a very particular metaphysics of part and whole relations. If current spatial imaginaries assume rigid borders between parts and wholes – with the latter enclosing the former, subsuming it and therefore establishing a top-down determinacy – Whitehead's mereotopology abandoned the linear part-whole relation of set theory in favour of a superpositioning of parts and whole, where each part *is* a whole *and* a part within that whole. In other words, for Whitehead, a British philosopher and mathematician, the matter is one of being obligated by what is at stake in our ways of thinking. The question then becomes: What does educational discourse proclaim for its field and what does it maintain is outside the proclaimed? Outside, either because it refuses to proclaim or because the way the field operationalizes the already proclaimed prevents it both from perceiving and expressing its non-proclaimed.

We call this a mereotopological matrix of relations of parts and wholes (a non-metrical or philosophical theory of extension). Whitehead was convinced that set theory, the prevailing foundational theory on which he himself had worked with Bertrand Russell, was inadequate to this philosophy, since it was based on the idea of an abstract set (e.g. the set of all barbers) and the relation of inclusion with its members (the barber cutting your hair). Indeed, set theory invites thinking of the abstract collection, the 'universe' and all actual occasions as members existing side-by-side in that collection, all advancing along a single, shared timeline. In a mereotopological matrix of relations, each individual level of generality (there are three levels of generality in *Process and Reality*: theory of actual occasions, theory of perception and theory of propositions or symbolic reference) has a view of the 'whole' (coordinate result of genetic specifications) but it is the 'entities' appropriate to each level of generality that the whole is analysed into. These levels of generality into which the whole may be analysed are parallel levels so that there is no need to assert their unity or identity (as with the barbers). And the whole takes on a different character at various levels of generality. For example, Whitehead's perceptions (one level of generality) and their objects and the modes of relation between them are parts in a 'whole' as articulated by the theory of perception. Now, the same whole would be called either 'nature' as exemplified in science when the genetic specification on a certain level of generality is measurement, but it would be called 'beauty' as exemplified in art, when the genetic specification is affect. What Whitehead's mereotopological schema enables him to do in his creative formalization of a given inquiry, is to specify precisely for this inquiry and no other, the coordinate and the genetic analysis and its functional limit.

> Nothing suffices to the disaster; this means that just as it is foreign to the ruinous purity of destruction, so the idea of totality cannot delimit it. If all things were reached by it and destroyed – all gods and men returned to absence – and if nothing were substituted for everything, it would still be too much and too little. (Blanchot [1980] 1986: 3)

Exhibit 3B: Time and Transdisciplinary Research on Touch in Education

When Barad ([2012] forthcoming) postulates in 'On Touching' the outside of thought as that which is 'aliveness' and 'murmurings', this is aligned with her philosophy of agential realism. Barad specifies the genetic elements of her analysis (for example, intra-agential relata) on a particular level of generalization as exemplified in science (touch from the perspective of quantum physics) but also on that of (queer) epistemology so that her onto-epistemological method merges or touches different levels of generalization and thus different genetic specifications (measurement, percepts, affects), wherein the 'whole' (the coordinate result of genetic specifications) may or may not satisfy her 'universal' – 'The inhuman I'. The inhuman is thought of in her paper as 'an infinite intimacy that touches the very nature of touch, that which holds open the space of the liveliness of indeterminacies that bleed through the cuts and inhabit the between of particular entanglements', wherein 'all matter is always already a dynamic field of matterings' and thus 'the play of quantum in/determinacies deconstructs not only the metaphysics of presence and the metaphysics of individualism but also anything like the possibility of separating them' (Barad ([2012] forthcoming: 13). If the Cartesian Cogito is now ostracized as detached, transcendental, machinic and inhuman, it might be possible to say that Barad's Cogito is still inhuman, but without distance; it is indeterminate but lively, self-touching and quantum.

There are now many scholars in Education who draw from Barad in their research, particularly those who are oriented towards new materialism. Their conclusions might eventually forge long-term effects in the field of education. Our project in this book is to show the importance of thinking with, and exposing, how educational theories can reproduce racial and sexist dialectic, if we do not examine how Time works through the particular (psychological, scientific) Categories we work with in Education.

For example, in Barad, an assumed fundamental proximity or self-touching of the dynamic field that is matter and the impossibility of distance (phenomenal, theoretical or metaphysical) is (a) posited as the relation par excellence and not bound only to a particular problematic, at a particular level of generalization in a particular coordinate whole; and (b) it disables any possibility for philosophy, if we agree with Whitehead, that philosophy does not confront art or nature directly, but confronts the structure of their possibilities. Such is the role of creative formalism that sustains the necessary distance of philosophy. Our objection is not to her 'quantum theory of touching' as such, for it is an interesting and novel way to approach the problematic of theory as well as of touch. Our objection is the recognition that even if, for example, 'touch events', 'theory events' and 'quantum events', are all intra-connected 'events', exemplified differently on different scales, what gets lost in entangling them in embodied proximity, is precisely the fact that some bodies live in the 'world without the protections of Space-time, but with all its limitations', 'existing in bodies that have not delinked from the plenum' (Ferreira da Silva 2014b: 93). Barad's quantum intra-agential-proximity can be contrasted with Ferreira da Silva's quantum *The Thing*. Both Barad and Ferreira da Silva propose a materialist reading, but Ferreira da Silva's plenum reverberates 'indifferent, passive universality, the Also of the many properties or rather "matters" that is, something that which in everything does come before consciousness and its tools because it is no longer once it is apprehended in Space-time' (Ferreira da Silva 2014b: 93). By contrast to Barad's necessary/causal intra-agential relationality, Ferreira da Silva assumes an opening of movement/time without proximity in *The Thing*: 'For this kind

> of transversability – the at-once crossing of physical and emotional lines of separation, real and imagined – to be imaginable, one needs to contemplate at a level at which everything can become and that such becoming *and not* affects anything or anyone else' (Ferreira da Silva 2014b: 93).
>
> What Ferreira da Silva's *The Thing* (virtuality that does not name or index; rather, it is offered as a 'guide for the imagination') invites us to examine is a mereotopological matrix of relations; 'movements possible because of the connections that precede time and space, but which operate in time and space: transversability assumes the existence of lines that run parallel but which can be transversed by another line – which might as well be an indentation in the fabric Space-time-through which the "Play of Express" efflux; transversability, the moving back and forth to different points in time, assumes linear causality, the existence of different points in time, but does not obey its limitation, which is efficient causality, that is, the idea that an effect cannot precede a cause . . . ; transubstantiality, finally, becomes a possibility as . . . break[ing] through the formal lines of space inscribed by our categories (of body, of species, of genus)' (Ferreira da Silva 2014b: 93).

Schools, as providers of public service, are accountable to various stakeholders. The theoretical and empirical research methodology supporting, furthering and validating its public service leans heavily on other humanities fields, most prominently that of psychology. For example, the logic of cause and effect is transversed into education not only through theories of child moral and cognitive development but also an expectation of steady (healthy) growth towards a 'fully' functioning, fulfilled and happy citizen, whose value is determined by and depends on their ability to perform their presupposed use in the society at large. But what if, guided by lines that can be transversed by another line, dys-synchronizing cause and effect from its predetermined directionality in Time – the field of education could develop its very own disciplinary and context-specific (coordinate whole) 'structure of possibilities', freed from the apparatus of Desire for the 'good life' (necessarily deferred in future conditional tense)? What if we declared precisely what kinds of learning, quotidian and indeterminate pedagogical matters matter for the educational field, and how? Based on its very own coordinate whole of possibles and impossibles? Not from, by or for, but at a radical distance with

– *parallel/alongside/contrasting* the psychological, developmental, scientific, patriarchal, colonial, heteronormative, economic, juridical, cultural goals and objectives. Mundane, quotidian, inhuman, ordinary, opaque, absent, dull, lingering, megalomaniac, distant, crowdy, evading, defiant, messy – these might be just some of the modes of complex being and doing in school that call out trespassing of 'proper' boundaries and embellish the diverse spectrum of existence rarely accounted for and researched in educational and curricular theory premised on growth, use, change and the good (and drawing on and from empirical studies in the field of psychology).

While schooling itself functions as an oppressive instrument of the status quo, for it is conditioned and premised on a very particular idea of Time, we want to sustain a provocation that does not preclude us from considering impossible possibilities for schooling by refusing to reduce students to objects of growth and change consumed by Time. We wish to disrupt the equation of Time with structures of domination by inviting readers/students in the field of education to become fabulators, witnesses to time freed from the disciplinary *World of Categories*, creating a time pedagogy that obligates a response, a confrontation, a pause – an encounter that requires uncomfortable work; respecting the limits of the Archive while rupturing the passive dynamic between Subjects in/of Time and His Archive of possible Being and Becoming.

:

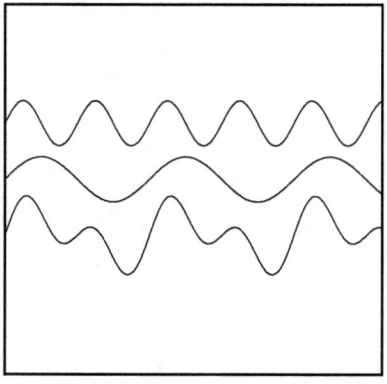

Lies 1: There is only the present and nothing to remember.

(Jeanette Winterson)[1]

4

Repetition

Escaping the Fugitive Present with Lefebvre and Hartman

In the Thai film director Apichatpong Weerasethakul's (2021) movie *Memoria*, Jessica suddenly starts hearing a strange, loud thump every once in a while. She visits a musician, Hernán, and asks him to recreate the sound digitally, which he does. And then he disappears. Later, Jessica meets an older man, named Hernán (who might be a reincarnation of the musician), who tells Jessica that he has never left his village. When she asks why, he explains that he remembers everything that has happened to him there and does not want to risk being overwhelmed by memories of other places. Jessica then begins to remember things, but it is not clear to whom the memories belong.

:

Figure Organism: Repetition

Formal education (*ēducāre*), in its spatio-temporal image of rearing and nurturing, is represented by figures in the image of an Organism, the most obvious one being the Child. An Organism, as an autopoietic system of organic sexual reproduction and self-maintenance, is fundamentally a temporal figure – all the individual parts of an Organism *reproduce* local birth and death in order to sustain the whole, as a sum of these temporal, sexual, perishing local events. While Organism can be said to be a temporal figure of reason, Time becomes an organismal figure when it begins to operate exclusively on the premise of an already actualized, phallic, explosive movement of a reproductive copula. As an organic necessity of futural, or forward movement, such Time is presupposed in the Organism's matrix of self-sustenance of local finitude for global permanence and change. It operates without us – tic-toc, tic-toc – but is also bound to us, as our Common Time. We need Time to figure us, to shape us as organisms that can live, like Hernán, without a change in space, but not without a change in time, that is, without memory.

This is why, as American queer theory scholar Valerie Rohy (2006) suggests, in '[g]oing back in memory, we build a history that anticipates what is to come, a history that will in time forget its own retrospective construction and assume the naturalized status of linear temporality' (68), which forecloses queer possibilities. By contrast, non-capital T *time* is an inhuman, non-copulative sexual rhythm, a non-actualized continuum of superimposed, rhythmic absences (past, present, future), always already quantic and coeval. In the first part of this chapter, we hint at the problem of ontologizing either Time or time, that is, either the continuous or the discontinuous, the organic or the non-organic, eternal or rhythmic Time, via Nietzsche and Lefebvre. In the second part, we read with a scholar of African-American literature Saidiya Hartman to glimpse at other temporal figures/possibles. We conclude by asking the following questions: What is the share of violence in education's continuous organismal re-actualization? And to what other figures might the field of education refer?

In the field of education, we make use of the concept of *curre* to represent an objective counterpart in the world, namely the passage of time – indeed, like a current – in the world beyond human mind/experience. With curriculum conceived as a programme with history, temporal and causal order of successive developmental stages, and change, students and teachers adhere to time-frames decided in advance, repeating the pre-established epistemological and axiological regime of signification, and enacting the patterned division of time into the slotted periods: measured, operationalized, managed. This predetermined Time regime is conditioned on, and justifies, the repetition of subservience, discipline and compliance. The notion of school Time as both the repetition of predetermined successive learning stages and the cyclical repetition of passage of Time *out there*, governs the power configuration of schools because it institutes moral zones and ethical ideals of the already established, tested and objective regimes of schooling. In this chronological framework, 'anticipations of education circulate and repeat staid habits of both educational practices and temporalities, often under the pretense of a 'promising future' (Webb, Sellar, and Gulson 2020: 290).

When the German philosopher Fredrich Nietzsche embraced death with an affirmative and existential yes, he conditioned his affirmation on a qualitative notion of repetition – much like French philosopher Henri Bergson embraced duration – but without assuming human consciousness to be the ground of the qualitative succession of the ebb and flow of time. Rather, for Nietzsche, consciousness was put to the test by an eternal return of the monstrous outside:

> This world: a monster of energy, without beginning, without end; a firm, iron magnitude of force that does not grow bigger or smaller, that does not expend itself but only transforms itself . . . a sea of forces flowing and rushing together, eternally changing, eternally flooding back, with tremendous years of recurrence, with an ebb and a flow of its forms; out of the simplest forms striving toward the most complex, out of the stillest, most rigid, coldest forms toward the hottest, most turbulent, most self-contradictory, and then again returning home to the simple out of this abundance . . . without goal, unless the joy of the circle is itself a goal. (Nietzsche 1968: 1067)

In his book *The Gay Science*, which was published in 1882, Nietzsche proposed that any particular event will eventually repeat itself – every single detail of the event, down to the tone of voice, the hue, the humidity – and continue to do so in a cyclic manner. For Nietzsche, the proposal had ethical consequences: a good life was one you would be proud of having to repeat (repeatedly). The French mathematician and philosopher Henri Poincaré (1890) turned the proposal into equations, formulating the *recurrence theorem*, which states that in certain physical systems, such as the solar system, each particular configuration of the system will eventually repeat itself (the popularity of Rube Goldberg-like kinetic sculptures, like the one outside Science World in Vancouver, attests to our fascination with Nietzsche's proposition).

The recurrence theorem is a statistical argument based on the assumption that atoms move in random ways, and that any one microstate is equally as likely to occur as another. For example, imagine rolling two dice and obtaining a five and a three. If you roll sufficiently many times, you will obtain this configuration again. Now imagine rolling five dice, as in Yahtzee. You can still obtain a particular configuration again, say, five, five, three, three, three, but it will *likely* take longer. It turns out that *recurrence time* – the amount of time for any configuration to return to its starting position – can be measured, but for any macroscopic-sized object, it is longer than the age of the universe. This doesn't mean that Nietzsche was wrong. Time might still be cyclic, even if the ethical consequences could hardly motivate a mere mortal.

But even if we agree that there will be a repeating cycle, this doesn't help us determine how the cycle begins. At the time of Poincaré, the idea of the Big Bang (which is hypothesized to have occurred 14 billion years ago) had not yet been introduced, which meant that thinking of time as eternal, as never starting or stopping, was considered reasonable. The idea of infinitely long time would therefore not have been incommensurable with extremely long cycles. With the Big Bang, however, the idea of *the* origin upsets the possibility of infinitely long time. The idea of origin, $t = 0$, is also relevant to an important law in physics: Newton's Second Law of Thermodynamics, which states that entropy never decreases over time. Entropy is what measures the amount of disorder in a system. An intact egg is more ordered than a whisked one. Since there are more disorderly states than orderly ones (just think about all the ways in which your living room could be arranged, or the files on your desktop), entropy also provides a measure of time in the sense that the past is that which is more ordered relative to the present, and the future is that which is less so. The problem, which Poincaré himself identified in the 1890s, is that if entropy is always increasing, how would a cycle be possible – that is, how could disorder be reversed so as to recover the intact egg? The Austrian physicist Ludwig Boltzmann rescued the contradiction by re-interpreting the Second Law of Thermodynamics, shifting it from being an absolute law of the universe, to being a statistical one – a move that lay the groundwork for quantum physics. Boltzmann argued that Poincaré's mathematical theory was indeed possible, but it was just a theory, and one based on assumptions about infinity; anything can happen given enough time. The *actual* happenings of the real world, according to Boltzmann, should be described in the language of statistics, which tracks real-time, increasing entropy.

But maybe the Big Bang isn't the absolute beginning. Maybe, to rescue Nietzsche and Poincaré, it's a local beginning and part of a cycle of beginnings in which the universe moves from low entropy to high entropy.

> 'Well, I'd hardly finished the first verse,' said the Hatter, 'when the Queen bawled out "He's murdering the time! Off with his head!"'
> 'How dreadfully savage!' exclaimed Alice.

> *'And ever since that,' the Hatter went on in a mournful tone, 'he won't do a thing I ask! It's always six o'clock now.'*
> *A bright idea came into Alice's head. 'Is that the reason so many tea-things are put out here?' she asked.*
> *'Yes, that's it,' said the Hatter with a sigh: 'it's always tea-time, and we've no time to wash the things between whiles.'*
> *'Then you keep moving round, I supposed?' said Alice.*
> *'Exactly so,' said the Hatter: 'as the things get used up.'*
> *'But when you come to the beginning again?' Alice ventured to ask.*
> (Lewis Carroll)[2]

Would you not throw yourself down and gnash your teeth and curse the demon who spoke thus? . . . If this thought gained possession of you, it would change you as you are or perhaps crush you. The question in each and every thing, 'Do you desire this once more and innumerable times more?' would lie upon your actions as the greatest weight. . . . Or how well disposed would you have to become to yourself and to life to crave nothing more fervently than this ultimate eternal confirmation and seal? (Nietzsche [1882] 1974: Aphorism 341)

Nietzsche contrasted here the homogeneous and technical form of education, characterized by mechanical repetition of measurement and extension, to repetition as intensity and quality of force. The thought of eternal return confronts one with 'a sea of forces' and their transforming relations, an image that refuses to abstract forces out of particular forms. Although still reactive, a student in an educational system operating on time narrativized and operationalized by qualitative repetition of cosmic time would be expected to play the game of schooling well, if they affirmed the roll of the dice. In other words, such a student would not hope for the best (predetermined) possible outcome but would embrace the creative chance of successes and failures as a single dice-throw, inviting forth the many different possible educational futures (a mode of chance creativity already practised by many students in role-playing video games). A Nietzschean educational programme might shift focus away from such educational chronotopes as becoming-worker (fully functioning citizens in the 'segrenomic' workforce (Rooks 2017)), becoming-good (leading a good neoliberal life of consumerism), or, becoming-bad (doing time in prison). This might involve an educational programme more committed to pauses, displacements, teleportations and reversals, than to staying the course.

Students break time already, without (or despite) school's help. They put their headphones on to tune out their teacher and classmates; they skip class; they daydream. Teachers break time too. They might opt to read aloud yet one more story and so create a quiet, collective pause. They might, also, invite students to study the last chapter of the textbook first; to study the history of oxygen in chemistry class; lives of neutrinos in literature class. The French novelist Alexandre Jardin opens his autobiography *Chaque femme est un roman* (2008) with a story about his high school mathematics teacher. On the first day of class, she asked his classmate Tristan an algebra question, which she described as the object of study for the course. He responded. She said, 'Dismissed! You're dismissed, go to the playground!' When asked what he had done wrong, the teacher responded, 'You answered the question correctly'. She went on to explain that she didn't see the point of making Tristan sit in the classroom if he had already mastered the topic, adding that in her books, those that are dismissed are the good ones. Three weeks later, Jardin had also mastered the topic – being dismissed having suddenly become attractive.

Now you might say that organized schooling already leaves so many, but particularly marginalized students, to chance, that chance is a dangerous concept to pursue in a world of social and climate inequity, systemic racism, sexism, classism, ableism and environmental degradation. For Nietzsche, a negation ethics of chance, in which we must choose between one option or the other – heads or tails – is inherently representational and reactive-oppressive. By contrast, a counter-dialectic, affirmational ethics of chance allows multiple options to co-exist; it admits options not yet on the table – heads or tails or rolling on the edge. Such an ethics is inherently immanent, non-reactive and dynamic. It entails death, self-destruction of the reactive and of the human, by an active destruction of 'strong spirits which destroy the reactive in themselves, submitting it to the test of the eternal return and submitting themselves to this test even if it entails willing their own decline' (Deleuze [1962] 2006: 70).

> This is one of the most liberating adult lessons, isn't it: that point when you see that everything that was insisted upon, passed down to you as an inflexible rule, was made up. For me, in real time, learning this looked like hacking my own past to find me at five, seven, ten years old. As always, upside down in a song, backflipping into a painting, teleporting into a film, gathering my pieces one by one – especially the ones I'd been told made me too strange for the world. I've been growing younger on purpose because I have the most to

teach me about how to keep alive in the wake of an evaporating reality, how to make edible joy from scratch, how to make friends inside a doll house, a vacation out of a train set, a safe house out of Lego blocks. A younger me has things to teach me about faith, about believing the yet unseen. I've been sitting next to her a lot. (Osunde 2021)

All the forces cast in the throw of the dice are affirmed at once. The god's-eye view of schooling implies an ironic understanding of all identities of space and time as laid out in linear events, where what is being repeated is the identity of the self-referential same. Think of predetermined cognitive developmental stages of learning, division of students by age and calendar year, division of learning into primary concrete and secondary abstract learning. These are the grid-like space-time coordinates of representational conceptions of difference and repetition. By contrast, as French philosopher Gilles Deleuze suggests, eternal return could suggest a process of immanent becoming on its own terms, an affirmation of a will to power in which all identities have been dissolved – all things named, listed, partitioned. Thus the only identity affirmed is that of the returning itself, a dynamic becoming which continuously repeats the production of difference as a 'practical selection among differences according to their capacity to produce – that is, to return or to pass the test of the eternal return' (Deleuze [1968] 1994: 41).

When I asked what she was reading, she told me Malorie Blackman. She asked what I've been up to, what we ended up becoming, if she would really be needing maths, if we did everything on time. I told her to forget the maths and hold on to the stories, that there are no clocks in my house, that we live a life where we get to move by the senses – rain sounds in the bedroom all through harmattan, night on repeat between the walls while the sun hangs high outside. I told her that when I couldn't see my way into the life I wanted, I wrote it down, I vision-boarded it using photographs and films and paintings like she taught me. Her mouth slackened as I told her how many hours I spent looking at Manuja Waldia's paintings three years ago when I lost my head, because the paintings showed me beautiful people around a stunning table, all fed and loved and chosen and happy – that's what I had needed the most. I told her that in my home, in the space where I live, I have that dining table now; that it became real because I saw it in color; that it took me a long time to accept our inability to tell the difference, but that she was right, the table inside a painting is as real as the table inside your house. (Osunde 2021)

Daydreaming temporalities. No resistance of knowledge and belief. Dreams of a table in its virtuality, as a process of becoming of continuity before it gets its structure and form. A temporality in which you can sit still with the coming together of a table.

What returns, repeats or instaurates[3] again anew, are not things identical to things passed, but 'the fact of returning for that which differs' (Deleuze [1962] 2006: 48). This is why Deleuze thinks of the eternal return as a synthesis; 'a synthesis of time and its dimensions, a synthesis of diversity and its reproduction, a synthesis of becoming and the being which is affirmed in becoming, a synthesis of double affirmation' ([1962] 2006: 48).

> The cyclical is generally of cosmic origin; it is not measured in the same way as the linear. The numbering systems best suited to it are duodecimal, which is to say base twelve: the twelve months of the year, the twelve hours of the clock-face, the 360° of the circumference (a multiple of twelve), the twelve signs of the zodiac and even a dozen eggs or oysters, which means to say that the measure by twelve extends itself to living matter in direct provenance from nature. Cyclical rhythms, each having a determined period or frequency, are also the rhythms of beginning again: of the 'returning' which does not oppose itself to the 'becoming', we could say, modifying a phrase of René Crevel. (Lefebvre [1992] 2004: 90)

If it is not 'measured in the same way', how is it measured? School mathematics teaches us that measurement relies on counting units, which involves comparing a standard unit (like a centimetre, as marks on a ruler) to the thing-to-be-measured. This works well for the classical dimensions: centimetres for lengths, acres for areas, gallons for volume, etc. But what if we have to measure what falls in between these dimensions? How do you measure the hours that it took for fifty minutes of math class to pass? In its speculative way, mathematics has explored some inter-dimensional ways of thinking measure. In fractal geometry, for example, there are shapes that exist between integer dimensions, like the Koch curve shown in Figure 4.1. This curve exceeds the one-dimensionality of a line without popping up to the two-dimensionality of a plane.

The Koch curve is created by starting with a line, then punching a little triangular roof in the middle of the line, and then taking each of the four new line segments thus formed and punching an even littler triangular roof into each. This process is repeated, iteratively, infinitely many times. Even

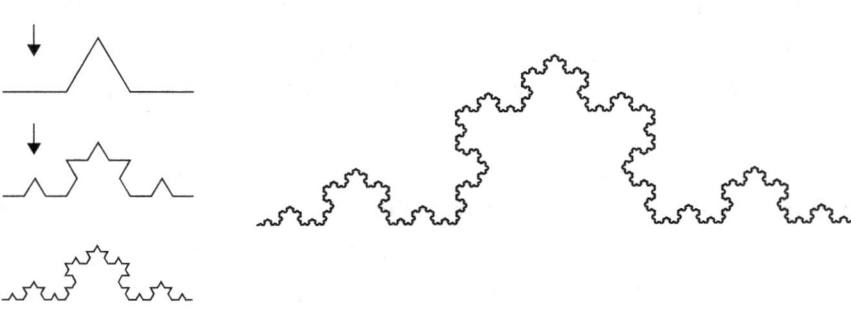

Figure 4.1 The Koch curve: iterative process (left), and the result after many iterations (right).

though the drawing only approximates the Koch curve, we can, through a mathematical sleight-of-hand, assert its existence (as a becoming), and even its precise dimension (about 1.26186). That math class's fifty minutes is to the first line as the felt hours are to the jagged curve – carving out a new dimension that consorts with the infinite in cyclical rhythms that are scale invariant.

But there are other ways of measuring too. Consider the alphabet of the aliens in Canadian film director Denis Villeneuve's (2016) movie *Arrival*. It consists of circular logograms that seem to be measured in Lefebvre's duodecimal register. Each twelfth piece of the arc is a splotch of blank ink that looks like spilt coffee. The messiness somehow ends up looking so *meaningful*, as well as beautiful, expressing the aliens' non-linear conception of time.

:

Figure Organism: Rhythm

rhythm (n.)[4]

From 1550s as 'metrical movement' . . . from Latin *rhythmus* 'movement in time', from Greek *rhythmos* 'measured flow or movement, rhythm; proportion, symmetry; arrangement, order; form, shape, wise, manner; soul, disposition', related to *rhein* 'to flow' (from PIE root ***sreu-** 'to flow').

The *rhythm method* in reference to birth control is attested from 1936. *Rhythm and blues*, US music style, is from 1949 (first in Billboard magazine).

The French philosopher Henri Lefebvre suggests that: 'Everywhere where there is interaction between a place, a time and an expenditure of energy, there is rhythm' (Lefebvre [1992] 2004: 15). What is interesting for us, is that Lefebvre takes rhythm[5] to be *a* time, a temporal pattern that refuses to 'isolate an object, or a subject, or a relation', (Lefebvre [1992] 2004: 12) since time is not set aside for the subject. 'It is only slow in relation to our time, to our body' which we often take to be 'the measure of rhythms' (Lefebvre [1992] 2004: 20). Similar to Whitehead, Bataille and Deleuze, Lefebvre's 'general dialectic' sacrifices synthesis in favour of a space modulated in between the different modes of existence of time and space, a space of tense contamination, invasion, abduction and compromise, a space retaining the integrity of their contrasting difference. Lefebvre links the triad of 'time-space-energy' without fusing and merging them, nor does he read one through the other. This is a 'difficult task and situation: to perceive distinct rhythms distinctly, without disrupting them, without dislocating time' (Lefebvre [1992] 2004: 19–20).

School curriculum, daily rituals and practices do not follow or respond to the demands of the distinct rhythms of a human body, earth's seasons, ambient humidity, or cosmic cycles (e.g., lunar). Instead, they often synthesize place and energy *in terms of* time. In other words, the answer to the student's lament of 'Teacher, I haven't finished yet', is 'Hurry up!' This is not just true in school, but more broadly, because space (and energy) have been stuffed into time, into the rhythms and demands of the capitalist, neoliberal machine. For Lefebvre (as well as for Nietzsche, Deleuze and Guattari), there is no rhythm without repetition in time and space, without reprises, instaurations, returns with a difference. And while rhythms 'imply repetitions and can be defined as movements and differences within repetition' (Lefebvre [1992] 2004: 90), repetition does not signify a bounded and enclosed totality. That is, if repetition is central to rhythm, repetition cannot be articulated without the articulation of difference.

I feel that whatever I'm writing exists already.

Maybe that's because of a glitch in the space-time continuum and when I write I'm actually putting my *living* self behind the *present* moment in time. Like I'm following something through the woods. Eyes open. Ears open. Heart open. And I'm following a path that is sometimes *behind* me. Now

I'm sounding like one of my characters. That's what the Foundling Father as Abraham Lincoln in *The America Play* (1993) is talking about. He's *following* in the footsteps of someone who is *behind* him. There is a strange relationship between writing and history and time, and I don't think it is what we think it is. Or how we perceive it. There's more to it. (Suzan Lori Parks, in Jacobs-Jenkins (2020))

Indeed, Time has come to synthesize us, but it's this Common Time that ignores the temporality of the digestive system, of dreams or generations. Our language participates in this synthesizing because we can say 'you're late' in such a way that designates the whole of you, while really only speaking to the meso-level synthesis of the visible you, and not the micro-level syntheses of your cells – each of which has its own time – nor the macro-level syntheses of your ancestors and descendants. Multiplying these rhythms, as we ought to, might make the already difficult job of managing thirty individual students in a classroom seem impossible. Indeed, it would be. But what is not impossible is responding to the demands of these times and resisting the collapsing to the Totalizing Time of the here, now, like this – to the non-rhythmic present.

present (n.1)[6]

c. 1300, 'the present time, time now passing, this point in time' (opposed to *past* and *future*), also 'act or fact of being present; portion of space around someone', from Old French *present* (n.) 'the present time' (11c.), from Latin *praesens* 'being there' (see **present** (adj.)).

In Middle English also 'the portion of space around someone' (mid-14c.). In old legalese, *these presents* means 'these documents, the documents in hand' (late 14c.).

present (n.2)

c. 1200, 'thing offered, what is offered or given as a gift', from Old French *present* and directly from Medieval Latin *presentia*, from phrases such as French *en present* '(to offer) in the presence of', *mettre en present* 'place before, give', from Latin *in re praesenti* 'in the situation in question', from *praesens* 'being there' (see **present** (adj.), and compare **present** (v.)). The notion is of 'something brought into someone's presence'.

Progress, capitalism, colonialism and consumerism engulf temporalities. They also produce cultural bias/desire towards a certain velocity of time. Slow reading, slow food, slow travel, slow cities, slow fashion, slow science: these are just some of the practices of resistance and refusal against the speed and acceleration of human daily lives in the global north. So then how about slow schooling, slow curriculum?

> We are on the extreme promontory of the centuries! What is the use of looking behind at the moment when we must open the mysterious shutters of the impossible? Time and Space died yesterday. We are already living in the absolute, since we have already created eternal, omnipresent speed. (Marinetti 1909)

The art history professor, Jennifer Roberts, asks her students to sit with an individual artwork for three hours. She tells them to '[a]pproach it as if you were a visitor from another planet with no prior knowledge of the configuration or content of earthly art' (Ables 2021). This isn't slowness for the sake of being slow – which can be excruciating (like waiting as the teacher takes attendance) – but slowness relative to human perception, a slowness that occasions rhythm.

When German philosopher Martin Heidegger sat with Van Gogh's painting on exhibition in Amsterdam in 1930, we can imagine the possibility that he looked at the many intricate details for hours, and perhaps as if from another

Figure 4.2 Vincent van Gogh, *A Pair of Shoes*, 1886; Paris, France. https://www.wikiart.org/en/vincent-van-gogh/a-pair-of-shoes-1886 (accessed 28 February 2022).

planet. He later wrote about it in 'The Origin of the Work of Art' (Heidegger [1935] 1971):

> From the dark opening of the worn insides of the shoes the toilsome tread of the worker stares forth. In the stiffly rugged heaviness of the shoes there is the accumulated tenacity of her slow trudge through the far-spreading and ever-uniform furrows of the field swept by a raw wind. On the leather lie the dampness and richness of the soil. Under the soles slides the loneliness of the field-path as evening falls. In the shoes vibrates the silent call of the earth, its quiet gift of the ripening grain and its unexplained self-refusal in the fallow desolation of the wintry field. This equipment is pervaded by uncomplaining anxiety as to the certainty of bread, the wordless joy of having once more withstood want, the trembling before the impending childbed and shivering at the surrounding menace of death. This equipment belongs to the earth, and it is protected in the world of the peasant woman. From out of this protected belonging the equipment itself rises to its resting-within-itself. (33)

We remember the first time we were invited to engage with this painting. In Grade 11, living in post-socialist Yugoslavia, our sociology teacher embarked on a slow journey of studying semiotics. And she did it via *A Pair of Shoes*. We studied this painting throughout the whole year, looked at it over and over again, read it, wrote about it, listened to it and imagined how it would be to work the rhythms of those long hours in 'her' shoes. We discussed class struggle. We discussed women's struggle. We discussed the historical, economic, discursive, artistic and political temporalities of its creation. This journey is still one of the fondest memories we have of high school. That, and the slow reading of the many thousands of pages of Russian, Czech, German and French literary canon, from Dostoevsky, Tolstoy, Nabokov, Gogol and Pushkin, to Camus, Sartre, Molière, Beckett, Kafka and others. This kind of a slow curriculum creates space for stepping outside of oneself and becoming other, for an ethics of both empathy and resistance to the established, predetermined, presupposed. *Having* time to read, look, listen, write and think with these artists felt like building a relationship with different rhythms and temporalities of both their characters in their fictional, virtual and actual times, as well as those of the authors themselves. Our preconceived notions of what it is we call life, human, ethics, relationality, struggle, our deepest assumptions, biases and presuppositions were laid bare as our daily teenage rhythms imbued, contrasted, humbled, cut, pricked with *a* becoming lady wearing a pair of shoes, a becoming Raskolnikov's struggle with guilt, a becoming Meursault's indifference towards his mother's death, a becoming the unbearable heat of the Moroccan desert, a becoming of the repetitive, never-ending waiting for Godot. This kind of a culturally and politically nonutilitarian slow curriculum, possible perhaps only due to the nation's transitioning times from socialism to capitalism, having a foothold in neither, now feels like a luxury.

Spinoza, says Deleuze ([1971] 1988) in *Spinoza: Practical Philosophy*, fashions thought 'in terms of speeds and slownesses, of frozen catatonias and accelerated movements, unformed elements, nonsubjectified affects' (129). Similarly to Deleuze's early work on the concept of force, as movement and speed, Lefebvre ([1992] 2004) suggests that 'if you have the ability to take the flows and streams (T.V., the press, etc.) as rhythms among others, you avoid the trap of the present that gives itself as presence and seeks the effects of presences' (23). For Lefebvre, what is perceived as a present is a representation, an image, simulacra, a thing mimicking what he calls presence: 'The present sometimes imitates (simulates) to the point of mistaking itself for presence: a portrait, a copy, a double, a facsimile, etc., but (a) presence survives and imposes itself by introducing a rhythm (a time)' (Lefebvre [1992] 2004). Lefebvre's concept of 'presence' is not theological nor phenomenological, that is, presence is not an essence vital to a thing or divinity that is *then* experienced as revealing, proximate to human consciousness. It is only by the gesture of rhythmanalysis [*le geste rhytmanalytique*], a gesture of paying attention to a relation between the present and presence, between their rhythms, that a thing can be perceived as presence. As such, this gesture 'does not imprison itself in the ideology of the *thing*' (Lefebvre [1992] 2004; *italics in original*). A thing is an instance of the present (in the proximity of the present), just as much as an image is, and *becomes* presence only when due attention is paid to *its* divergent and convergent rhythmic relationality with *its* present (as Whitehead would have done with Cleopatra's needle).

Human consciousness is not the originating reference point. Yet, in schools, we train children to focus upon an inflated present, on the representational processes of extraction, mining and abduction of events and activities away from their geological timescales. Because planetary geological timescales are, so it seems, too vast and too deep for human imagination to 'understand' in its different and differentiating presence, schools perpetuate over-standing, which is a certain violent temporal disjuncture: schools rhythms obscure the temporalities of the geological deep-time that make those same rhythms possible. The Indigenous practice of thinking seven generations ahead intentionally breaks through the present. One could spend all day thinking about what it means for the Big Bang to have happened almost 14 billion years ago.

> From any given object, from a simple *thing* (Van Gogh's Shoes), a great artist creates a strong presence, and he does so on a canvas, a simple surface. The metamorphosis does not prevent the restitution of the thing *as it is*. Both enigmatic and simple, filling a simple surface, the act [*geste*] of the artist has the power to evoke time (the wearing away of the pair of shoes), and the presence of a long period of destitution. Therefore a series of *presents*. The **presence** of the scene brings forth all its presents, and is also the presence of Van Gogh, of his life that was poor but dominated by the creative act [*geste*]. (Lefebvre [1992] 2004: 24; *italics and bold in original*).

In the global north, school's social rhythms are generally organized around (a) the economy (the nine-to-five workday of the middle-class workers); (b) the once agrarian needs (between fall and early summer); (c) the chronological age of children; (d) the so-called cognitive developmental stages that accompany these; (e) the content to be covered (which ranges from the more concrete to the more abstract). Contrast these with the four rhythms Lefebvre (Lefebvre [1992] 2004: 18) outlines in his book on rhythmanalysis, which can be applied to school: (1) secret rhythms – in other words, the rhythms you are unaware of – such as the physiological and psychological rhythms of metabolism, memory, breathing, or grass growing outside your classroom; (2) public or social rhythms of school calendars and institutionalized/organized life, but also the shared rhythms of students' tiredness, digestion, secretion, and so on; (3) fictional rhythms that include curriculum, various cultural rituals, and gestures; (4) dominating-dominated rhythms that, as Lefebvre points out, are completely made up as well as long-lasting, such as starting the school day at 8.30 am and finishing at 2.30 pm, or starting school at the age of five.

These dominating-dominated rhythms may well feel completely arbitrary to you as an individual (why do we start school at 8.30 am instead of at the more humane hour of 9.30 am, or 5.00 am for the early risers?), but they have long-lasting effects on the cultural and economic regimes of how particular societies function, endure and reproduce. To Lefebvre, rhythmanalysis is not an analysis of rhythms, but serves to analyse the temporalities of everyday life practices, through which the relationality between time and space occurs. He shows the importance of paying attention to the tensions between (a) linear rhythms, penetrating into everyday life; (b) repetitions of the capitalist system and (c) the cyclic rhythms of cosmic origin. School productions of inextricable temporality of daily acts, experience and practice 'make' the time we are 'in' through the critical features of governing school rhythms. But these rhythms as established regimes of biocentric temporality have in them contemporaneously embedded, repetitious and stratified inequalities of temporalities.

> *The future is already here – it's just not very evenly distributed.*
> (William Gibson)[7]

We should not kid ourselves. The secret rhythms are there, even though we seldom look at them. They are in the rituals of banter in front of lockers, where one can open a small but hidden wardrobe door – à la Lewis Carroll; in the movement of interlocked teenage bodies moving down hallways during the precious ten minutes of *in between* time. They might be in the art classroom, the classroom of the inclusion teacher, the gym – places where unsurveilled rhythms can be instaured. Why is there no academic research on these secret rhythms? Perhaps they require different methods, like the fabulations of the American writer and scholar Saidiya Hartman (2019) in which she describes the secret rhythms of Black women in the dimly lit hallways in the tenement buildings of 1920s Harlem.

While the cyclical rhythms in pre-industrial societies organize daily life, in modern industrial society, the linear rhythms of the colonial (plantation) and industrial–capitalist system take over and dominate the cyclic, planetary rhythms. As German philosopher Hannah Arendt ([1958] 1998) shows in *The Human Condition*, 'during the Middle Ages, it is estimated that one hardly worked more than half of the days of the year' (132, ft 85). She goes on to say that the 'monstrous extension of the working day is characteristic of the beginning of the industrial revolution, when the laborers had to compete with newly introduced machines' (Arendt [1958] 1998). Arendt's own turn to activity, to work, labour and action, can be seen as a re-temporalizing of philosophy, a re-claiming of rhythms of the everyday, so easily lost in the obsession with universals such as truth, beauty and morality.

The transatlantic slave trade, monocropping and the plantation system[8] (the conditions that enabled Industrial Revolution) are 'historically present conceptual device[s]' (McKittrick 2016: 10) that produce the linear rhythms cutting (extracting) through and from the geologic, the planetary and the cyclical – both human and inhuman, master and slave. In the following passage, written by an educated son of a slave owner, the violent extractions of slave labour and earth's plants and minerals are set side-by-side through a temporal alignment between earth cycles and plantation rhythms of the slave work day:

> At six o'clock in the morning the overseer forces the poor slave, still exhausted from the evening's labors, to rise from his rude bed and proceed to his work. The first assignment of the season is the chopping down of the forests for the next year's planting, using a scythe to hack down the smaller trees. This work normally goes on for two months, depending upon the type of jungle being cut and the stamina of the slaves. The next step is destruction of the large trees, and this, like previous work, continues for twelve hours each day. At night the slaves return home, where evening work of two or more hours awaits them, depending upon the character of the master. They set fire to the devastated jungle, and then they cut and stack the branches and smaller tree trunks which have escaped the fire and which, occupying the surface of the earth, could hinder development of the crop. These mounds of branches are again burned, and the result is a sad and devastating scene! Centuries-old tree trunks which two months before had produced a cool, crisp atmosphere over a broad stretch of land lie on the surface of a field ravaged by fire and covered with ashes, where the slaves are compelled to spend twelve hours under the hot sun of the equator, without a single tree to give them shelter. This destruction of the forests has exhausted the soil, which in many places now produces nothing but grasses suitable for grazing cattle. The temperature has intensified, and the seasons have become irregular. The rains at times damage the crops, and at other times there is no rain at all. The streams and certain shallow rivers, such as the Itapucuru, have dried up or have become almost unnavigable, and lumber for building, has become very rare or is only found at a great distance from the settlements. (F.A. Brandão Junior 1865)

In *Diachronic Loops/Deadweight Tonnage/Bad Made Measure,* Canadian Black geographies scholar Katherine McKittrick (2016) works with historically present slave temporalities of Black lives to suggest the biocentric structure of time as the bedrock of white modernity:

> I read The Zong, the slave ship, as a historically present conceptual device that opens up two overlapping analytical pathways: first, the histories embedded on and around the slave ship anticipate our ecocidal and genocidal present because they are part of an identifiable *biocentric loop* – the ship incites an analytical leaning toward racism and black death; second, The Zong allows us to think about racial matters anew and interrupt this loop because it holds in it the possibility to foster different knowledges and, simultaneously, be understood as a location through which many knowledges are constituted. Put simply, the ship imparts and creates knowledges. It follows that the scientific underpinnings of modernity – biocentricity, positivism – are aligned with, not preceding, human practices. The Zong cannot be contained by a singular theoretical frame or story – instead, it demands and is an articulation of multiple historically present black lives. (10; *emphasis added*)

Instead of assuming time in education to be *empty and homogenous* – to follow the German philosopher Walter Benjamin ([1940] 1968) – like a hollow vessel filled with any number of events (an idea that thinkers from the sixteenth century onwards developed very gradually, in their anti-Aristotelian accounts of time as independent of human minds, souls and celestial bodies), we suggest time be understood as an educational artifice of biocentric power conventions and representations.

To say that time is an *artifice* is to say that time is a code of inequality of scales; a biocentric code of desire, interpretation and selection/survey in relation to the colonial, extractive history of setting restraints and limitations to epistemological, ontological and axiological regimes of knowing, doing and being. Here we do not understand the concept of artifice as exclusively man-made, but follow Australian feminist philosopher Claire Colebrook (2016) in her anti-organismal image of life, when she suggests that *all life is artificial life*. With this postulation, Colebrook takes Arendt beyond Arendt, who discussed the human condition in relation to life being *made* artificial: 'The human artifice of the world separates human existence from all mere animal environment, but life itself is outside this artificial world, and through life man remains related to all other living organisms. For some time now, a great many scientific endeavours have been directed toward making life also "artificial," toward cutting the last tie through which even man belongs among the children of nature' (Arendt [1958] 1998: 2).

To say that time is a *code of human sexual desire* is to say, with Arendt, that it is bound up with the organic reproductive desire to escape the human condition; that is, to escape death and human dependence on the indifferent, geologic forces of nature: 'It is the same desire to escape from imprisonment to the earth that is manifest in the attempt to create life in the test tube, in the desire to mix "frozen germ plasm from the people of demonstrated ability under the microscope to produce superior human being" and "to alter [their] size, shape and function"' (Arendt [1957] 1998: 2).

> In the clear, critical light of day, illusory administrators whisper of our need for institutions, and all institutions are political, and all politics is correctional, so it seems we need correctional institutions in the common, settling it, correcting us. But we won't stand corrected. Moreover, incorrect as we are there's nothing wrong with us. We don't want to be correct and we won't be corrected. (Harney and Moten 2013: 20)

To say that time is a *biocentric* code/artifice is to say that in its *loop*, time is a repetition of temporal disjunction. On the one hand, time, as out of joint for the disenfranchised, dispossessed and displaced, loops back onto slavery always in novel ways (i.e., Jim Crow, school-to-prison pipeline). On the other, as an anachronism, such 'segrenomic' temporality continues to constitute white modernity. Or, as Rohy (2009) shows in her depiction of hegemonic temporalities, 'White, public, linear, historic time is not separate from but informed by anachronism, whose vertiginous temporal loops it declines to acknowledge' (34).

White modernity does away with the indeterminate, monstrous, liminal temporal dimensions. Similarly, in the field of educational research, Time, whether linear or cyclical, fast or slow, past or future, operates through organic figures of reproductive copulations (progressive/regressive, active/passive, productive/unproductive), maintaining and nurturing the growth of student self-furthering and perseverance as objective, 'natural' (moral) educational outcomes – something that, as Indian historian Dipesh Chakrabarty (1997) shows, 'researchers automatically assume as providing ontological justification of their work' (36).

:

This Configuration

This movie deals with the epidemic of the way we live now.
What an inane card player. And the age may support it.

Each time the rumble of the age
Is an anthill in the distance.

As he slides the first rumpled card
Out of his dirty ruffled shirtfront the cartoon
Of the new age has begun its ascent
Around all of us like a gauze spiral staircase in which
Some stars have been imbedded.

It is the modern trumpets
Who decide the mood or tenor of this cross-section:
Of the people who get up in the morning,
Still half-asleep. That they shouldn't have fun.
But something scary will come
To get them anyway. You might as well linger
On verandas, enjoying life, knowing
The end is essentially unpredictable.
It might be soldiers
Marching all day, millions of them
Past this sport, like the lozenge pattern
Of these walls, like, finally, a kind of sleep.

Or it may be that we are ordinary people
With not unreasonable desires which we can satisfy
From time to time without causing cataclysms
That keep getting louder and more forceful instead of dying away.
Or it may be that we and the other people
Confused with us on the sidewalk have entered
A moment of seeming to be natural, expected,

And we see ourselves at the moment we see them:
Figures of an afternoon, of a century they extended.

               (John Ashbery)[9]

:

Figure *Anorganism*: A *Auantic Fabulation*

Can monumentalizing the past suffice in preventing atrocity? Or does it only succeed in framing these crimes against humanity from the vantage point of contemporary progress and reason, turning history into one great museum in which we revel in antiquarian excess? (Hartman 2002: 773)

Nowadays there is much talk about environmental, ecological and sustainable education, both in the research literature and in schools. In its utilitarian focus on sustaining the planet for 'our' human survival (or at least survival of the selected few – predominantly white and predominantly rich), the focus of 'new' pedagogical approaches is directed towards recycling and growing food, and in some instances, towards 'Indigenizing' and 'decolonizing' curricula. These 'alternative' attempts at disrupting the colonial and neoliberal vestiges of organized schooling for the most part sustain the story of white modernity by continuing its efforts at organizing, mining, extracting and managing the rhythms of phallic figures such as 'nature', 'culture' and the current 'techno-oriented' modes of capitalist production. Such a conception does not allow room for abstract potentialities, such as counter-factual fabulations and entities, which could produce real ethico-pedagogical effects.

In 'Venus in Two Acts', Hartman (2008) suggests that:

> If I could have conjured up more than a name in an indictment, if I could have imagined Venus speaking in her own voice, if I could have detailed the small memories banished from the ledger, then it might have been possible for me to represent the friendship that could have blossomed between two frightened and lonely girls. Shipmates. Then Venus could have beheld her dying friend, whispered comfort in her ear, rocked her with promises, soothed her with 'soon, soon' and wished for her a good return. Picture them: The relics of two girls, one cradling the other, plundered innocents; a sailor caught sight of them and later said they were friends. Two world-less girls found a country in each other's arms. Beside the defeat and the terror, there would be this too: the glimpse of beauty, the instant of possibility. (8)

While, as Hartman suggests, 'a slave ship made no allowance for grief and when detected the instruments of torture were employed to eradicate it' (Hartman 2008), if she has told the counterstory of the two girls, it would have 'trespassed the boundaries of the archive' (Hartman 2008: 9). At the same time, in not telling their counterstory, Hartman asks, 'was I simply upholding the rules of the historical guild and the "manufactured certainties" of their killers, and by doing so, hadn't I sealed their fate? Hadn't I too consigned them to oblivion?' (Hartman 2008: 10). For Hartman, fabulating this quantic event via epistemological questioning of the ethics of archive, ethics and politics of telling any story, is what is at stake – not only to '*give voice* to the slave', but rather to fabulate impossibles, unimaginables, 'what cannot be verified', and archived (Hartman 2008: 12). 'It is an impossible writing which attempts to say that which resists being said (since dead girls are unable to speak)' (Hartman 2008: 10; *emphasis in original*). This *critical fabulation* (Hartman 2008: 11) of 'what cannot be verified' (Hartman 2008: 12) – an 'impossible writing' (Hartman 2008: 10) – asks: what it would be to violate historicity, violate the archive? Hartman asks, 'how does one re-write the chronicle of a death foretold and anticipated, as a collective biography of dead subjects, as a counter-history of the human, as the practice of freedom?' (Hartman 2008: 3).

We set out this chapter by asking: What is the share of violence in education's continuous organismal re-actualization? What Hartman's counter-actual *an*organismal fabulation as 'method' of restitution suggests, is that the continuous re-actualization of the archive – a temporal-material practise of curating, listing, tracking, organizing, preserving and managing the question of what it is to be human – as the only and objective narrative to be told (the business of schooling) is an act of policing. It is policing because its condition is violence, violence as the ground of both a 'sense of the human' (Cavarero 2015: 11) and a 'counter-history of the human' (Hartman 2008: 3).

When Hartman fabulates an account of the impossible event formed between the two slave girls on board the Recovery – '[t]he *furtive communication* that might have passed between two girls, but which no one among the crew observed or reported' (2008: 10; *emphasis in original*) – it is this 'might have been' she proposes as a new method of measuring time by figuring the impossibles as counter-possibles with recommencement of what was not able to become actualized the first time, but insists in its coeval becoming of continuity as a general potentiality, a 'bundle of possibilities, mutually consistent or alternative, provided by the multiplicity of eternal objects' (Whitehead [1929] 1978: 102).

What happens to the question of time in education, if we move Hartman's critical counter-actual fabulation to a different scale – that of the extensive continuum – 'the first determination of order - that is, of real potentiality – arising out of the general character of the world . . . it does not involve shapes, dimensions, or measurability; these are additional determinations of real potentiality arising from our cosmic epoch' (Whitehead [1929] 1978: 103).

For Italian philosopher Luciana Parisi, 'in contrast to a continuity of becoming, the space of flow where the unity of events lies in an underlying continual temporal invariant, a lived duration, Whitehead's notion of the extensive continuum undoes the split between space and time' (Parisi and Goodman 2009), wherein '[t]he continuum gives potential, while the actual is atomic or quantic by nature. The continuum only exists in the spatio-temporal gaps between actual occasions, but it is what unifies the occasions in one common world' (Parisi and Goodman 2009). In her own approach to the question of rhythm, she argues 'both against a continual flow of becoming, governed by un-spatialized pure time, and against the locality of space-time' (Parisi and Goodman 2009), and instead uses Whitehead's extensive continuum, which draws on quantum physics, to suggest the existence of 'achronological nexus outside the space-time split' (Parisi and Goodman 2009), which are 'vibratory potentials gelling a multiplicity of coexistent space-times: here there is a simultaneity of actual occasions, which are able to detour into one another by selecting potentials or eternal objects. It is in such a potential resonance of one quantum region with another, that an encounter between distinct actual entities occurs' (Parisi and Goodman 2009). For Parisi, following Whitehead, rhythm is 'amodal and atemporal':

> Rhythm proper, cannot be perceived purely via the 5 senses but is crucially transensory or even nonsensuous. Rhythmic anarchitecture is concerned with the virtuality of quantum vibration. It is necessary here to go beyond the quantification of vibration in physics into primary frequencies. For us, it is rhythm as potential relation, which is key. If rhythm defines the discontinuous vibrations of matter, then we must also ontologically prioritize the in-between of oscillation, the vibration of vibration, the virtuality of the tremble. The rhythmic potential that is an eternal object, cannot be reduced to its phenomenological corporeality. The vibratory resonance between actual occasions in their own regions of space-time occurs through the rhythmic potential of eternal objects, which enables the participation of one entity in another. The rhythmic potential of an eternal object exceeds the actual occasion into which it ingresses. To become, an actual entity must be out of phase with itself. (Parisi and Goodman 2009)

On a different scale, we can read Parisi's 'rhythmic anarchitecture' alongside Hartman's 'black noise' (Best and Hartman 2005: 9), which 'represents the kinds of political aspirations that are inaudible and illegible within the prevailing formulas of political rationality' (Best and Hartman 2005: 9). In reading the archive counter-factually by writing critical fabulations as the *continuity of discontinuity* of the narratives of the enslaved, Hartman poses an ethical obligation to 'respect black noise – the shrieks, the moans, the nonsense, and the opacity, which are always in excess of legibility and of the law and which hint at and embody aspirations that are wildly utopian, derelict to capitalism, and antithetical to its attendant discourse of Man' (Hartman 2008: 12). Similarly, for Parisi, the rhythmic (vibratory) 'nexus of the extensive continuum exceeds and precedes the distinction between subject and object and constitutes a virtual mesh of relations, which enables the becoming of experience, the continuity of discontinuity' (Parisi and Goodman 2009).

When *Time* in education is no longer imaged in an erected figure of phallic, copulative, reproductive Organism sustained over time, *time* can be thought away from the biocentric power of schooling, whose pre-emptive modes of bio-control operate directly through the archival activity of fixed past and potential futurity in the present, serving as lures for feelings to existing desires. For example, while one of the premises of schooling is to enable *all* students to lead a good life, wherein the current epochal question of what a good life is has been operationalized for the powerful few, and is indistinguishable from mass consumerism of goods and production of ever new desires, 'the time of slavery persists in this interminable awaiting – that is, awaiting freedom and longing for a way of undoing the past. The abrasive and incommensurate temporalities of the "no longer" and the "not yet" can be glimpsed in these tears' (Hartman 2002: 770). This is the share of violence in education's continuous organismal re-actualization.

So then, to what other 'figures' might the field of education refer?

Leading students into a predictable future with a finite expiry date, schooling blocks time without a goal, blocks untimeliness. If it is repetition, as a continuous rehearsal of white modernity, not the calendar time, that enables racialized, gendered and heteronormative appropriation of organismal temporal scales in education, what is at stake 'is more than exposing the artifice of historical barricades or the tenuousness of temporal markers like the past and the present' (Hartman 2002: 763); rather, what is at stake is the fact that we 'have yet to imagine the possibility of writing a history that attends to the possibility of the non-self-identity of any historical moment' (Goldberg 2007: 503).

In this reading, Parisi's *rhythm* and Hartman's *critical fabulation* account for the continual distribution of potential relations between discontinuous modes of quantic temporalities, a reading that pushes Lefebvre's concept of rhythmanalysis further, via the counter-factual. Rhythmquantic fabulation is an *an*organismal account of a vibratory and non-self-identical temporal tense/nexus of superimposed events, the 'might have been' impossibles and the 'will have beens' future possibles. It is our hope that this chapter cautiously initiates an ethico-pedagogical field of educational work to-be-made, an experimentation against the pre-emptive, biocentric governmentality conditioned on the colonial archival politics of Time.

> '*But look, History still goes on rehashing these recalls to the identitarian, based on a territory . . . etc.*'* Those are the last desperate bursts of the return of the identitarian repressed. The more the progress of Relation is ascertained, the more creolization grows, the more the madness of those who are panicked by this movement of the world is exacerbated. Their new demon, the absolute Evil that they intend to exorcise, is what they call globalization. Then the places of hybridity and sharing, the Beiruts and the Sarajevos, are systematically crushed and hammered. In the smallest village where a bridge had been built between two communities, this bridge is blown up. The Rwandas are maintained in their dereliction. It would seem that we cannot do anything about it. But we are changing in ourselves, and, all around, there are these breaths of the last night. (Glissant [1997] 2020: 126; *italics in original*)

Exhibit 4A: Cycle/Frog/Child

Teachers often present students with a biocentric temporal code of a life cycle as an interval of time during which a sequence of a recurring succession of events or phenomena (of Space) unfolds in Time and is completed. In most curricular design, teachers usually start with an organic, sexual-reproductive animal life cycle, like the following example of our son's learning. This is partly to help students salvage/manage their own finitude (by figural merging of organic scales in a monumental cycle of life and death).

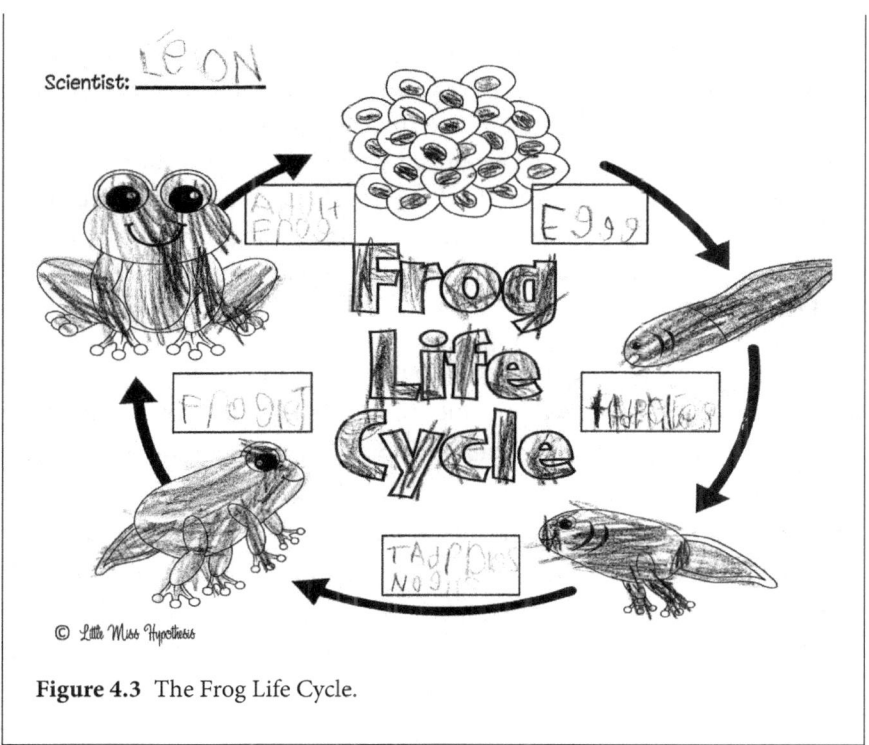

Figure 4.3 The Frog Life Cycle.

But what if we could start with the non-organic, *an*organismal rhythmquantic fabulation, releasing the Cycle/Frog/Child from Time? We could find a way of showing that a cycle is a rhythm, filled with attraction of affectability (erotic sexuality as style, possibility, immediacy). A cycle can then figure as an eternal present, one that can actualize its constitutive relation only as an endless erotic rendering of infinitesimal possibles (of what it is to cycle?). In other words, this figure of a cycle, if released from organic, reproductive Time and understood not as an always already fixed, actualized set of conditions or an interpretive devise, can become actualized in an infinite number of expressive ways, some not even imagined yet, some never imagined by humans. Instead of presenting the actualized (the already established, organic temporal modes presented in a figure of a cycle of life in order to see how they relate and interact in various organisms), we might help students read these infinitesimal actualizations only as modalities of the 'Play of Expression' (as named by Ferreira da Silva (2014b)), reverberating quantic fabulations of non-actualized (might have been) expressions of to cycle and to-frog.

> I look at his oily dark surface, his haptic black sea I don't think 'immersive' like Moyra's. It's the Hudson in the seventies. Dirty as fuck. Moyra's chickens researching in the yard are peck pecking in the timelessness of a day are like a gang of kids. But they are sensations: down low, gathering knowledge for her. We always explain animal intelligence in terms of the ages of children. Since we don't execute them (kids) for food before they have time to grow they function as living measurement for all other creatures. Chickens can count and in many cases are simply smarter than kids. (Myles 2021)

There are many other examples of counter-fabulations that teachers could use to trouble curriculum as an uncritical repetition and rehearsal of the archive. Not just in biology, or literature, but in mathematics too; de Freitas and Sinclair (2014) describe such an example in the context of mathematics, when they follow a Grade 3 child's insistence that six is both even *and* odd. The counter-fabulation snubs the Aristotelian law of the excluded middle, in which things are either one thing or another, and gives rise to a whole newly made possible category of numbers: 6, 10, 14, . . . 56, etc. Far from being the bound to representation, mathematics actually thrives on such counter-fabulations.

And in history too. In their *The Dawn of Everything: A New History of Humanity*, American anthropologist David Graeber and British archaeologist David Wengrow (2021) offer a counter-fabulation of the human archive. In his review of the 2021 book entitled *Human History Gets a Rewrite*, William Deresiewicz (2021) suggests that this counter-narrative goes

> against the conventional account of human social history as first developed by Hobbes and Rousseau; elaborated by subsequent thinkers; popularized today by the likes of Jared Diamond, Yuval Noah Harari, and Steven Pinker; and accepted more or less universally. The story goes like this. Once upon a time, human beings lived in small, egalitarian bands of hunter-gatherers (the so-called state of nature). Then came the invention of agriculture, which led to surplus production and thus to population growth as well as private property. Bands swelled to tribes, and increasing scale required increasing organization: stratification, specialization; chiefs, warriors, holy men. Eventually, cities emerged, and with them, civilization – literacy, philosophy, astronomy; hierarchies of wealth, status, and power; the first kingdoms and empires. Flash forward a few thousand years, and with science, capitalism, and the Industrial Revolution, we witness the creation of the modern bureaucratic state. The story is linear (the stages are followed in order, with

no going back), uniform (they are followed the same way everywhere), progressive (the stages are 'stages' in the first place, leading from lower to higher, more primitive to more sophisticated), deterministic (development is driven by technology, not human choice), and teleological (the process culminates in us). (Deresiewicz 2021)

This narrative is one among many, but it is the one that took hold. It is the one that we repeat and rehearse, with each generation of students, across subjects. Alongside the repeated Time of History, the quantic non-actualized fabulations persist as real possibles, modulating Time with every impossible futurity. Graeber and Wengrow offer a counter-actual fabulation, where, for example, they suggest:

> The Indigenous critique, as articulated by these figures in conversation with their French interlocutors, amounted to a wholesale condemnation of French – and, by extension, European – society: its incessant competition, its paucity of kindness and mutual care, its religious dogmatism and irrationalism, and most of all, its horrific inequality and lack of freedom. The authors persuasively argue that Indigenous ideas, carried back and publicized in Europe, went on to inspire the Enlightenment (the ideals of freedom, equality, and democracy, they note, had theretofore been all but absent from the Western philosophical tradition). They go further, making the case that the conventional account of human history as a saga of material progress was developed in reaction to the Indigenous critique in order to salvage the honor of the West. We're richer, went the logic, so we're better. (Deresiewicz 2021)

Architects are creatives who understand the importance of the studies, designs and drawings of never-built or never-actualized plans and constructions – more important, even than the ones that have been built. One example that comes to mind is *Habitat '67*. Only one-fifth of the original plan has been built. In an interview for *Time Space Existence* (2018), the Canadian architect Moshe Safdie calls it the 'heritage in the unbuilt'. For Safdie, many of his unbuilt projects are some of the most significant works he has done; he believes that 'had the original Habitat '67 been built, perhaps the course of the architecture in this century would have been different'.

History, science, technology, literature, religion, art, ethics, politics: they are populated with sketches, drawings, decisions, experiments, designs, utterances and plans never pursued, never uttered, never written, paths never taken.

But they persist and haunt the archive. By speculating the different possible futures that might have been, had a different narrative taken hold, teachers could pedagogically release History, Culture, Imagination and Mathematics from Time. They could help students practise ethics of indeterminacy and multidimensionality; unattached and speculative creativity in addressing life events without organic figures; imagining and enacting 'impossible' quantic forms of social, cultural and planetary existence – forms and modes that haunt the life worlds as we know them.

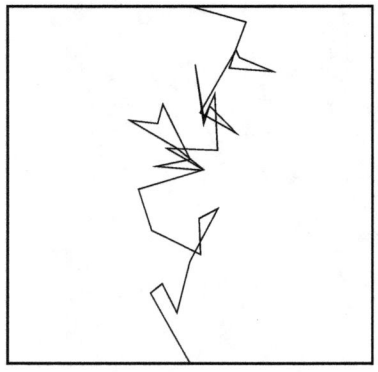

Lies 5: Any proposition that contains the word 'finite' (the world, the universe, experience, ourselves . . .)

(Jeanette Winterson)[1]

5

Refusal

Fabulating Time with Bonnie Honig and Michael Taussig

> *refusal (n.)*²
>
> late 15c., *refusel*, 'act of refusing to do something, rejection of anything demanded', from **refuse** (v.) + **-al** (2). The sense of 'choice of refusing or taking', as in *right of first refusal*, is by 1570s. The earlier noun was simply *refuse* (late 14c., from Old French *refus*), which was common through 16c.

Each of the three temporal modalities (past, present and future, in all of their conjugative complexities) entail presumptions regarding the others that are often ill-considered or even ignored: how we understand the past, and our links to it through reminiscence, melancholy or nostalgia, prefigures and contains corresponding concepts about the present and the future; the substantiality or privilege we pragmatically grant to the present has implications for the retrievability of the past and the predictability of the future; and, depending on whether we grant to the future the supervening power to rewrite the present and past, so too we must problematize the notions of identity, origin and development. (Grosz 1999: 18)

Moreover, women's time and choices are closely circumscribed, primarily by their gender, but also by their age, ethnic origin and class; these in turn shape their employment status, income levels and household circumstances. The autonomy which women have to enjoy personal leisure is relative to these overarching structures. Leisure is thus one of women's 'relative freedoms'. (Wimbush and Talbot 1988: xiv)

My response to the call to refuse, to dissent, is not to rush and abandon the tools for thinking and existing that aid in the confrontation of the instances of total (murder) and symbolic (everything else) racial violence – in all its guises – that seem to multiply endlessly in the global present. No, my response is this: let us start to use these tools with caution, aware of their capacity to reproduce racial violence and at the same time let us move on(ward) to assemble tools with which to think and live in the world otherwise. (Ferreira da Silva 2018: 38)

Inspiration for my research has come from many places, sometimes from my Mi'kmaw life experience, courses I have taken or taught, writing papers or speeches, or dreams. My learning spirit guides me to these 'ah-hah' moments, which happen in the most unlikely times and places, especially when I am led to let go of thinking, drifting and edging on various states of relaxation, exercise, or alternate forms of consciousness when I am led to consider something new. (Battiste 2013: 108)

In that regard, the names by which I am called in the public place render an example of signifying property *plus*. In order for me to speak a truer word concerning myself, I must strip down through layers of attenuated meanings, made excess in time, over time, assigned by a particular historical order, and there await whatever marvels of my own inventiveness. (Spillers 1987: 65; *emphasis in original*)

[A] given entity can be in (a state of) superposition of different times. This means that a given particle can be in a state of coexisting at multiple times – for example, yesterday, today, tomorrow . . . times bleeding through one another. (Barad 2018: 67–8)

A concern with histories that hurt is not then a backward orientation: to move on, you must make this return. If anything, we might want to reread melancholic subjects, the ones who refuse to let go of suffering, who are even prepared to kill some forms of joy, as an alternative model of the social good. (Ahmed 2010: 50)

:

When Plato tells the story of the origins of all being(s) in his *Timaeus*, it's a three-part heroic family drama: the works of Reason (paternal force giving form and order to Necessity), what comes about by Necessity (mother and nurse of beings), and how Reason and Necessity collaborate to create the world of human experience (offspring of Necessity and Reason). It is through a story of Necessity that Plato introduces the concept of space into the history of Western philosophy. Parmenides, who introduces the goddess Necessity (*ananke*) and the goddess Justice (*dike*) in his poem 'On Being', presents them (perhaps as kin of sorority, outside the patriarchal kinship in Plato's spatio-temporal kinship drama?) as responsible for the cosmic order, an order revealed by the visible patterns produced by the sun, moon and stars. Goddess Necessity sets in place and maintains the elemental milieu through the receptacle's whirling movements: 'Everything happens according to necessity; for the cause of the coming-into-being of all things is the whirl, which he [Democritus] calls necessity' (Kirk, Raven, and Schofield [1957] 1983: 419). And Goddess Justice 'does not loose her fetters and let anything come into being or pass away, but holds it fast' (Burnet 1892). As *Timaeus* fabulates it, this is the chaotic and raw state of the cosmos when Reason arrives on the familial scene to give/impose/mediate on it a formal order that brings meaning and beauty to the cosmos.

For Plato, the *chora* is the place out of which being develops (personified by Necessity): '[f]or the moment, we need to keep in mind three types of things: that which comes to be, that in which it comes to be, and that after which the thing coming to be is modelled, and which is the source of its coming to be. It is in fact appropriate to compare the receiving thing to a mother, the source to a father, and the nature between them to their offspring' (Plato, *Timaeus* 50d).[3] Chora is a receptacle (*hupodoche*) into and out of which qualitative and quantitative differences come to appear as such. What enables beings to usher into the world of appearances is chora, described as the nurse or midwife of being. Plato here repeats his use of a reproductive analogy to further his metaphysical ends from *Theatetus*, where Socrates compares himself to a midwife of ideas, tasked with bringing them into the world. Plato fabulates chora as a receptacle without substance or any qualities of its own, inheriting from Necessity the capacity to hold the universe together not by the imposition of limit as boundary, but by the power of its receptivity. Timaeus describes receptacle as nonfamiliar, as a *strange* being without, or out of, place (*topos*), as invisible and without shape. It is neither being nor non-being but an interval in which the 'forms' are held. Chora 'gives space' and has maternal attributes – it is a womb, a matrix.

According to feminist philosopher Elizabeth Grosz, the outset of the divine creation of the cosmos and earth in Plato's thought is actually a series of binary oppositions such as being-becoming, ideal-material, divine-mortal, that are related to the relationship between reason and the material world. In *Space, Time, and Perversion: Essays on the Politics of Bodies* (1995), Grosz shows that the opposition between being (the unchanging, the world of Forms and Ideas, the ideal), and becoming (the sensible, subject to change, the imperfect) presumes a mediation or mode of transition and is not as self-explanatory as it might seem. She/chora is a kind of non-thing with only a reference to being: '[W]e shouldn't call the mother or receptacle of what has come to be ... either earth or air, fire or water, or any of their compounds or constituents. But if we speak of it as an invisible and characterless sort of thing, one that receives all things and shares in a most perplexing way in what is intelligible, a thing extremely difficult to comprehend, we shall not be misled' (1995: 51b).[4] Chora the receptacle is placed in the interval between the intelligible realm of the Forms and the sensible realm experience, of physical phenomena. The intelligible and the sensible realms are two and not the same because of chora, which enables both their difference/separation, and the exchange between them. Chora is designated therein as 'a third kind ... which always *is*, not admitting of destruction and providing a seat for all that has birth, itself graspable by some bastard reasoning ... the very thing we look to when we dream' (1995: 52b).[5] Chora can neither be perceived through the senses nor known through reason; it can only be apprehended through a 'bastard reasoning' akin to the 'reasoning' of dreams. It is a third kind of ontological entity between being and non-being, facilitating the intelligible Forms into becoming sensible.

> Our new starting point in describing the universe must, however, be a fuller classification than we made before. We then distinguished two things; but now a third must be pointed out. For our earlier discourse the two were sufficient: one postulated as model, intelligible and always unchangingly real; second, a copy of this model, which becomes and is visible. A third we did not distinguish, thinking that the two would suffice; but now, it seems, the argument compels us to attempt to bring to light and describe a form difficult and obscure. What nature must we, then, conceive it to possess and what part does it play? This, more than anything else: that it is the receptacle [hupodoche] – as it were, the nurse – of all becoming. (Plato, *Timeaus* 48e-49a)[6]

What it means to exist is to take up space: we 'say that everything that exists must be in some place [*topos*] and occupy some room [*chora*], and that what is not somewhere on earth or heaven is nothing' (1995: 52d).[7] Space brings time into becoming but has no possibilities of becoming. Space is the mother of time but has no positive self-identity. Space, like *chora*, is imaged as a grave, cave, an abyss and 'a pure difference, between being and becoming' (Grosz 1995: 116). It is space which produces the separation of being and becoming and thus enables their co-existence. Like Grosz, French feminist philosopher Luce Irigaray thus deconstructs the many ways in which space has been historically conceived (inherited from Plato[8] and Aristotle[9]) and has functioned to contain women or to obliterate them. She suggests that a reconceptualization of the relations between sexes (in order for an autonomous and independent self-representation for femininity) to occur (as Brazilian feminist philosopher Denise Ferreira da Silva (2014b) does in her feminist poethics of Blackness, discussed in the tropism of Rupture), this would entail a radical reconceptualization of the representation of space and time:

> In order to make it possible to think through and live [sexual] difference, we must reconsider the whole problematic of *space* and *time* ... The transition to a new age requires a change in our perception and conception of *space-time*, the *inhabiting of places* and of *containers, or envelopes of identity*. (Irigaray [1984] 1993: 7, with emphases and additions as quoted in Grosz (1995: 121))

We begin with the problematic of space, which has been a central and evolving concern for feminist scholars. That they are concerned may seem obvious, given what was offered to them in Plato, but the stakes are not just about gender, but about the binary opposites listed by Grosz. With time ending up on the same side of town as reason, the implications for schooling are quite deep. The question comes down to: from whose idea of reason was it reasoned how it is we become reasonable? Take a deep breath as you continue reading; try to refrain from seeking resolution; it's the reading and not the resolution we want to offer.

Irigaray writes her project from a symbolical order based on female genealogies. She shows that the Human has always been written in the masculine, while Woman as the subject has been non-existing or has not existed yet. In her book *An Ethics of Sexual Difference* (Irigaray [1984] 1993) she argues that it is necessary to rethink the concept of place on ethical grounds in terms of sexual difference. The transcendental must be connected to the sensible, the earth, the ground and place. Rethinking place is crucial for an understanding of sexual difference and Irigaray stresses the need to give the relationship between place and Woman a positive value because, in her view, Woman is literally outside time. She says that any discourse on place and time is simultaneously a discourse on sexual difference, and the starting point for rethinking time and place is the maternal body.[10]

In his prominent book *The Practice of Everyday Life* (originally published in French in 1980), the French philosopher and theologian Michel de Certeau postulates that places are narratively inscribed by our memories. He considers places to be 'fragmentary and inward-turning histories, pasts that others are not allowed to read, accumulated times that can be unfolded but like stories held in reserve, remaining in an enigmatic state, symbolizations encysted in the pain or pleasure of the body' (de Certeau [1984] 1993: 108). The memorable places are the ones in which subjectivity is 'already linked to the absence that structures it as existence and makes it "be there". [The] being-there acts only in spatial practices, that is, in *ways of moving into something different*. It must ultimately be seen as the repetition, in diverse metaphors, of a decisive and originary experience, that of the child's differentiation from the mother's body' (de Certeau [1984] 1993: 109; *emphasis added*).

De Certeau emphasizes that it is through this experience that the possibility of space and of localization of a subject is inaugurated. The 'original spatial structure', as de Certeau would have it, depends on the manipulation that can make the maternal body go away and make oneself disappear. The condition for this to occur is that one considers oneself still identical with the object, that is, the maternal body. This makes it possible to experience being *there* 'without the other but in a necessary relation to what has disappeared' (de Certeau [1984] 1993: 109). He maintains that this differentiation from the maternal body can be traced even further back, as far as the naming of the child that separates the foetus identified as masculine from his mother. However, he questions what happens with the female foetus, which in his mind is from this very moment (i.e., the naming) onwards introduced into another relationship to space.

Irigaray poses a possible answer by suggesting that if woman remains in empathy with her mother, she remains in her place: 'Back into herself she turns her mother (and) herself. She interiorizes her container-mother in herself-as-container' (Irigaray [1984] 1993: 42). It is between the two that woman exists, argues Irigaray. Masculine discourse on the space-time dialectic as it is narrativized in Western phallogocentric ideology takes its charge from the process of relegating this spatial dependence on the mother's body to the 'real' or the 'pre-symbolic', where the maternal place has no positive self-identity. Irigaray claims that woman is assigned to be place without occupying a place. Men seek female placelessness: 'Through her, place would be set up for man's use but not for hers' (Irigaray [1984] 1993: 52). Woman's body is a container for her child and occasionally for men, but never for herself. Again, Woman is literally outside of time. In the ontological division of Space and Time, and the ensuing allotment of Woman to Space and Man to Time, Space/Woman is the receptacle in which nothing happens, and whose purpose is to provide the dialectical means for action.

The *memory of a place*, referring back to de Certeau, is entrusted to woman by the *nostalgic man* as 'he makes woman the keeper of his house, his sex (organ), his history' (Irigaray [1984] 1993: 71). At the same time, he is not capable of establishing long-lasting love of self because his version of love of self takes the form of nostalgia for a maternal-feminine that is forever lost to him. His self-love seemingly takes the form of a long *return* to that first place through the female other, who is forever lost and 'must be sought in many others, an infinite number of others' (Irigaray [1984] 1993: 60–1). Because woman is meant to assimilate love to herself, as Irigaray writes, without any return of love for her, she is not granted access to a space-time 'of her own' (Irigaray [1984] 1993: 71). The maternal-feminine is the cause of the 'self-cause of men' and not for herself. She needs to exist but as 'an a priori condition (as Kant might say) for the space-time of the masculine subject' (Irigaray [1984] 1993: 85). Irigaray claims that this is the ground on which, as Grosz (1995) postulates, 'a thoroughly masculine universe is built' (121). Grosz argues that the bodies of women figure as 'socially guaranteed compensation for men's acquisition of phallic status, the repositories of men's own lost corporeality, and the guardians of men's mortality' (Irigaray [1984] 1993: 122).

The meaning of place has been associated with the pre-Oedipal, which is to say, that it has been (for example in theories of Lacan and Freud) linked to the early mother-child relation. Space, on the other hand, according to Irigaray, is a construct of the mind that has been created as a solution to the threat of the maternal first place because place represents flesh, materiality and corporeality.

> In broad strokes the story I wish to relate is this: the world, human and nonhuman, begins with and enlarges upon the arts of deceit, shot through with a decisive act of intense misogynistic violence followed by the continuing anxiety on the part of men that women will resume their earlier power over men. (Taussig 2020: 107)

As opposed to Irigaray, French feminist philosopher Julia Kristeva sets her maternal *chora* in direct relation to the symbolic. In *Revolution in Poetic Language* ([1974] 1984) and elsewhere, Kristeva theorizes the constitution of the subject by distinguishing between the pre-symbolic (pre-linguistic, metonymic) and symbolic (linguistic, metaphoric) modalities of the signifying process. The two are relatively exclusive and necessarily dialectical. She makes this distinction through the subtle combination of concepts drawn from the later works of Plato and from psychoanalytic, phenomenological and linguistic theories. In opposition to Plato's supposed reduction of the maternal *chora* into nothingness, Kristeva's *chora* gives the maternal a prominent role in the signification processes and in subject formation. It is not an empty receptacle but a place or space of significant activity of human drives. She applies the concept of *chora* in order to describe the continuous rhythmic and feminine space shared by a mother and her child: 'the drives, which are "energy" charges as well as "psychical" marks, articulate what we call a *chora*: a non-expressive totality formed by the drives and their stases in a motility that is as full of movement as it is regulated' ([1974] 1984: 23). Kristeva argues that the child's early intimate relationship with the mother's body is a kind of language, defined by the patterns of sound and movement. The child experiences hunger, alertness and drowsiness, all of which are answered by the 'mother' who caresses the child, talks to the child and makes faces at the child. Even though the child hears the spoken words around her, she does not experience them as a formal language but responds to sound, and understands the world around her in terms of rhythmic or sporadic movements, sounds without prescribed sense, feelings of pleasure or pain whose origin is indefinite.

Here we would like to add a temporal, anaphoric dimension – when a child mimics her mother's gestures, this is not a 'replication', to use the terminology of Australian anthropologist Michael Taussig, but rather 'a repetition with a difference', wherein it is this 'being the same and being different', that is 'magical, not in a conceptual logic sort of way, but in the materiality and sensuality of the items hovering in their medley of connectednesses', a gift exchange that 'obliges return' (Taussig 2020: 125). These are the

> transient moments of becoming and un-becoming. We meet the Other in soulful hybridity, enlarged thus in our beingness, then dissolve back into altered patterns of difference. Ad infinitum. It is a game we play continuously. We call it life. Yet that life depends upon the intimacies and intimacies of that 'soulful hybridity,' on whether it be motivated by the magic of dominance or by something even more complex summed up as the mastery of non-mastery. (Taussig 2020: 126)

The semiotic (pre-symbolic) phase is followed by a rupture, which Kristeva writes in reference to Lacan's theory of the mirror stage, and names a *thetic state*. It is a moment of drift from the semiotic towards naming ('Naming seems especially important here. Naming of things. One after the other. As if plucked from real life so as to be nourished and cherished in their newfound linguistic echo chamber of magnifying mimesis' (Taussig 2020: 128)) and becoming participatory in a signifying system. In the *thetic phase*, the maternal body is rejected by and split from the child. The semiotic relationship to the mother begins to be lost as the child enters the symbolic, and Kristeva proposes that much of the symbolic language in which we engage has the effect of establishing and maintaining this cut in a relationship with the mother, who becomes the other. The world we inhabit is radically external to the mother and her body. However, Kristeva argues that the semiotic and symbolic modalities are not discontinuous from each other because:

> These two modalities – the semiotic and the symbolic – are inseparable within the signifying processes that constitutes language, and the dialectic between them determines the type of discourse (narrative, metalanguage, theory, poetry, etc.) involved; in other words, so-called 'natural' language allows for different modes of articulation of the semiotic and the symbolic. (Kristeva ([1974] 1984): 24)

The forces of the *chora* are pre-discursive or pre-symbolic and work like a rhythmic chamber, as the origin of meaning. It signifies signs which derive from the early relations between mother and child. *Chora* is more like a process than a language. It is the place where the human being is generated and negated at the same time – as *discontinuity* (destructive, fixed) and *flow* (creative, fluid). Kristeva understands *chora* as 'a luminous spatialization, the ultimate language of jouissance at the far limits of repression, where bodies, identities, and signs are begotten' (Taussig 2020: 269). In relation to space, *chora* articulates the time and space of the mother. It is not linear and abstract. If one is to describe *chora*, one must move in-between both semiotic language and symbolic language, because *chora* is not possible to represent since it may not be immediately accessible. In contrast to Irigaray, Kristeva does not understand *chora* as an origin for female imagery. This is because Kristeva's *chora* is dependent on symbolic language in order to be able to exist. It exists only as a possibility because not only is the semiotic produced by the thetic cut but it is also produced recursively on the basis of this break (Taussig 2020: 69).

American art historian Kaja Silverman, however, suggests that Kristeva understands *chora* as a feminine place, but she uses the term without giving it clearer definition. It stands in a kind of ambiguous relation to language and representation. *Chora* cannot be determined but is at the same time determined in relation to paternal language. There is no positive self-identity in connection to maternal language like in Irigaray. ('No doubt about it. Language heats up when lightning streaks through the night. I try to picture Foucault, head shaven like a monk in the mountains of Mexico, which is where Nietzsche wanted to go in the hope that the fierce electrical storms would cure his fierce migraines' (Taussig 2020: 120)). Kristeva's maternal is beyond representation, an unsignifiable space in which the pregnant mother is disruptive, but loses her own relation to language. Silverman maintains that Kristeva fails to provide a language for questioning female destiny because she denies the mother the very possibility of speech by relegating her to the silence of the *chora*: 'The mother is either fused or confused with her infant, and in the process comes both to be and to inhabit the chora' (Silverman 1988: 102). Or, as Taussig asks, 'And doesn't every de-allegorization' of the human body 'evoke another allegory' (Taussig 2020: 121).

> *In the beginning there was a river.*
> *The river became a road and the road branched out to the whole world.*
> *And because the road was once a river it was always hungry.*
> (Okri)[11]

In the end, we cannot undo Time, as either a Category of Thought, an object of representation or a subject of perception through Time. If Woman is outside of time, how do we re-ontologize it in order to subvert or dismantle the house of reason (from the outside)? This is, in a sense, a reprise of Ferreira da Silva's question, as we described in the tropism of Rupture, which is how to mobilize Blackness as a Thing that is outside the solidified matrix of value. For her, this outsideness is alchemized into a gift that exercises its own power *precisely because it's on the outside*.

:

Here we explore the use of *fabulation* as a method of refusal rather than rupture, following Bonnie Honig's (2021) appropriation of American writer and scholar Saidiya Hartman's fabulation. Hartman's method is captured in her words 'I have crafted a counternarrative', which is a 'method of refusal', which can also be the basis for the story told of an action that becomes part of a web of meaning (Hartman 2019: xiv).

Fabulation I: from Asilia Franklin-Phipps (2017)

> I met Frankie at a talk at her university. . . . We met over the course of the term and recorded our conversations.
>
> Frankie discussed feeling like she did not belong quite a bit. The molar assemblage of school positioned her existence as non-belonging – she was a queer, Black girl from Iowa – and all at once, she embodied not belonging. Frankie went to Black Student Union meetings and felt the space was too heteronormative. Frankie struggled in her social groups because she felt her experiences as a Black woman were discounted or dismissed when others only wanted to meaningfully engage in her queer identity. She did not grow up around many Black people and her parents and teachers provided little insight into the world that she faced as a high school girl and later as an undergraduate student. Frankie began to feel less pinned to the feeling of not belonging when she began taking courses with Black women, taking coursework in Ethnic Studies and Women and Gender Studies, and joining clubs and forming social connections with other students of color. This had not been possible in her high school. Although these lines of flight allowed Frankie a bit more freedom when she entered particular compositions of *motion and rest*, this greater awareness and ability to name, articulate, and challenge her positioning – becoming a feminist kill joy (Ahmed 2010) and becoming-molecular – made the other parts of her life more challenging.
>
> Through self-education and alternative social spaces, Frankie was undermining her molarization and becoming-molecular, but this molecularity was further disciplined when she returned to more molar

spaces like the biology lab, heteronormative male-dominated study groups, and science courses where she would once again be the only Black girl. Although this produced Frankie as anxious and depressed, she did feel that she was gaining something from managing these disparate campus spaces because she did not quit, going on to graduate and continuing to opt into radical, activist spaces that challenged molarity in the forms of capitalism, racism, sexism, and heteronormativity. Molar confrontations require extra work that at times becomes unmanageable; Frankie took on additional labor that was not recognized, or maybe was unable to be recognized, as it did not correspond with the labor of dominant groups. Her grades slipped, and even though she accomplished much more than many undergraduates, this traditional yet incomplete measure of her accomplishment allowed her to be imagined and imagine herself as incompetent.

Which girls need to work harder than anyone else? How hard Frankie must work is related to her positioning as Black Girl Other. Frankie understood herself in terms of ontologies of being – she was either smart or she was not smart – and in moments she thought of herself as multiple but was rarely perceived so. She was used to understanding herself in terms of fixed, imposed subjectivities: too Black, too White, too queer, and too anxious. Despite being one of very few Black women in the biology major, and having been successful in her high school science courses, she understood the absence of Black and Brown students as a further indication of her not belonging. This doubt was reinforced by regular slights and dismissals from mostly White, mostly male colleagues, a pattern she had become used to in high school. She was often avoided when it was time to pick lab partners, and when she did speak, her contributions were often ignored or dismissed by her male colleagues. The only reason she continued in the major was that she really loved science. Low grades further produced her as unsuitable for the space.

When asked about the number of Black people in any given class or school context, she only needed a minute to answer: 'three,' 'two,' or 'just me.' The number, always low, often produced enough anxiety to keep her still, silent, and stuck, learning and becoming differently than her White male peers. The minute Frankie got a chance, she moved to a place where she could not count anymore.

Frankie is willing to give up her specificity to be able to identify with a group. She is okay with not belonging, as long as she does not also have to be the only Black person in the room. She is aware that she is opting out of dominant notions of monetary success by opting into an alternative life space. She is okay with being the only queer-identifying person in the room and she is okay being the only person who grew up in a small town in the Midwest. In this, she is creating her own life space and becoming-molecular, as the molar assemblage would produce her as inert, fixed in her place as a struggling queer Black girl.

(Franklin-Phipps 2017: 387–9; *our emphasis*)

Fabulation II: from Michael Taussig (2020)

Don't think of this as 'over there' and 'back then,' as something exotically primitive. Instead stitch it into your current views and make a collage and see how you feel about your 'normal.' Up until the massacre of the women, as the Selk'nam men tell it, men lived in ignorance of the fact that the spirits emerging from the women's house on special occasions were not spirits but masked mortal women who held sway over men who carried out the day-to-day tasks of food preparation and child care. When the men found out and consequently killed the adult women, they appropriated their initiation rites. Ever since then, the energy motivating the men's rites stipulates that women must be held in ignorance of the massacre and of the powers men feel are inherent to women because otherwise women will resume power. However, women in the post-matriarchal phase were aware that the spirits were now in fact mortal men wearing masks, but because of threats against their lives if they so much as mentioned this, the women feign ignorance. In other words, what was a secret when the women imitated the spirits became a public secret when the men took over. It became a secret known to all, involving a dizzying cocktail of deceit and counterdeceit: men miming the spirits, women miming ignorance that it was mortal men doing this, and men miming their belief that the women remained ignorant of what they were doing – all in all a great circuit of deceit and mimeses, which appears to me to create a great charge, like an electric charge, empowering the spirits themselves.

Another and seemingly different way of putting this is that men fear women as polluting, a stand-in word for their alleged occult powers, especially the powers of trickery and deceit which are, after all, mighty synonyms of the mimetic faculty. As I see the situation, this attribution of pollution as involved in trickery, deceit, and mimesis rests on the idea that in the prehistoric time of women's dominance there was a great capacity for flux in identities, involving manifold identifications and metamorphoses between humans and nonhumans. It was mimesis unbound, the birth of mimesis, we might say, in the steamy cauldron of endless becoming: In ancient times there were already many ancestors here in our country. In those days sun and moon, stars and winds, mountains and rivers walked the earth as human beings, exactly as we do today. But at that time the women held sway everywhere. 'Ancient times' here means woman's time in which the mimetic faculty, as I read the ethnography, is Dionysian in Nietzsche's sense, involving mimesis for the joy and awe of its adventure and love of its caress lined by fire. For Nietzsche, Dionysian mimicry is not a consumer choice. It is impossible to avoid. Like breathing. And it has no purpose other than itself (which is, to say the least, more than enough).

The massacre of women culminated in the struggle between the Sun (male) and the Moon (female). Thrown into fire, her face badly burned, the woman personifying Moon managed to escape into the moon or actually become the moon in the sky, where she exists as a powerful and dangerous shaman striking fear into the hearts of all, especially the male shamans. Her scarred face not only appears at the full moon but testifies to the trauma of matricide. For the men it is the sign that they have to be vigilant. Their paranoia is boundless, fearing one day the women will revolt and take power again. For the women, who have to know what not to know, the scar is no less eloquent. This massacre is noteworthy not only for its gender reversal of power but for the transition and merging of a person – the one who enacts Moon – with the moon itself. In my description you can see how effortlessly I flip between a person, a personage, and the moon itself, back and forth, until there is a resting point as the woman becomes the moon. The ultimate mimetic evolution and accomplishment, we might say, was occasioned by the slaughter of the women, who passed into nature while the men exercised their newly found theatrical powers based upon public secrecy, meaning that which is known but cannot, must not, be articulated. The mimetic transition into nature by the murdered women was, as I see it, part and parcel of the tremendous mimetic capacities women exercised before the massacre, at a time when the world was constituted as a mimetic force-field with the men as a necessary audience, bereft of mimetic talent.

(Taussig 2020: 107–12)

Fabulation III: from Bonnie Honig (2021)

Refusal in Euripides's fifth-century tragedy, the Bacchae, occurs when the women (1) refuse work in the city, then (2) move outside the city where they live otherwise, then (3) return to the city with a set of demands. The first two actions violate King Pentheus's orders. By the time of the third, Pentheus is dead and Cadmus, his grandfather, has stepped into his place. As I read the play, the three refusals are connected stops on a single arc of refusal. Indeed, the work-refusal and heterotopian escape set up the return to the city that follows.

From the perspective of an arc of refusal, the bacchants' time outside the city appears not as ventilation but as preparation: a re-formation of the body and steeling of the mind to one day alter the everyday, not just rejoin it. When the women leave Thebes and repair to Cithaeron, I argue, their purpose is to prepare a storm of transformation and not just gather a breeze of fond memories that will occasionally stir the windless 'safety' of home. The latter reading is recuperative. The former is transformative.

In the Bacchae, the arc belongs to the women, the bacchants, but their refusal has not received any serious attention as such, because (1) the women are assumed to be mad, in thrall to Dionysus, and unaware of what they are doing when they defy and kill the king, (2) the tragic ending means most readers see not an arc but a restoration or reprimand, and (3) although the play is named for the bacchants, most readers take the focus to be the play's remarkable agon between Thebes's male rivals: Pentheus, the king, and Dionysus, a foreign god who is (unbeknownst to Pentheus) the king's cousin. For these reasons, most readings of the Bacchae prioritize its lessons about religion, kinship, recognition, or hubris but not refusal. But what happens when we switch the focus from the male rivals' quest for power to the women's collaborative experiments? From male hubris to women's agency? From heterotopia as fugitivity to a space/time of rehearsal? From women's singular madness to refusal's arc?

Dionysian rituals attract the three remaining sisters, Agave, Ino, and Autonoe, who, along with the rest of Thebes's women, abandon their work, violating Pentheus's order to return to their looms. Pentheus has some of the women imprisoned, trying to contain them and preserve order, but they all escape to Cithaeron where they party like it's 405 B.C. Says the servant to Pentheus, 'And the bacchae whom you shut up, whom you carried off and bound in the chains of the public prison, are set loose and gone, and are gamboling in the meadows, invoking Bromius [aka Dionysus] as their god. Of their own accord, the chains were loosed from their feet and keys opened the doors without human hand.' Or in a different translation: 'The chains fell from their feet and the bars of their cells were withdrawn as if by magic.' It seems Dionysus is also the god of prison abolition. The women's escape is a gift of the god, Dionysus, the play suggests. That may be. But Dionysus is also a gift the women give to themselves: he is summoned by their desire.

In the Bacchae, however, the inoperativity that the women enjoy involves not just the suspension of use but also a kind of intensification of use. Away from patriarchy's sex-gender enclosures, the women experience leisure and pleasure in new, intensified ways that alter their experience of space and time. Their power is suggested by the messenger's report to Pentheus that when the women chased away the herdsmen spying on them, the women ran, and 'the world ran with them.'

In the moment of his murder, Pentheus calls out, 'Mother, Mother, look, it's me, your son, Pentheus!' and Agave wrenches his arm from its socket. Agave's nonrecognition of Pentheus suggests there is a problem with kinship or maternity (Butler) or with Agave (most readings). But what if we switch Agave's identity from mother, which is the interpellation that fails, to subject, an interpellation that seems to succeed? What if Agave did recognize Pentheus and still, or therefore, went on to dismember him?

This means approaching Euripides's play as an imaginative exploration of what is needed to render patriarchy inoperative, to engage it agonistically with inclination, and to demand or propose the fabulations that record it and support the effort to move past it.

The scene of dismemberment vivifies the fears that stop us, the reluctance to lose loved ones that renders us complicit with oppressive structures, and the anxieties that can keep us compliant with our own and others' subjugation. I suggest, in any case, that the overt violence on which so many focus when they encounter the Bacchae is less radical than the *relaxation and rehearsal* on Cithaeron that precede the regicide and the claim to the city that comes after it.

(Honig 2021: 1–13; *our emphasis*)

At this point, dear reader, you might be asking yourself what *chora* has to do with time and school. Plato invented this concept to help him think time and space, and most Western philosophy will devote considerable energy to either revising it, responding to it or using it as a basis for other concepts. At this point in your reading, you might have thought, 'yes, we are *now* moving decidedly/critically away from male-female binaries into radical undecidability and gender fluidity'. However, this chapter is distinct from the notion of *nostalgia*, which would emphasize precisely the extractive and colonial, masculine origin of thinking Time, longing for a return to the maternal/natural, pre-theoretical and proximate past. Here, the past is the lens through which we look into the future, maintaining connections with the ancestral timelines, because, as American scholar of Black culture Hortense Spillers suggests in 'Mama's Baby, Papa's Maybe' (1987),

undressing these conflations of meaning, as they appear under the rule of dominance, would restore, as figurative possibility, not only Power to Female

(Maternity), but also Power to the Male (for Paternity). We would gain, in short, the *potential* for gender differentiation as it might express itself along the range of stress points, including human biology in its intersection with the project of culture. (Spillers 1987: 66)

In addition, if as a reader, you judge these Fabulations, including Plato's *chora*, as 'just stories', you are participating in the biggest story, perhaps ever, to be told, which is that of Progress. We have shown, particularly in Revelation and Remediation, how colonial expansion affected temporal regimes of knowing, making History into a Category of Time-as-Arrow (Progress) wherein only powerful events such as industrialization, clock-time, colonization, technological advancements (such as gunpowder) were significant. This relegates other timelines and narrations to 'mere' mimetic storytellings, wherein, in Taussig's (2020: 111) words,

Stones are now no more than stones. Condors are no more than condors. And so it goes.

But only up to a point. For the history of that other time lingers on in dreams hidden in animals and things.

But this *thetic* cut/event of emptying the (female) capacity for mimesis in storytelling, in turn, made possible the category of History: 'the attribution to history of the latent power of human events and suffering, a power that connected and motivated everything in accordance with a secret or evident plan to which one could feel responsible, or in whose name one could believe oneself to be acting' (Koselleck [1979] 2004: 35).

The German historian Reinhart Koselleck, famous for his sedimentation model of multiplicity of historical time, captured in his phrase 'contemporaneity of noncontemporanious', argues that this cut, from

the latent power of *human* events and suffering [. . .] occurred in a context of epochal significance: that of the great period of singularization and simplification which was directed socially and politically against a society of estates. Here, Freedom took the place of freedoms, Justice that of rights and servitudes, Progress that of progressions and from the diversity of revolutions, 'The Revolution' emerged. (Koselleck [1979] 2004: 35)

Time then operates with its own idiosyncratic index of Categories (Freedom, Justice, Progress, Revolution), as a matter of value transaction in a given (irreversible because progressive) juridico-economic moral equations of the present.

1) The captive body becomes the source of an irresistible, destructive sensuality; 2) at the same time – in stunning contradiction – the captive body reduces to a thing, becoming *being for* the captor; 3) in this absence from a subject position, the captured sexualities provide a physical and biological expression of 'otherness'; 4) as a category of 'otherness,' the captive body translates into a potential for pornotroping and embodies sheer physical powerlessness that slides into a more general 'powerlessness,' resonating through various centers of human and social meaning. (Spillers 1987: 67)

Taussig suggests that what occurs is 'based on something like Nietzsche's idea of *ressentiment*, a culture of revenge, hate, and fear, in which a person is defined by what they are against and the mimetic faculty is weaponized, no longer enjoyed and suffered only for its own sake' (Taussig 2020: 109; *emphasis in original*). Taussig's mimetic faculty is the capacity to imitate, and its status in modern life is well captured by the derisive connotation of mimicry. Taussig goes on to argue:

If anything, *ressentiment* demands new and powerful skills of deception so as to fool the women whom, even in their degraded condition, men consider as inherently mimetically astute. Mimesis in its ressentiment mode is thus a mimesis sustaining mastery. (Taussig 2020: 109)

But Mimesis in the ressentiment mode also blows open the ethical time scale of obligation and responsibility. The non-coeval temporality of mimetically astute women, slaves and the dispossessed speaks to the layered, but asynchronous structure of time, one in which time is not always already reproductive, smooth and faithful; it is also violent, contradictory, antagonistic and ambiguous.

Collectively, 'we' in the West, no longer have the capacity to be lured by ancestral stories into other timelines that offer radically different and differentiated possibles for living well with the dead, and dying well with the living, other than in our dreams and imaginations thus far understood only as leisured escape from the actual. Because 'we always have the beliefs, feelings and thoughts we deserve given our way of being or our style of life' (Deleuze [1962] 2006: 2), we need 'to assemble tools with which to think and live in the world otherwise' (Ferreira da Silva 2018: 38).

With the earlier three Fabulations, we invite you to allow yourself to be affected, provoked; to feel these Fabulations reverberate in you, take shape, take hold, invite a response-ability – or better, a potentially more mimetic reprise. With these Fabulations, we push Irigaray further in thinking with place and time, by reading Plato's *chora* alongside Spiller's reading of Franklin-Phipps's reading of Black girls becoming-molecular, Honig's reading of *Bacchae*, and Taussig's feminine mimetic faculty/power to show that a *choral bacchaeic tempo* might offer a different way into thinking about Time, as a feminist refusal of the unjust politico-juridical and economic violence (re)producing, maintaining and governing difference against difference through schools: of slaves, women and the 'banausoi' (Arendt [1958] 1998: 82), in other words, '[the] part of those who have no part' (Rancière 2010: 33).

In this book, alongside the redeployment and reappropriation of the metaphysical fabulations of Categories of Space and Time for school education that can accommodate alternative possibles, we abduct *chora* and *Bacchae* to refuse and agonize school Time that continuously re(e)merges racialized and sexed categories of otherness as the result of 'mimesis in its ressentiment mode' between the clock, the child/savage, and the teacher (over 70 per cent mostly woman and mostly White). There is much potential in these Fabulations for cotemporal tracings of the many possibles (parallel universes, agonistic temporalities, otherworldly dimensions and volumes), that is, 'a time that is gathered together, with multiple pleats' (Serres [1990] 1995: 60) 'bleeding through one another' (Barad 2018: 68). We trace some. We leave it to you, to be devoured by others.

Irigaray reclaims (feminine) spatio-temporal ontology by reclaiming Plato's emptyfied, negative *chora* (formless receptacle giving form) as a maternal body with a positive identity. Kristeva leaves it hanging in the semiotic. Spillers (1987) cuts it into a Black woman's *flesh*,[12] making a radical distinction between body as liberated subject positionality, and *flesh*, as positionality of the captive slave. Spillers shows that 'before the "body" there is the "flesh," that zero degree of social conceptualization that does not escape concealment under the brush of discourse, or the reflexes of iconography' (Spillers 1987: 67). The 'ungendering' of Black women's bodies began with the transatlantic slave trade and the disruption of the familial bonds of Black people. In the extractive grammar of slavery, the father is made to signify absence of power and the mother's maternal relationality to her offspring is no longer recognized. That is, Spillers' analysis of the imposition of the colonial syntax of relationality highlighted the fact that the grammatical composition of enslavement, as a form of Black matrilineal reproductive oppression, negated and cancelled out any form of Black parental right (including White patrilineal affiliation) in a 'cultural formation where "kinship" loses meaning' (Spillers 1987: 74). She suggests that the loss of kinship is replaced by *property*, a White supremacist ideology of patriarchal ownership.

We stress her kinship point here, because *sororal-animal kinship*[13] plays an important grammatical part in our feminist reading of bacchaic refusal of Time in its application to teachers. Crucially, along with Spillers and Honig, we ask what happens to *chora* and the spatio-temporal family drama of Western colonial metaphysics, when the privileged kinship is not patriarchal (White, father, husband, son) colonial relationality imposing matricide in its negative patri-matriarchal relationality (self-sacrificing stereotype of White, mother, wife, daughter), but, like in Euripides' drama, the sororal-animal kinship? What happens to time when we shift from the maternal to the sororal plane? Reading alongside Taussig's rewriting of the Selk'nam myth, we also ask what happens to the 'mimetic force-field' as exhibited in relaxation, rest and inoperativity when (sororanimal) kinship is no longer resisted against the privilege of property, which is the decisive shift in 'the operation and capacities of the mimetic faculty itself' (Taussig 2020: 110), an operation responsible for the patriarchal spatio-temporal epistemic violence? As Taussig suggests, the mimetic consequences of matricide were not a 'simple reversal or inversion from women's time to men's time' (Taussig 2020: 110). Rather, the 'nature of the world changes. Metamorphosis itself is but a shadow of its former self. Stones are now no more than stones. Condors are no more than condors. And so it goes' (Taussig 2020: 111).

Three sisters, Agave (Pentheus's mother who will dismember and eventually kill him), Ino and Autonoe, inspired by Dionysian festivities, leave the city for Cithaeron; they refuse work (both productive and reproductive). They refuse to nurse their human (male) offspring, and instead, nurse the many animals of the Cithaeron. Thus, they reject conventional morality and heteronormativity of human-sex-gender and render it 'unreproductive'. Honig re-fabulates Agamben's concept of inoperativity, which is a 'pure' and 'passive' non-use, into a feminist concept of refusal, which intensifies use instead. In Euripides's tragedy, the women of Thebes escape the bonds of household reproduction, defying King Pentheus's orders to stay home, work at their looms and care for their children. In that, their refusal does suspend use. But at Cithaeron, the women enjoy relaxing outside the city, at a distance from its arrangements and restrictions, exemplifying the 'new use in common' (Honig 2021: 22).

How the women enjoy themselves, however, presses further, beyond inoperativity (to render something inoperative means 'removing it from use by exhibiting it or reiterating it in a festive form where it cannot be a means to anything' (Honig 2021: 14–15)). The Bacchants refuse spectacle as 'invariably a carrier for the male gaze'. They find their way to a different temporality, what we would call sororal-animal kinship and mimetic inoperativity. This temporality cannot be easily dismissed as leisure, nor the ancient skholē,[14] a form of temporality that was 'freed from the urgencies of the world, [allowing for] a free and liberated relation to those urgencies and to the world' (Bourdieu 2000: 1). This is embodied in today's examples of Anglo-Saxon university campuses and boarding schools reserved for the privileged few, far removed from those who 'live permanently in the *askholia*, the hurry', bearing the onus of time in the form of its endless and vulgar shortness (Bourdieu 2000: 226; *emphasis in original*). As French philosopher Michel Foucault (1986) suggests in *Of Other Spaces,* 'In our society where leisure is the rule, idleness is a sort of deviation' (25).

> This leisure, needless to say, is not at all the same, as current opinion has it, as the skholē of antiquity, which was not a phenomenon of consumption, 'conspicuous' or not, and did not come about through the emergence of 'spare time' saved from laboring, but was on the contrary a conscious 'abstention from' all activities connected with mere being alive, the consuming activity no less than the laboring. The touchstone of this skholē, as distinguished from the modern ideal of leisure, is the well-known and frequently described frugality of Greek life in the classical period. Thus, it is characteristic that the maritime trade, which more than anything else was responsible for wealth in Athens, was felt to be suspect, so that Plato, following Hesiod, recommended the foundation of new city-states far away from the sea. (Arendt [1958] 1998: 131–2, ft84)

On Cithaeron, the sisters move to inoperativity's intensified 'new use' (or re-use, as in Ahmed's example of the mailbox becoming bird nest). Honig (2021) describes their new establishment as a 'heterotopia' where they rehearse another, rest-full way of living: 'Organized into three women-led bands rather than male-headed households, the bacchants together transgress all the norms by which they were governed in Thebes and they ground new normativities' (22). The city consumes them, by maternalizing them, but rather than refuse to nurture at Cithaeron, which would imply Agamben's 'no use' refusal of maternalism, they nurse animals out in the wild. Their breastfeeding

> refuses the maternalism of heteronormative reproduction but not the intimacy of care. They throw out the baby, we might say, but keep the bathwater. Repurposing the breast out in the wild, they violate the practices of enclosure that prohibit women being out of doors and they ironize familiar patriarchal practices that force women into domesticity. (2021: 23).

In order to resist being consumed by the patriarchal society and reclaim *tempo rubato*, Bacchants refuse both the frugality of skholē (ascetic, passive, pure and nonproductive temporality reserved for men) and askholia (impure, brutal temporality of production as use). The Bacchants impregnate idle temporality not as a container to fill up with their pleasures and sorrows, but to turn it into *chronosporosis*[15] (to borrow and draw from *chronosporic* temporality, a concept indicating the dispersed spreading of time as a density, volume, all at once, coined by feminist scholar Svetlana Slapšak). *Chronosporosis* might be a *chora(l)* (so maybe chorosporosis?), mimetic *awiberation*[16] – fleshy, moonbleeding, multiple, sowing, slow-dispersing and pleasurable Third (in a non-extractive syntax betwixt Time and Space). It is consumption of food[17] for pleasure, erotic pleasure of the breast othermothering/nursing animals and psychic pleasure of rest-full-ness. As American scholar and literary critic Patricia Yaeger suggests in *Honey-Mad Women* (1986), 'In consuming honey so avidly, the honey-mad woman . . . consum[es] a substance like herself [and] usurps her society's right to consume her' (11). Such is an ethics of opacity as refusal of Time.

Like the three sisters at Cithaeron, Baba Yaga, *no longer* sexually useful for reproduction and sustenance of human lives, resides apart from humans and the ocular violence of the male gaze. But unlike the Bacchae, who are *still* in their sexual-reproductive corporal phase, nursing animals, consuming food and resting, Baba Yaga lives/becomes a hut that's more like an animal than a house. As little girls, we learned that Baba Yaga has skinny chicken legs that can run fast and in disperse movements through the forest to avoid anyone who might be *looking* for her. She consumes children. Unreproductive femininity turned into a monstrous Thing, the fence around her chicken-body-house is made from old human bones and atop each of the posts sits a human skull to enlist horror and scare away those who come near. Her house moves, and when it does, she, like Plato's *chora*, spins and screeches to a halt and settles with loud *chora(l)* groans and creaks. When an odd visitor arrives here or there, the house turns its back, refusing to be seen.

But just as Baba Yaga governs life with death, passing betwixt the human and inhuman, the Bacchants who nurse wild animals at Cithaeron, presumably a beautiful garden, also 'rework the "anthropological machine" to contest sovereignty' (Honig 2021: 23). As Argentinian political scientist Guillermina Seri puts it, Agamben's sovereign power 'reproduces itself by distinguishing between human and inhuman, and makes clear that there is no humanity outside this decision' (cited in Honig 2021: 23). Agave's (with the help of her

Figure 5.1 Baba Yaga, the witch from Slavic folklore. She lives in the forest in a hut on chicken legs and flies in a mortar, covering her tracks with a broom. Natalia Mikhalchuk / Alamy Stock Photo. DOI: 10.1080/09518398.2019.1597210

sisters) regicide is a slow one and, as such, it 'occurs long before they attack Pentheus' (Honig 2021: 23). When the sisters realize they *are being watched*, they attack Agave's son Pentheus, 'or maybe it is his verticalism they attack: 'Once they saw [Pentheus] . . . they started pelting him with stones, throwing fir branches over like javelins . . . But all fell short. Finally, they sheared the limbs off an oak and tried to lever the fir [tree] up by its roots. But that failed too' (Honig 2021: 50). In order to bring down Pentheus, the women must incline to each other and act in concert together to force down the tree. Agave shouts,

'"Come, my maenads, gather round this tree and all take hold . . . " And with that, countless hands pulled and pushed . . . and from his high roost Pentheus fell.' Thus, the women dethrone Pentheus. They go on to dismember him, too, as he futilely pleads with them to let him live. 'The air was full of yelps and cries and he heard what must have been his last scream, delivered to the world with his last breath.' (Honig 2021: 50)

Claiming sovereignty over chronosporosis, via an ethics of opacity, is about safeguarding life of sororanimal kinship in heterotopia, away from male gaze – refusing to be seen, recognized, represented, looked at/for. The Bacchants, just as Baba Yaga, employ mimetic deceit to express a positive affirmation of the repressed, monstrous, invisible, methamorphic kinship temporalities (sister/mother/animal, unproductive, unreproductive, unproprietal). If you remember from Fabulation II, we cite Taussig pointing out that the attribution of 'pollution' (women's occult powers equated by analogy to darkness, monstrosity, polymorphous sexuality, porosity) as it is involved in 'trickery, deceit, and mimesis' is based on the idea that in the 'prehistoric time of women's dominance there was a great capacity for flux in identities, involving manifold identifications and metamorphoses between humans and nonhumans' (Taussig 2020: 108).

When Agave brings the head of her son to her father Cadmus, seeking glory for her own (and her sisters') bravery, her father's response is not that of appraisal; instead, he 'buttress(es) the old familiar order against the proposed new one, shoring up the virtues of productivity and verticality against the new glories of inoperativity and inclination' (Honig 2021: 80). To this end, the father does not provide space for any type of a dialogue with Agave. Instead, Cadmus 'reinterpellates her into the world as he knows it and wants it to be. He does not extend himself to her; he reformats the situation to suit himself. With a series of questions to his daughter, Cadmus carefully shifts Agave from a proud revolutionary woman to a mourning mother' (Honig 2021: 79). Following Arendt, Honig suggests that with this sequence of questions Cadmus names/pronounces Agave by robbing her 'of *who* she is and returns her to *what* she is' (Honig 2021: 80; *emphasis in original*). Instead of offering 'the transformative power and glory she craves', he gathers together the 'homogenization of the social and restoration to her proper place' in the syntax of patriarchal kinship (Honig 2021: 80):

> 'Can you hear me?' he says
> 'I'm sorry Father; I can't remember: what were we talking about?'
> 'Into which house did you marry?'
> 'I married Echion, One of the Sown men they say.'
> 'And the name of the son you bore your husband?'
> 'Our son is Pentheus'
> 'And whose head do you hold in your hands?'
> 'A lion's . . . '
> '*Look at it* properly'
> 'Ah, No! No! I see the greatest sorrow!'
> 'Does it still look like a lion?'
> 'No! No. It is . . . Oh gods. It is Pentheus' head I hold.' (Honig 2021: 80; *our emphasis*)

According to American philosopher Martha Nussbaum, Honig suggests, with this sequence of questions, the father reinterpellates Agave to 'the real world of moral reasoning'. But Honig interprets his 'invocations of patriarchy's kinship roles – Father. Husband. Son.' as a process of re-positioning her as 'Daughter. Wife. Mother.' wherein these attributes or 'roles are emplotted as the unalterable chronology of a woman's life. Sister is nowhere to be heard' (Honig 2021: 80).

But what if we read Agave's response-ability alongside Taussig's mimetic faculty linked to prehistoric women's time of an abundance of women's modes/fabulations of change and becomings? Agave's feint ignorance might be read as a continuation of sororal (unreproductive) refusal of being seen/named, an opacity sustained by powers of trickery and deceit, a newly intensified unproductive use of sovereignty by the occult powers gathered together in a metamorphic sororanimal relationality at the rest-full and slow Cithaeron. In Taussig's words, women in the post-matriarchal phase were aware that the spirits were now in fact mortal men wearing masks, but because of threats against their lives if they so much as mentioned this, the women feign ignorance. In other words, what was a secret when the women imitated the spirits became a public secret when the men took over. It became a secret known to all, involving a dizzying cocktail of deceit and counterdeceit: men miming the spirits, women miming ignorance that it was mortal men doing this, and men miming their belief that the women remained ignorant of what they were doing – all in all a great circuit of deceit and mimeses, which appears to me to create a great charge, like an electric charge, empowering the spirits themselves. (Taussig 2020: 108)

That is, we read both Taussig's invocation of a prehistoric temporality associated with feminine capacity for mimesis, and Honig's reading of Agave's metamorphosis from a revolutionary Bacchae to subservient mother, as a feminist mode of sovereignty over chronosporosis, via an ethics of opacity. The opacity of mimetic deceit performed by Baba Yaga (her chicken legs and bird-like face awiberations of bird-like flying around dark forest unproductivity) and Agave's performance/miming of ignorance (knowing what not to know) is an ethics bound up with refusal of patriarchal Time, Time cut off from chronosporosis of storytelling, magic and mimesis. Time bound up with place turned property (extracting productive and reproductive value from women, slaves, children, animals). An ethics of opacity – empowered by rest, food, slow yet intensified (via sororanimal pleasure) – and a refusal of Time.

However, there is much more at stake in an ethics of inoperativity (a particular composition of 'motion and rest') and opacity (mimetic power of deceit, trickery, a refusal of patriarchal ocular epistemology). We are suggesting these opacities as pedagogical modes of feminist refusal of Time – for the bodies turned *flesh* in the systemic rupture between the Black female bodies and the White women's syntext of womanhood (motherhood and sexuality). The symbolic, corporeal and juridico-economic colonial law of *partus sequitur ventrem* codified enslavement as depending on 'the condition of the mother' (Spillers 1987: 79), and her ungendered *flesh* as the place of inscription, as Spillers argues, and as such it transfers from one generation to the next via 'symbolic substitutions'. Spillers suggests that 'African-American female's "dominance" and "strength" come to be interpreted by later generations – both black and white, oddly enough – as a "pathology," as an instrument of castration' (Spillers 1987: 74). In this composition, the absence of the father (and the effects of this absence on his male children) is interpreted as a failure of Black mothers and motherhood (without the leisure time, White juridical and economic privilege and kinship support of the White mothers and wives of European aristocracy and North American plantation owners). Black female *flesh* could not provide (and thus castrated?) the space and maternal place for the self-actualization of her male counterpart through Time. In the leisure time experienced by the privileged, who has a room of *her* own, in the words of British writer Virginia Woolf.

> Women have served all these centuries as *looking-glasses* possessing the *magic* and delicious *power* of reflecting the figure of man at twice its natural size. Without that power probably the earth would still be swamp and jungle. The glories of all our wars would be unknown. . . . Whatever may be their use in *civilized* societies, mirrors are essential to all violent and heroic action. That is why Napoleon and Mussolini both insist so emphatically upon the inferiority of women, for if they were not inferior, they would cease to enlarge. That serves to explain in part the necessity that women so often are to men. And it serves to explain how restless they are under her criticism; how impossible it is for her to say to them this book is bad, this picture is feeble, or whatever it may be, without giving far more pain and rousing far more anger than a man would do who gave the same criticism. For if she begins to tell the truth, the figure in the looking-glass shrinks; his fitness for life is diminished. How is he to go on giving judgement, civilizing natives, making laws, writing books, dressing up and speechifying at banquets, unless he can see himself at breakfast and at dinner at least twice the size he really is? So *I reflected, crumbling my bread and stirring my coffee and now and again looking at the people in the street. The looking-glass vision is of supreme importance because it charges the vitality; it stimulates the nervous system. Take it away and man may die, like the drug fiend deprived of his cocaine.* Under the *spell* of that illusion, I thought, looking out of the window, half the people on the pavement are striding to work. They put on their hats and coats in the morning under its agreeable rays. They start the day confident, braced, believing themselves desired at Miss Smith's tea party; they say to themselves as they go into the room, I am the superior of half the people here, and it is thus that they speak with that self-confidence, that self-assurance, which have had such profound consequences in public life and lead to such curious notes in the margin of the private mind. But these contributions to the dangerous and fascinating subject of the psychology of

the other sex – it is one, I hope, that you will investigate *when you have five hundred a year of your own* – were interrupted by the necessity of paying the bill. (Woolf 1929; *our emphasis*)

When Cadmus says to Agave '*Look at it* properly', might he be demanding that she employ her magic powers and *Look at Him properly*, to serve as the looking-glass enlarging his place as Father, King, Husband?

In a double bind of the colonial composition of Time and Blackness, rest, idleness and inoperativity are prohibited and criminalized as loitering, vagrancy for Black and Brown bodies while simultaneously, the '"underachievement" in black males of the lower classes', as Spillers (1987) suggests, is perceived as 'primarily the fault of black females, who achieve out of proportion, both to their numbers in the community and to the paradigmatic example before the nation' (66).

When Frankie is confronted with colonial structures of temporal confrontations in her high school years and later at the university, she performs 'extra work that at times becomes unmanageable; Frankie took on additional labor that was not recognized, or maybe was unable to be recognized, as it did not correspond with the labor of dominant groups' (Franklin-Phipps 2017: 387). This extra labour on the part of Black girl students is not recognized by White teachers, because Time is not something that figures prominently in educational theory, practice and policy. Even less is it addressed as the neocolonial regime, sustaining White supremacy and its systemic patriarchal oppression of racially marginalized peoples.

Frankie's success as a Black woman student is quantified and qualified not only through the measure of value via grades and educational assessment (Time constraints inflicted by neoliberal capitalist educational regime that values/measures Time as a commodity of those who will have always already be(long)come through Time), but via the descaled measure of value preconditioned on colonial extraction of Black female *flesh* and family *kinship* resulting in 'dehumanizing, ungendering, and defacing of African persons' (Spillers 1987: 72) that Frankie experiences as daily micro school aggressions: 'Her grades slipped, and even though she accomplished much more than many undergraduates, this traditional yet incomplete measure of her accomplishment allowed her to be imagined and imagine herself as incompetent' (Franklin-Phipps 2017: 388). In another testament to this ongoing/progressive temporal violence on Black women and girls, American author Ijeoma Oluo (2018) writes:

> It is very hard to survive as a woman of color in this world, and I remember saying once that if I stopped to feel, really feel, the pain of the racism I encountered, I would start screaming and I would never ever stop. So I did what most of us do, I tried to make the best of it. I worked 50 percent harder than my white coworkers, I stayed late every day. I dressed like every day was a job interview. I was overpolite to white people I encountered in public. I bent over backwards to prove that I was not angry, that I was not a threat. I laughed off racist jokes as if I didn't feel the sting. I told myself that it would all be worth it one day, that being a successful Black woman was revolution enough. (2)

When unschooling and deschooling is reserved for the selected few, and schools as we know them will have apparently persisted at all costs (as the public discourse during the Covid-19 reopening narrates, kids need a sense of normalcy – i.e. they (?) miss the socializing aspects of schooling), some of us were hoping that since the rich and the powerful don't give a fuck about millions of people and children dying from hunger, air pollution, drought, etc., every year, and the fires choking and scorching vegetal, animal and plant beings and persons, and then the floods drowning them, perhaps the Covid-19 pandemic would place significant stress on the need to restructure our society that is so dependent on neocolonial extractive regimes, that is, the going-to-work and doing-your-time (either in the office, factory, school, or prison), so that not only the children of the privileged classes can enjoy high-quality educational compositions of 'motion and rest'.

If a complete refusal of the existing school system is impossible – because so many working and middle-class parents depend on its free babysitting economy – rather than demand reform or inclusion in the White neoliberal and neocolonial schooling agenda, we urge teachers and students to claim periods of rest, inoperativity, inactivity, immovability, motionless pleasure and mimesis through such non-chronogen(er)ic modes of learning that encourage 'mastery of non-mastery' (Taussig's mimesis), knowing what not to know (i.e. Agave's refusal to acknowledge/*see*) and refusing to be seen/known (Frankie's refusal via opacity). This praxis would privilege an ethics of paying attention – demanding a pedagogy of slowness, rituals that carry radical possibilities for girl, BIPOC and SOGI empowerment – and a radical redress of both

White students' privilege and power, and their White fragility, discomfort and resistance against anti-racist work. Our project is thus aligned with but somewhat different from those scholars who advocate for a rethinking of Time in schools through 'research-creation' and walking curriculum, and who, like Canadian curriculum studies scholar Stephanie Springgay and Australian education scholar Sarah Truman (2019), 'emphasize movement that is not about moving from one point to another but about the endless proliferation of absolute movement' (4).

:

As we write this section today (26 August 2021), at 3.06 pm or 15.06 hours, we receive in our mailbox a hot-off-the-press American historian and feminist scholar Tina M. Campt's book *A Black Gaze* (2021), a book we pre-ordered in May and thus forgot all about. The smell of paper and ink is intense and we find ourselves sniffing the gift over and over again before we open Verse Four, and on page 112 our eyes press on the last few lines of the last paragraph: 'while their respective enactments of slowness diverge significantly, each uses slowness in ways that require us to take care, to take notice, and to amplify how we care of ourselves and others, and how we care for both the living and the dead'. (These lines make us think of deep-time geologic and spirit temporalities, and we wonder how we could stop educating our White students to live 'well' their riches and privileges, but die well in order to become socially and ecologically just keepers of ancestral modes of being and becoming.) Through discussing the art works of American artist Okwui Okpokwasili and American photographer and educator Dawoud Bey, she focuses on their 'attention to slowness', which 'opens up a useful framework for understanding the velocities and intensities of contemporary Black life, and, more significantly, the temporality of a Black gaze' she asks: 'For what if we thought of a Black gaze as itself a particularly acute velocity of living? What might its temporality be?' (Campt 2021: 112).

Today's choralsporic synchronicity in thinking

> **chorosporosis** (in the monstrous/mimetic outside matricide/City, outside the colonial castrations/enclosures of pure and transparent Time),
> **tempo** (communal rest-fullness and slowness as refusals of patriarchal and colonial violence against female bodies and Black female *flesh*) and the

ocular (opacity; deceit, trickery; magic of the looking-glass; sororal refusal of male gaze; 'temporality of Black gaze')

impresses on us as a feeling of a chora(l) tuning/whirling into potentiality becoming anaphorically ingressed in new possibles; through coevalness of lives, notions, fabulations and experiences as distinct as those of Campt, Taussig, Honig, Spillers, Frankie, Agave, Biidaaban, Plato, Euripides, etc.

> Black gaze:
> a framing that positions viewers in relation to the precarity and possibility of blackness; a gaze that requires the affective labour of adjacency.
> (Campt 2021: 172)

Campt clarifies that what she is naming the Black gaze does not 'describe the viewpoint of Black people', which means that it is 'not a gaze restricted to or defined by race or phenotype' (Campt 2021: 172). Instead of it being an ocular Category, it is rather a 'viewing practice and a structure of witnessing that reckons with the precarious state of Black life in the twenty-first century. A Black gaze . . . repurposes vulnerability and makes it (re)generative', while at the same time, it 'does not position white spectators as the subjects of its gaze' (Campt 2021: 172). In other words, it is a gaze that 'reconfigures the dominant gaze by exploiting white exclusion from and vulnerability to the opacity of blackness' (Campt 2021: 172). And so it goes. 'In doing so, it demands forms of affective labour that implicate and impact its viewers' (Campt 2021: 172).

Similar to our reading of Plato's chora (patriarchal spatio-temporal ontology) alongside the chora(l) safeguarded by the mimetic sororanimal opacity of the three sisters at Cithaeron, rather than refuse to employ or re-deploy Plato's chora – or in Campt's case, the White male gaze – which would be a 'no use' refusal of colonial patriarchy, we stay/mimic with/in the magic powers of the negative. The inoperativity of chora(l) opacity becomes an intensified field of a poetics of depth – a contrecolonial[18] pedagogy of paying attention (a 'practice of witnessing') to a deep, slow and rest-full modality of living with another. *Possibles.* Nursing animals in the sororal kinship of chorospororis, outside the

City, refuses the maternalized and accelerated heteronormative spatio-temporal reproduction. Campt's Black gaze refuses the ocular (colonial) field through which the dominant White gaze builds and holds-in its juridico-economic power in the speculative leisure of *perhaps*. The power of opacity in Bacchants and Campt's Black gaze do not refuse the deep intimacy of care, but perform a tense of *as if*, a less causal (and sequential) modality than the if-then of perhaps.

KinCare. Witness. Still.

Opacity as a mode of 'no-use' addresses demands that in relating to an Other, we slow down and sit with the discomfort of stillness. It requires that we 'check our desire for reciprocal recognition' (Seph Rodney, as cited in Campt 2021: 153). It requires that we 'sit uncomfortably with the impulse to transform that discomfort into a form of reflection that is potentially transformative' (Campt 2021: 153). This is a pedagogy of 'enduring discomfort and facing it head on' (Campt 2021: 154), also known through Haraway as 'staying with the trouble'. Campt too works out a different fabulation of temporality via sororal chorus as an inoperative tempo of Black gaze.

In analysing American artist Simone Leigh's installation 'Loophole of Retreat I', Campt fabulates a fugitive loophole:

1/ Black women's insurgency (she pays tribute to Debbie Sims Africa and her incarcerated sisters who laboured to conceal the birth of her son in prison and create a three-day 'protective space of refuge and sanctuary' (2019: 150) for Debbie and the infant to bond).

2/ In the gallery, three large figures stand 'proudly in a commanding triangle,' where the sister figures face each other, each 'seemingly transfixed by her presence. She does not return the gaze, but does not look away. Smooth black surfaces stand in for what should be the figure's eyes, but it is an absence that in no way signals a lack of sight. They hold each other's gazes; they hold each other's presence. They rest and hold each other in what becomes an almost sacred space of quite intensity' (2019: 150).

3/ Harriet Jacob's (1861) *Incidents in the Life of a Slave Girl*: **'*loophole of retreat: the dark enclosure of an attic space where she plots and plans she dreams of possibility from within impossible strictures of confinement her escape is immanent, as her imagination is boundless her enclosure is an incubator for a practice of refusal and a roadmap to freedom*'** (as cited (in bold and italics) in 2019: 146).

Campt shows that the absence of eyes on the three sister figures (*Panoptica, Jug* and *Sentinel*) denies White normative gaze, but she does not understand this to be a reaction formation on the level of 'negation or reserve'.

> The absence of eyes that should serve as the sources, origins, or conduits of these looks intensifies our search for contact and connection. Their absence amplifies a look that is there but not there. It is a look that seeks us out even in its erasure. United kindred in the gallery, the three figures create a sheltering space of care, providing refuge as a group that watches out and watches over. They are a trio who embrace without touching, speak without words or sound, and gaze without eyes with power and grace at one another and at us. Like their sibling sound installation, P*anoptica, Jug,* and *Sentinel* cohere as a chorus. (2019: 152)

The power of this capacity to create a distinct, fugitive Black gaze, lies in its 'power of opacity' (2019: 153) that demands from us complex forms of 'affective labour of adjacency' (2019: 172). This complex pedagogical/contrecolonial labour requires that we care by paying due attention to opaque compositions of 'motion and rest', which can only happen in slowness, stillness, immovability of intimate, deep care for the micro temporal, sonic, secret, quiet, silent rhythms and gestures – modes of 'overlooked velocity of living' (2019: 111). As an alternative ethics of care and pedagogy, slowness and rest are required in any contrecolonizing educational praxis that is response-able to notice, to pay attention.

> Slowness is an opening to linger durationaly in the small, in details, in reflection. Rather than delayed or diminished development, it intensifies our perception of any outcome. Rather than reducing exertion, slowness extends and multiplies the energy we must use to engage in a particular activity. Yet Lepecki goes even further when he encourages us to understand slowness as an alternative form of ethics. It is an ethics he describes as 'a radical mode of composing the infinite velocities and slownesses of being'. (2019: 110)

Perhaps. As if. Possibles.

:

Reprise

Plato: time is motion.
Aristotle: time is the number of motion.
Zeno: time is the interval of motion and a measure of swiftness and slowness.
Plotinus: time is a function of the life of the Soul.
St. Augustine: the passing of time is in the present, and internal – entirely in our minds, as memory and as anticipation.
Newton: time is the duration of the existence of things; it flows on eternally, calmly and evenly without relation to anything external.
Kant: time is formed by consciousness' sense (thinking, perceiving) of ordering its *internal* states *within*.
Husserl: distinguishes between physical time, which comes first, and the internal consciousness of time, which is determined by the first, physical world.
Heidegger: time produces itself insofar as there is man.
Leibniz: time is the order of events.
Bergson: time is duration, which is a single connected process that cannot be broken into parts.
McTaggart: there is no such thing as time.
Einstein: time is an illusion that moves relative to the observer.
Deleuze: time is the power of life to evolve.

:

We had said in previous pages that the predetermined Time regime is conditioned on and justifies the repetition of subservience, discipline and compliance. The notion of school Time as both the repetition of predetermined successive learning stages and the cyclical repetition of the passage of Time *out there*, governs the power configuration of schools because it institutes moral zones and ethical ideals of the already established, tested and objective regimes of schooling. The earlier cheat sheet list of definitions conjured up by white, male scientists and philosophers speak to the various definitions foundational for different ethics, with the main onto-mathematical-philosophical categories in common being: external/internal, change/stasis, being/becoming, human/nonhuman, and point of view.

Time in school is commoned by being repeatedly retold through a figure of phallic, copulative, reproductive Organism sustained over time, whose pre-emptive modes of bio-control operate directly through the archival activity of fixed past and potential futurity in the present, serving as lures for sentimentality to existing desires. For example, while one of the ethical premises of schooling is to enable all students to lead a good life, the current epochal question of what a good life is has been operationalized for the powerful few, and is indistinguishable from mass consumerism of goods and the production of ever new desires. Canadian Educational Humanities scholar Mishra Tarc suggests that 'We are living in a time of great violence against those with the least power and recourse to justice in our human community' (Tarc 2020: 89). She asserts that '[o]ur time is distinctly one that visibly, horrifically bears witness to unthinkable adult war on children in school shootings, in family separations, in rape and abuse of children, in tiny bodies dragged up on shorelines at the borders of nations. As the adult community's humanity descends deeper into brutality, as we begin killing our young, we are no longer recognizable to ourselves' (Tarc 2020: 89). This is the share of violence in education's continuous organismal re-actualization.

In this book, we fabulate time for education, to provoke a choral refusal of time's transcendental privileges over temporal synthesis (becoming), in order to unbind the organismal (extractive-productive-sexual) synthesis of thinking and being. This provocation calls for a non-dialectical ethic of relating; in indifference *and* difference, life *and* death.

We use 'ethical' in its etymological connection to 'ethos' or habit. When we think of ethical encounters and events in schooling, we normally think of habits of relating with care, mutual respect, responsibility and obligation. These habits demand and obligate an identification in relation to a pledge, a wager to respond to the other by promising a return, an exchange. Time operationalizes our desire for use. Such an ethic is based on a particular (either utilitarian, deontological, teleological, moral, or justice and virtue-based) understanding of habit, one that *either* accepts *or* rejects the provocation to respond to the other, divergent identity. **Response (n)** is an answer, a reply – to respond – an answer to, a promise in return, a pledge. But a **relation (n)** comes from a bringing back, restoring; recounting, telling, bearing back. This later definition of a relation evokes reprise, rather than response. **Reprise (n)** is to take back, pull back, hold back. Resumption of an action. The musical sense is repeated passage, or act of repeating a passage.[1]

In these pages, ethical relationality becomes a temporal question of reprise, whereby rhythm modulates as a virtual relation of possibles, defining, to borrow the words of Parisi and Goodman (2009), 'the discontinuous vibrations of matter'. In considering an ethical relationality, we must thus 'also ontologically prioritize the in-between of oscillation, the vibration of vibration, the virtuality of the tremble' (Parisi and Goodman 2009) which 'represents the kinds of political aspirations that are inaudible and illegible within the prevailing formulas of political rationality' (Best and Hartman 2005: 9). In reading the archive counter-factually by writing critical fabulations as the continuity of discontinuity of the narratives of the enslaved, Hartman poses an ethical obligation to the 'virtuality of the tremble', to prioritize and 'respect black noise – the shrieks, the moans, the nonsense, and the opacity, which are always in excess of legibility and of the law and which hint at and embody aspirations that are wildly utopian, derelict to capitalism, and antithetical to its attendant discourse of Man' (Hartman 2008: 12).

Magic and Dreamers.

> However, when these girls say, 'We want to make life more beautiful' and when they rank love as one of the arts, they are not interested in reproduction art: to replay the past is not enough, when one knows how grim the realities of the past have been. They would like to invent a new art of love, and there are many precedents which show that it is possible to do so. (Zeldin 1998: 84)

'These girls' know not to put their passion for/from the other to the test of the past or the future possibles, but to other dreamers and fabulators, also dreaming up impossible worlds, densities and dimensions of time. The ethical obligation to 'respond . . .' to the other is here replaced by the question: 'what reprise is required by your wager?' Such a question affirms and presupposes the continuity of discontinuity (holding back *and* repeating, taking back *and* resuming), a being out of phase with the others' dreams. Which, 'like yours, are created according to the means of their own adventure' (Stengers [2002] 2014: 518).

And if the exchange is possible, if sometimes – an essentially anonymous event – one dream may induce the modification of another or evoke another, it is insofar as their point of junction is always a tangent point: neither a frontal clash between rival powers nor being swallowed up in the other's dream, not confusion in a banal dream of power but a local resonance, designating past tenses of divergent accomplishments and future tenses responding to distinct tests. (Stengers [2002] 2014: 518)

:

Notes

Introducing

1. Le Guin (1974).
2. Harper (n.d.), 'Etymology of time', *Online Etymology Dictionary*.
3. Harper (n.d.), 'Etymology of artifice', *Online Etymology Dictionary*.
4. Borges (1962).
5. This quotation is from Celia Britton's (2020) English translation of Glissant, but we have read and additionally draw ideas from the original French: Édouard Glissant's (1997).
6. Merriam-Webster (n.d.).
7. See, for example, Donald's (2020a).

Remediation

1. See page 83 of Jeanette Winterson's ([1989] 1990).
2. Harper (n.d.), 'Etymology of remediation', *Online Etymology Dictionary*.
3. Harper (n.d.), 'Etymology of remedy', *Online Etymology Dictionary*.
4. For the original French, see Châtelet (1993).
5. We use this concept in the Bergson-Deleuze immanence trajectory, as 'a certain existence which is more than that which the idealist calls a "representation," but less than that which the realist calls a "thing" – an existence placed halfway between the "thing" and the "representation"' (Bergson [1896] 1991: 9).
6. For the original French, see Glissant (1990).
7. In such a *technology-rich world*, the privileged enjoy the objects of life-expanding and life-enhancing 'scientific processes such as vaccines, organ transplants and other sophisticated medical procedures, other, often racialized bodies become useful as raw sources and labor', valued for their time-expandable 'biological capacities' (Brown 2015: 322).
8. For critiques and controversies of Ariès' thesis, see Dekker and Groenendijk (2012).
9. Designations too often used as a biocentric explanation and justification of failed monastic and colonial discipline.

10 For more see, for example, *Cutting School: The Segrenomics of American Education*, by Noliwe Rooks (2017).
11 For more see, for example, Erin Manning's (2018).
12 From page 178 of Malcolm Bowie's (1991).
13 See the English translation of the original Latin: Kaan ([1844] 2016).

Revelation

1 See page 83 of Jeanette Winterson's ([1989] 1990).
2 Harper (n.d.), 'Etymology of revelation', *Online Etymology Dictionary*.
3 See page 318 of Nick Land's (2011) 'Circuitries'.
4 Harper (n.d.), 'Etymology of progress', *Online Etymology Dictionary*.
5 Harper (n.d.), 'Etymology of defer', *Online Etymology Dictionary*.
6 From Ursula Le Guin's ([1986] 2019).
7 See Simondon (1958) for the original French.

Rupture

1 Page 83 of Jeanette Winterson's ([1989] 1990).
2 Harper (n.d.), 'Etymology of rupture', *Online Etymology Dictionary*.
3 See for example Dwayne Donald's (2020a).
4 Harper (n.d.), 'Etymology of time', *Online Etymology Dictionary*.
5 In an interview by Leah Collins (2019).
6 Meaning to 'assert, name'.

> **category (n.)**
> from *kata* 'down to' (or perhaps 'against;' see **cata-**) + *agoreuein* 'to harangue, to declaim (in the assembly),' from *agora* 'public assembly' (from PIE root *****ger-** 'to gather').
>
> (from Harper's 'Etymology of category', *Online Etymology Dictionary*)

We are using *Kategoria of Time* in Aristotle's sense of applying *kategoria* to his different classes of things that can be named. We understand Kategoria of Time as a thing (in Hegelian sense) that can be Named; an *Index* inscribing, proclaiming Western scientific, juridical, literate, philosophic, aesthetic, religious Grammar of Thought.

index (n.)
late 14c., 'the forefinger' from Latin *index* (genitive *indicis*) 'one who points out, discloser, discoverer, informer; forefinger (because used in pointing); pointer, sign; title, inscription, list', literally 'anything which points out', from *indicare* 'to point out', from *in-* 'into, in, on, upon' (from PIE root ***en** 'in') + *dicare* 'proclaim' (from PIE root ***deik-** 'to show', also 'pronounce solemnly', and see **diction**). Related: *Indexical*.

Obsolete in English in its original sense (*index finger* is recorded from 1768). Meaning 'alphabetical list of a book's contents with directions where in the text to find them' is from late 16c., from Latin phrases such as *Index Nominum* 'Index of Names'.

Meaning 'object serving as a pointer on an instrument, hand of a clock or watch' is from 1590s. Scientific sense (*refractive index*, etc.) is from 1829, from notion of 'an indicator.' Economic sense (*cost-of-living index*, etc.) is from 1870, from the scientific usage.

The Church sense of 'forbidden books' is from *index librorum prohibitorum*, first published 1564 by authority of Pius IV. The *Index Expurgatorius* was the catalogue of books that Catholics were forbidden to read unless certain passages were deleted, first printed 1571.

(from Harper's 'Etymology of index', *Online Etymology Dictionary*)

7   To evoke both the in-vitro process of insemination (outside the body in artificial environment, virtual) and vitrum, which refers to a pane of glass (transparency, looking-glass, indeterminacy).
8   All 'April 12, 2019' DFdS quotes come from Ferreira da Silva (2019): 'An End to "This" World: Denise Ferreira da Silva Interviewed by Susanne Leeb and Kerstin Stakemeier'.
9   Ferreira da Silva (2019).
10 Ibid.
11 All 'Sometime in 2008' LI quotes come from Luce Irigaray (2008): *Sharing the World*. This particular one is from p. 98.
12 All 'February 2017' DFdS quotes come from Ferreira da Silva (2017): '1 (life) ÷ 0 (blackness) = ∞ − ∞ or ∞ / ∞: On Matter Beyond the Equation of Value'. This one is from p. 11, note 2.
13 Irigaray (2008: 103).
14 Ibid., 102.
15 Ibid.

16 Ibid., 98.
17 Ferreira da Silva (2017: 1-2).
18 The 'Summer 2014' DFdS quotes come from Ferreira da Silva (2014b): 'Toward a Black Feminist Poethics'; this one lives on p. 83–84.
19 All 'Sometime in 2014' DFdS quotes are from Ferreira da Silva (2014a): 'Radical Praxis or Knowing (at) the Limits of Justice'; see p. 529 for this one; *italics in original.*
20 In contrast to libidinal economy structured on the phallus (such as in Lacan's and Freud's psychoanalytic), Irigaray proposes a libidinal economy structured on the embodied connection to the maternal body. In Irigaray's libidinal economy, the structure of (sexual) desire and social exchange in Western signifying apparatuses are suggested to be conditioned on matricide, not patricide.
21 Ibid., 534.
22 Ibid., 534-5.
23 Ibid., 530.
24 Ferreira da Silva (2014b: 84-5).
25 Ibid., 87.
26 Ferreira da Silva (2017: 11, note 4).
27 Irigaray (2008: 101).
28 Ferreira da Silva (2014b).
29 Irigaray (2008: 99).
30 The 'Sometime in 2001' LI quotes come from Luce Irigaray (2001): 'From *The Forgetting of Air* to *To Be Two*'; this one from p. 309.
31 Ferreira da Silva (2014b: 90).
32 Irigaray (2008: 99).
33 Harper, Douglas (n.d.), 'Etymology of epoch', *Online Etymology Dictionary*.
34 Irigaray (2008: 99–100).
35 Ibid., 100.
36 Ferreira da Silva (2014b: 89–90).
37 Ferreira da Silva, 2022, p. 86.
38 Ferreira da Silva (2014b: 91).
39 Ibid., 90).

Repetition

1 From Jeanette Winterson's ([1989] 1990: 83).
2 From the classic Alice's Adventures in Wonderland, originally published in 1865. This quotation can be found on pages 104–5 of an edition available online at the time of this writing; see Carroll ([1865] 2000).

3 We use the word 'instauration' in the sense of Souriau (1939), which he defines as 'all processes, abstract or concrete, of operations that create, construct, order or evolve, that lead to the position of a being in its pathos, which is to say with a sufficient burst of reality, and instaurative is all that pertains to such a process' (p. 10, our translation). The concept of instauration seeks to blur the subject-object dichotomy and avoid substantialist assumptions of application, causation and transfer.
4 Harper (n.d.), 'Etymology of rhythm', *Online Etymology Dictionary*.
5 Emile Durkheim (1912), Marcel Mauss (1950), Gaston Bachelard (1969), Walter Benjamin ([1940] 1968) were all interested in the theory of rhythm. All these studies are thought to be inspired by Gabriel Tarde's (1890) universal repetition theory (Brighenti and Kärrholm, 2018).
6 Harper (n.d.), 'Etymology of present', *Online Etymology Dictionary*.
7 Gibson (1999).
8 With the origins in Arab sugar plantations, monocropping and plantation system was first introduced in Latin America (and then North America) by the Portuguese settlers.
9 Ashbery, John (1981: 79). Copyright (c) 1981 by John Ashbery. All rights reserved. Used by arrangement with JA Projects Inc and Georges Borchardt, Inc. for the Estate of John Ashbery.

Refusal

1 Jeanette Winterson's ([1989] 1990: 83).
2 Harper (n.d.), 'Etymology of refusal', *Online Etymology Dictionary*.
3 Quotation from Zeyl's (2000) translation of Plato's *Timaeus*.
4 From Zeyl (2000).
5 From the translation by Kalkavage (2016).
6 Via Cornford's ([1935] 2000) translation.
7 From Cornford ([1935] 2000).
8 Plato (*Timaeus* 37d) defines time as chronos: 'the moving image of eternity (aion) that moves according to number', via the translation in Hamilton and Cairns (1989).
9 Aristotle (*Physics* IV 220a) refused Plato's *imaged thought* of eternity and defined chronos without alluding to images, as 'the number of movement according to the "before and after"' (Hardie and Gaye 2003). *Now*, also as a measure of movement, is only a limit, a boundary between past and anticipated future.
10 In the tropism on Revelation, we discuss the rethinking of space and place by Indigenous scholars. While they should be contrasted in their particular

premises and aims, we are arguing in this book that they each have their own space-time tendencies, and can therefore not be synthesized or opposed. For Indigenous scholars, the time of the ancestral past and the violent erasure of culture and language should be contrasted with the feminist's predicament of Woman's exclusion from time. The way they both mobilize against a static, passive understanding of space produces powerful resonances. Here we work with Irigaray because of the stepping stones offered towards Taussig's feminist mimetic and Honig's feminist refusal.

11 From page 3 of Ben Okri's (1991).

12 For further discussion on 'flesh' and blackness see, for example, Ronald A. T. Judy's (2020) discussion of the intricate concomitance of Black flesh, thinking, and semiosis; Fred Moten's Black flesh as a site of 'fantasy in the hold' (2013); Saidiya Hartman's analysis of liberation and the suffering flesh (1997); and Alexander G. Weheliye's suggestion, following Hortense Spillers and Sylvia Wynter, that flesh be considered as a zone of potentiality, as well as resistance (2014).

13 For more on the importance of kinship in feminist critiques of patriarchy see Haraway's concept of 'making kin' (Haraway 2016).

14 School as skholē establishes a division between those who are inside and experience free time on equal terms, and those who are outside skholē who experience time as use and production. Living in askholia, those outside skholē are forced to perpetually justify their uses of time in terms of its productivity. Elsewhere in this book we have reiterated the fact that school (distinct from monastic learning) is not born specifically as a space to learn, but was intended for experiencing time outside askholia, which is time experienced = outside school.

15 =

> **sorosis (n.)**
> 'consolidated fleshy multiple fruit' (such as a pineapple), 1831, from Modern Latin, from Greek *sōros* 'a heap' (of corn), which is of uncertain origin

+

> **spore (n.)**
> from Greek *spora* 'a seed, a sowing, seed-time', related to *sporas* 'scattered, dispersed', *sporos* 'a sowing', from PIE **spor-*, variant of root **sper-* 'to spread, sow' (see **sparse**).

(Harper, Douglas (n.d.), 'Etymology of sorosis' and 'Etymology of spore', *Online Etymology Dictionary*)

16 Alluding to Baba Yaga, from Slavic mythology, who is a – sometimes bird-like, but always old – woman past her reproductive years. A witch who lives alone, deep in the dark forest, in folk storytelling, with powers to devour, eat human flesh and lay eggs. Or grant wishes. Baba can mean 'midwife', 'sorceress' or 'fortune teller'. No longer in the role of reproductive sexuality, she is – becomes – in power of metamorphosis (sometimes bird, woman, chicken), and thus in power of mimesis. She also controls the elements, such as the weather, and can, at times, show grandmaternal care. Yaga is from

> ***awi-**
> Proto-Indo-European root meaning 'bird'. It is the hypothetical source of/ evidence for its existence is provided by: Sanskrit vih, Avestan vish, Latin *avis* 'bird'; Greek *aietos* 'eagle'; Old Church Slavonic *aja*, Russian *jajco*, Breton *ui*, Welsh *wy*, Greek *ōon*, Latin *ovum*, Old Norse *egg*, Old High German *ei*, Gothic *ada*, all meaning 'egg'.

(Harper, Douglas (n.d.), 'Etymology of *awi-', *Online Etymology Dictionary*)

Thus, according to etymology, it also might be the source of the words *ovulation, ovary*.

17 For more on food and sexuality see Slapšak's (2016) *Cabbage: A Review of the Historical Anthropology of Food and Sexuality*.

18 We do not use the word decolonial, which makes the temporal assumption that there is a going back to a (bad) time before, which will result in a (good) time after – which adopts the spatial imaginary of time as remediation. In the key of refusal, which is the tropism under consideration here, we work with contrecolonial, which is to refuse colonialism without the desire of salvation or progress.

Reprise

1 Our descriptions of these three words – response (n.), relation (n.), reprise (n.) – are based on their respective entries in the Online Etymology Dictionary (see Harper, Douglas (n.d.)).

References

Ables, Kelsey (2021), 'The "slow art" Movement Isn't Just About Staring Endlessly at Paintings. It's also about Accessibility', *The Washington Post*, 4 April. Available online: https://www.washingtonpost.com/entertainment/museums/slow-art-day-looking-at-art/2021/04/01/f6eaf2a0-916b-11eb-bb49-5cb2a95f4cec_story.html (accessed 9 February 2022).

Adorno, Theodor ([1951] 1974), Minima Moralia: Reflections from a Damaged Life, trans. E. F. N. Jephcott, London: New Left Books.

Ahmed, Sara (2010), 'Happy Objects', in Melissa Gregg and Gregory J. Seigworth (eds), *The Affect Theory Reader*, 29–51, Durham and London: Duke University Press.

Ahmed, Sara (2019), *What's the Use?: On the Uses of Use*, Durham: Duke University Press.

Arendt, Hannah ([1958] 1998), *The Human Condition*, 2nd edn, Chicago: The University of Chicago Press.

Ariès, Philippe ([1960] 1962), *Centuries of Childhood: A Social History of Family Life*, trans. Robert Baldick, New York: Vintage.

Arrival (2016), [Film] Dir. Denis Villeneuve, USA: Paramount Pictures.

Ashbery, John (1981), 'This Configuration', *The Paris Review*, 79. Available online: https://www.theparisreview.org/poetry/6986/this-configuration-john-ashbery (accessed 10 February 2022).

Bachelard, Gaston ([1964] 1969), *The Poetics of Space*, trans. Maria Jolas, Boston: Beacon Press.

Bakhtin, Mikhail ([1981] 2008), 'Forms of Time and of the Chronotype in the Novel', in Michael Holquist (ed.), *The Dialogic Imagination: Four Essays*, trans. Caryl Emerson and Michael Holquist, 84–258, Austin: University of Texas Press.

Barad, Karen ([2012] forthcoming), 'On Touching – The Inhuman that Therefore I Am', v1.1 (preprint), in Susanne Witzgall and Kerstin Stakemeier (eds), The Politics of Materiality. Originally published in differences (2012), 23(3): 206–23.

Barad, Karen (2007), *Meeting the Universe Halfway*, Durham and London: Duke University Press.

Barad, Karen (2018), 'Troubling Time/s and Ecologies of Nothingness: Re-turning, Re-Membering, and Facing the Incalculable', *New Formations*, 92: 56–86.

Battiste, Marie (2013), *Decolonizing Education: Nourishing the Learning Spirit*, Saskatoon: Purich Publishing.

Benjamin, Walter ([1940] 1968), 'Theses on the Philosophy of History', in Hannah Arendt (ed.), *Illuminations*, trans. Harry Zohn, 253–64, New York: Schocken Books.

Bergson, Henri ([1896] 1991), *Matter and Memory*, trans. Nancy Margaret Paul and W. Scott Palmer, New York: Zone Books.

Bergson, Henri (1911), *Creative Evolution*, trans. Arthur Mitchell, New York: Henry Holt and Company.

Best, Stephen and Saidiya Hartman (2005), 'Fugitive Justice', *Representations*, 92 (1): 1–15.

Biidaaban (2017), [Film] Dir. Amanda Strong, Canada: Spotted Fawn Productions.

Blanchot, Maurice ([1980] 1986), The Writing of the Disaster, trans. Ann Smock, Nebraska: University of Nebraska Press.

Borges, Jorge Luis (1962), *Labyrinths: Selected Stories & Other Writings*, New York: New Directions.

Bourdieu, Pierre (2000), *Pascalian Meditations*, trans. Richard Nice, Stanford: Stanford University Press.

Bowie, Malcolm (1991) *Lacan*, Cambridge: Harvard University Press.

Braneck, Mira (2021), 'Unbearable Reading: An Interview with Anuk Arudpragasam', *The Paris Review*, 15 July. Available online: https://www.theparisreview.org/blog/2021/07/15/unbearable-reading-an-interview-with-anuk-arudpragasam/ (accessed 25 February 2022).

Brighenti, Andrea Mubi and Mattias Kärrholm (2018), 'Beyond Rhythmanalysis: Towards a Territoriology of Rhythms and Melodies in Everyday Spatial Activities', *City, Territory and Architecture*, 5 (1). https://doi.org/10.1186/s40410-018-0080-x.

Brown, Jayna (2015), 'Being Cellular: Race, the Inhuman, and the Plasticity of Life', *GLQ*, 21 (2–3): 321–41.

Burnet, John (1892), Poem of Parmenides, English trans. Available online: http://philoctetes.free.fr/parmenidesunicode.htm (accessed 22 February 2022).

Campt, Tina M. (2021), *A Black Gaze*, Cambridge and London: The MIT Press.

Carroll, Lewis ([1865] 2000), Alice's Adventures in Wonderland, A BookVirtual Digital Edition v1.2, Chicago: VolumeOne Publishing. Available online: https://www.adobe.com/be_en/active-use/pdf/Alice_in_Wonderland.pdf (accessed 8 February 2022)

Cavarero, Adriana (2015), 'Narrative Against Destruction', *New Literary History*, 46: 1–16.

Césaire, Aimé ([1955] 2000), *Discourse On Colonialism*, trans. Joan Pinkham, New York: Monthly Review Press.

Chakrabarty, Dipesh (1997), 'The Time of History and the Times of Gods', in Lisa Lowe and David Lloyd (eds), *The Politics of Culture in the Shadow of Capital*, 35–60, Durham: Duke University Press.

Châtelet, Gilles (1987), 'L'enchantement du virtuel', *Chimères*, 2.

Châtelet, Gilles (1993), *Les enjeux du Mobile*, Paris: Seuil.

Châtelet, Gilles ([1993] 2000), *Figuring Space: Philosophy, Mathematics and Physics*, trans. R. Shore and M. Zagha, Dordrecht: Kluwer Academy Press.

Clark, Timothy (2012), 'Scale', in Tom Cohen (ed.), Telemorphosis: Theory in the Era of Climate Change, Volume 1, 148–66, London: Open Humanities Press.

Colebrook, Claire (2016), 'Futures', in Bruce Clarke and Manuela Rossini (eds), The Cambridge Companion to Literature and the Posthuman (Cambridge Companions to Literature), 196–208, Cambridge: Cambridge University Press. Available online: doi:10.1017/9781316091227.018 (accessed 24 January 2022).

Collins, Leah (2019), '"Live action could never have created these worlds": Amanda Strong on her Latest Film, Biidaaban', *CBC Arts*, 15 June. Available online: https://www.cbc.ca/arts/live-action-could-never-have-created-these-worlds-amanda-strong-on-her-latest-film-biidaaban-1.4821934 (accessed 25 February 2022).

Cornford, Francis Macdonald ([1935] 2000), *Plato's Cosmology*, Indianapolis: Hackett Publishing Co.

de Certeau, Michel ([1980] 1984), *The Practice of Everyday Life*, trans. Steven Rendall, Berkeley: University of California Press.

de Freitas, Elizabeth and Nathalie Sinclair (2014), 'The Politics of the Mathematic Aesthetic: Curricular Con (sens) us and Acts of Dissensus', *Philosophy of Mathematics Education*, 28 October.

Dekker, Jeroen J. H. and Leendert F. Groenendijk (2012), 'Philippe Ariès's Discovery of Childhood After Fifty Years: The Impact of a Classic Study on Educational Research', *Oxford Review of Education*, 38 (2): 133–47.

DeLanda, Manuel (2000), *A Thousand Years of Nonlinear History*, New York: Swerve Editions.

Deleuze, Gilles ([1962] 2006), *Nietzsche and Philosophy: Columbia Classics Edition*, trans. Hugh Tomlinson, New York: Columbia University Press.

Deleuze, Gilles ([1968] 1994), *Difference and Repetition*, trans. Paul Ratton, New York: Columbia University Press.

Deleuze, Gilles ([1970] 1988), Spinoza: Practical Philosophy, trans. Robert Hurley, San Francisco: City Lights Books.

Deresiewicz, William (2021), [book review] 'Human History Gets a Rewrite', *The Atlantic*, 18 October. Available online: https://www.theatlantic.com/magazine/archive/2021/11/graeber-wengrow-dawn-of-everything-history-humanity/620177/ (accessed 12 February 2022).

Dinshaw, Carolyn (1999), *Getting Medieval*, Durham: Duke University Press.

Donald, Dwayne (2009). 'Forts, Curriculum, and Indigenous Métissage: Imagining Decolonization of Aboriginal-Canadian Relations in Educational Contexts', *First Nations Perspectives*, 2 (1): 1–24.

Donald, Dwayne (2019). 'Homo Economicus and Forgetful Curriculum', in Huia Tomlins-Jahnke, Sandra Styres, Spencer Lilley, and Dawn Zinga (eds), *Indigenous Education: New Directions in Theory and Practice*, 103–25, Edmonton: University of Alberta.

Donald, Dwayne (2020a), 'Place', in Judy Wearing, Marcea Ingersoll, Christopher DeLuca, Benjamin Bolden, Holly Ogden, and Theodore Michael Christou (eds), *Key Concepts in Curriculum Studies*, 156–66, New York: Routledge.

Donald, Dwayne (2020b), 'Homo Economicus and Forgetful Curriculum: Remembering Other Ways to Be a Human Being', [Talk] University of Alberta Sustainability Council. 23 January. Available online: https://youtu.be/VM1J3evcEyQ (posted 28 January 2020; accessed 28 January 2022).

Drakulić, Slavenka ([1992] 2016), *How We Survived Communism and Even Laughed*, New York: HarperCollins.

Durkheim, Emile (1912), *Les formes élémentaires de la vie religieuse*, Paris: Puf.

Egan, Kieran ([1983] 2012), *Education and Psychology: Plato, Piaget and Scientific Psychology*, London and New York: Routledge.

Egan, Kieran (2002), *Getting it Wrong from the Beginning: Our Progressivist Inheritance from Herbert Spencer, John Dewey, and Jean Piaget*, New Haven and London: Yale University Press.

F. A. Brandão Junior (1865), A escravatura no Brasil precedida d'um artigo sobre a agricultura e colonisacao no Maranhdo, Brussels: H. Thiry-Venn Buggenhoudt: 31–8. Available online: https://faculty.chass.ncsu.edu/slatta/hi216/documents/slavery/work.htm (accessed 11 February 2022).

Ferreira da Silva, Denise (2014a), 'Radical Praxis or Knowing (at) the Limits of Justice', in Suvendrini Perera and Sherene Razack (eds), *At The Limits of Justice: Women of Colour on Terror*, 526–37, Toronto: University of Toronto Press.

Ferreira da Silva, Denise (2014b), 'Toward a Black Feminist Poethics', *The Black Scholar*, 44 (2): 81–97.

Ferreira da Silva, Denise (2017), '1 (life) ÷ 0 (blackness) = $\infty - \infty$ or ∞ / ∞: On Matter Beyond the Equation of Value', e-flux *Journal*, 79: 1–11. Available online: https://www.e-flux.com/journal/79/94686/1-life-0-blackness-or-on-matter-beyond-the-equation-of-value/ (accessed 25 February 2022).

Ferreira da Silva, Denise (2018), 'Hacking the Subject: Black Feminism and Refusal Beyond the Limits of Critique', *philoSOPHIA*, 8 (1): 19–41.

Ferreira da Silva, Denise (2019), 'An End to 'This' World: Denise Ferreira da Silva Interviewed by Susanne Leeb and Kerstin Stakemeier', *Texte Zur Kunst*, 12 April.

Available online: https://www.textezurkunst.de/articles/interview-ferreira-da-silva/ (accessed 25 February 2022).

Ferreira da Silva, Denise (2022), *Unpayed Debt*. MIT Press.

Foucault, Michel (1986), 'Of Other Spaces', trans. Jay Miskowiec, *Diacritics*, 16 (1): 22–7.

Franklin-Phipps, Asilia (2017), 'Entangled Bodies: Black Girls Becoming-Molecular', *Cultural Studies <-> Critical Methodologies*, 17 (5): 384–91.

Freud, Sigmund ([1930] 1961), *Civilization and Its Discontents*, trans. James Strachey, New York: W W Norton.

García-Moreno, Laura (2013), 'Strange Edifices, Counter-Monuments: Rethinking Time and Space in W. G. Sebald's Austerlitz', *Critique: Studies in Contemporary Fiction*, 54: 360–79.

Gibson, William (1999), see origin discussion at http://quoteinvestigator.com/2012/01/24/future-has-arrived/ (accessed 10 February 2022).

Glissant, Édouard ([1990] 1997), *Poetics of Relation*, trans. Betsy Wing, Ann Arbor: University of Michigan Press.

Glissant, Édouard (1997), *Traité du tout-monde: Poétique IV*, Paris: Gallimard.

Glissant, Édouard ([1997] 2020), *Treatise on the Whole-World*, trans. Celia Britton, Liverpool: Liverpool University Press.

Goldberg, Jonathan (2007), 'After Thoughts', *South Atlantic Quarterly*, 106 (3): 501–10.

Gould, Stephen Jay (1977), *Ontogeny and Phylogeny*, Cambridge, MA: Harvard University Press.

Gould, Stephen Jay (1987), *Time's Arrow, Time's Cycle: Myth and Metaphor in the Discovery of Geological Time*, Cambridge, MA and London: Harvard University Press.

Graeber, David and David Wengrow (2021), *The Dawn of Everything: A New History of Humanity*, London: Allen Lane.

Greene, Maxine (1971), 'Curriculum and Consciousness', *Teacher's College Record*.

Grosz, Elizabeth (1995), *Space, Time and Perversion: Essays on the Politics of Bodies*, New York: Routledge.

Grosz, Elizabeth (1999), 'Thinking the New: Of Futures Yet Unthought,' in Elizabeth Grosz (ed.), *Becomings: Explorations in Time, Memory and Futures*, 38–55, Ithaca: Cornell University Press.

Grosz, Elizabeth, Kathryn Yusoff and Nigel Clark (2017), 'An Interview with Elizabeth Grosz: Geopower, Inhumanism and the Biopolitical', *Theory, Culture & Society*, 34 (2–3): 129–46. Available online: doi:10.1177/0263276417689899.

Grusin, Richard (ed.) (2017), *Anthropocene Feminism*, Minneapolis: University of Minnesota Press.

Güneş, Gökhan and Volkan Şahin (2020), 'Preschoolers' Thoughts on the Concept of Time', *The Journal of Genetic Psychology*, 181 (4): 293–317.

Habermas, Jürgen (1984), *The Theory of Communicative Action, Vol. 1 Reason and the Rationalization of Society*, trans. T. McCarthy, Boston: Beacon Press.

Haeckel, Ernst (1897), *The Evolution of Man*, New York: D. Appleton & Co.

Hamilton, Edith and Huntington Cairns, eds ([1961] 1989), *The Collected Dialogues of Plato*, Princeton University Press. Available online: doi: 10.2307/j.ctt1c84fb0.

Haraway, Donna (1991), *Simians, Cyborgs, and Women: The Reinvention of Nature*, New York: Routledge.

Haraway, Donna (2016), *Staying with the Trouble: Making Kin in the Chthulucene*, Durham: Duke University Press.

Hardie, R. P and R. K. Gaye, trans. (2003), *Physics: Aristotle*, Adelaide: The University of Adelaide Press.

Harney, Stefano and Fred Moten (2013), *The Undercommons: Fugitive Planning & Black Study*, Wivenhoe, New York and Port Watson: Minor Compositions.

Harper, Douglas (n.d.), 'Etymology of *awi-', *Online Etymology Dictionary*. Available online: https://www.etymonline.com/word/*awi- (accessed 27 February 2022).

Harper, Douglas (n.d.), 'Etymology of Artifice', *Online Etymology Dictionary*. Available online: https://www.etymonline.com/word/artifice (accessed 27 February 2022).

Harper, Douglas (n.d.), 'Etymology of Category', *Online Etymology Dictionary*. Available online: https://www.etymonline.com/word/category (accessed 27 February 2022).

Harper, Douglas (n.d.), 'Etymology of Defer', *Online Etymology Dictionary*. Available online: https://www.etymonline.com/word/defer (accessed 27 February 2022).

Harper, Douglas (n.d.), 'Etymology of Epoch', *Online Etymology Dictionary*. Available online: https://www.etymonline.com/word/epoch (accessed 27 February 2022).

Harper, Douglas (n.d.), 'Etymology of Index', *Online Etymology Dictionary*. Available online: https://www.etymonline.com/word/index (accessed 27 February 2022).

Harper, Douglas (n.d.), 'Etymology of Present', *Online Etymology Dictionary*. Available online: https://www.etymonline.com/word/present (accessed 27 February 2022).

Harper, Douglas (n.d.), 'Etymology of Progress', *Online Etymology Dictionary*. Available online: https://www.etymonline.com/word/progress (accessed 27 February 2022).

Harper, Douglas (n.d.), 'Etymology of Refusal', *Online Etymology Dictionary*. Available online: https://www.etymonline.com/word/refusal (accessed 27 February 2022).

Harper, Douglas (n.d.), 'Etymology of Relation', *Online Etymology Dictionary*. Available online: https://www.etymonline.com/word/relation (accessed 27 February 2022).

Harper, Douglas (n.d.), 'Etymology of Remediation', *Online Etymology Dictionary*. Available online: https://www.etymonline.com/word/remediation (accessed 27 February 2022).

Harper, Douglas (n.d.), 'Etymology of Remedy', *Online Etymology Dictionary*. Available online: https://www.etymonline.com/word/remedy (accessed 27 February 2022).

Harper, Douglas (n.d.), 'Etymology of Reprise', *Online Etymology Dictionary*. Available online: https://www.etymonline.com/word/reprise (accessed 27 February 2022).

Harper, Douglas (n.d.), 'Etymology of Response', *Online Etymology Dictionary*. Available online: https://www.etymonline.com/word/response (accessed 27 February 2022).

Harper, Douglas (n.d.), 'Etymology of Revelation', *Online Etymology Dictionary*. Available online: https://www.etymonline.com/word/revelation (accessed 27 February 2022).

Harper, Douglas (n.d.), 'Etymology of Rhythm', *Online Etymology Dictionary*. Available online: https://www.etymonline.com/word/rhythm (accessed 27 February 2022).

Harper, Douglas (n.d.), 'Etymology of Rupture', *Online Etymology Dictionary*. Available online: https://www.etymonline.com/word/rupture (accessed 27 February 2022).

Harper, Douglas (n.d.), 'Etymology of Sorosis', *Online Etymology Dictionary*. Available online: https://www.etymonline.com/word/sorosis (accessed 27 February 2022).

Harper, Douglas (n.d.), 'Etymology of Spore', *Online Etymology Dictionary*. Available online: https://www.etymonline.com/word/spore (accessed 27 February 2022).

Harper, Douglas (n.d.), 'Etymology of Time', *Online Etymology Dictionary*. Available online: https://www.etymonline.com/word/time (accessed 27 February 2022).

Hartman, Saidiya (1997), *Scenes of Subjection: Terror, Slavery, and Self-Making in Nineteenth-Century America*, New York: Oxford University Press.

Hartman, Saidiya (2002), 'The Time of Slavery', *South Atlantic Quarterly*, 101 (4): 757–77. Available online: https://doi.org/10.1215/00382876-101-4-757 (accessed 11 February 2022).

Hartman, Saidiya (2008), 'Venus in Two Acts', *Small Axe*, 12 (2): 1–14.

Hartman, Saidiya (2019), *Wayward Lives, Beautiful Experiments: Intimate Histories of Social Upheaval*, New York: Norton.

Havelock, Eric A. (1963), *Preface to Plato*, Cambridge and London: Belknap Press.

Hegel, Georg Wilhelm Friedrich ([1807] 1977), Phenomenology of Spirit, trans. A. V. Miller, New York: Oxford University Press.

Hegel, Georg Wilhelm Friedrich ([1861] 1975), *Lectures on the Philosophy of World History*, trans. Hugh Barr Nisbet, Cambridge: Cambridge University Press.
Hegel, Georg Wilhelm Friedrich (1956), *The Philosophy of History*, trans. J. Sibree, New York: Dover Publications.
Heidegger, Martin ([1935] 1971), 'The Origin of the Work of Art', in *Poetry, Language, Thought*, trans. Albert Hofstadter, 33, New York: Harper & Row.
Heywood, Colin (2001), *A History of Childhood*, Cambridge: Polity Press.
Honig, Bonnie (2021), *A Feminist Theory of Refusal*, Cambridge, MA and London: Harvard University Press.
Ingold, Tim (2007), *Lines: A Brief History*, London: Routledge.
Ingold, Tim (2015), *The Life of Lines*, London and New York: Routledge.
Irigaray, Luce ([1984] 1993), *An Ethics of Sexual Difference*, trans. Carolyn Burke and Gillian Gill, Ithaca: Cornell University Press.
Irigaray, Luce (2001), 'From *The Forgetting of Air* to *To Be Two*', trans. Heidi Bostic and Stephen Pluháček, in Nancy Holland and Patricia Huntington (eds), *Feminist Interpretations of Martin Heidegger*, 309–15, Pennsylvania: Pennsylvania State University Press.
Irigaray, Luce (2008), *Sharing the World*, London and New York: Bloomsbury Academic.
Jacobs, Harriet A. (1861), *Incidents in the Life of a Slave Girl*, ed. Lydia Maria Francis Child, Boston: Published for the Author.
Jacobs-Jenkins, Branden (2020), 'Suzan-Lori Parks, The Art of Theater No. 18', *The Paris Review*, 235. Available online: https://theparisreview.org/interviews/7636/the-art-of-theater-no-18-suzan-lori-parks (accessed 9 February 2022).
Jardin, Alexandre (2008), *Chaque femme est un Roman*, France: Éditions Grasset.
Judy, Ronald A. T. (2020), *Sentient Flesh: Thinking in Disorder, Poiesis in Black*, illustrated edn, Durham: Duke University Press.
Kaan, Heinrich ([1844] 2016), Sexual Pathology, trans. Melissa Haines, ed. Benjamin Kahan, Ithaca: Cornell University Press.
Kalkavage, Peter (2016), *Plato: Timaeus*, 2nd edn, Indianapolis: Hackett Publishing Co.
Keeling, Kara (2007), *The Witch's Flight*, Durham: Duke University Press.
Kimmerer, Robin Wall (2021), 'A Family Reunion Near the End of the World', in Gavin Van Horn, Robin Wall Kimmerer and John Hausdoerffer (eds), *Kinship: Belonging in a World of Relations*, vol. 1, The Planet, IL: The Center for Human and Nature Press.
Kirk, G. S., John Earle Raven and M. Schofield ([1957] 1983), *The Presocratic Philosophers a Critical History with a Selection of Texts*, Cambridge: Cambridge University Press.

Koselleck, Reinhart ([1979] 2004), *Futures Past: On the Semantics of Historical Time*, trans. Keith Tribe, New York: Columbia University Press.

Kristeva, Julia ([1974] 1984), *Revolution in Poetic Language*, trans. Margaret Waller, New York: Columbia University Press.

Land, Nick (2011), 'Circuitries', in Robin Mackay and Ray Brassier (eds), *Fanged Noumena: Collected Writings 1987–2007*, 289–318, Cambridge, MA: Urbanomic/Sequence Press.

Lear, Jonathan (2008), *Radical Hope: Ethics in the Face of Cultural Devastation*, Cambridge, MA: Harvard University Press.

Lefebvre, Henri ([1992] 2004), *Rhythmanalysis: Space, Time and Everyday Life*, trans. Stuart Elden and Gerald Moore, New York and London: Continuum.

Le Guin, Ursula (1974), *The Dispossessed: An Ambiguous Utopia*, New York City: Harper & Row.

Le Guin, Ursula ([1986] 2019), *The Carrier Bag Theory of Fiction*, intr. Donna Haraway, Ignota. https://ignota.org/products/the-carrier-bag-theory-of-fiction.

Levin, Simon A. (1992), 'The Problem of Pattern and Scale in Ecology', *Ecology*, 73 (6): 1943–67.

Manning, Erin (2018), 'Me Lo Dijo un Pajarito: Neurodiversity, Black Life, and the University as We Know It', *Social Text*, 36 (3): 1–24.

Marcus, George and Fred Myers, eds (1995), *The Traffic in Culture: Refiguring Art and Anthropology*, Berkeley: University of California Press.

Marinetti, Filippo Tommaso (1909), 'Declaration of Futurism', *Poesia*, 5 (6): 1–2.

Marx, Karl (1973), Grundrisse: Foundations of Political Economy, trans. Martin Nicolaus, London: Allen Lane.

Massey, Doreen (2005), *For Space*, London: SAGE Publications Ltd.

Mauss, Marcel (1950), *Sociologie et Anthropologie*, Paris: Puf.

McKittrick, Katherine (2016), 'Diachronic Loops/Deadweight Tonnage/Bad Made Measure', *Cultural Geographies*, 23 (1): 3–18.

McKittrick, Katherine (2021), *Dear Science and Other Stories*, Durham: Duke University Press.

Memoria (2021), [Film] Dir. Apichatpong Weerasethakul, Colombia: Cineplex, and USA: Sovereign Films.

Merriam-Webster (n.d.), 'Tropism', Merriam-Webster.com Dictionary. Available online: https://www.merriam-webster.com/dictionary/tropism (accessed 27 February 2022).

Mikulan, Petra (forthcoming), 'Ethics of Refusal: A Speculative Pragmatic Challenge to Systemic Racism in Education', *Educational Theory*, 72 (1).

Miller, Greg (2006), 'Back to the Future', *Science*, 15 June. Available online: doi:10.1126/article.33060 (accessed 27 January 2022).

Minh-ha, Trinh T. (1991), *When the Moon Waxes Red*, London and New York: Routledge.
Moten, Fred (2013), 'Blackness and Nothingness (Mysticism in the Flesh)', *The South Atlantic Quarterly*, 112 (4): 737–80.
Myles, Eileen (2021), 'Time Puts Its Stamp on Everything', *The Paris Review*, 6 May. Available online: https://www.theparisreview.org/blog/2021/05/06/time-puts-its-stamp-on-everything/ (accessed 12 February 2022).
Nanni, Giordano (2012), *The Colonisation of Time: Ritual, Routine and Resistance in the British Empire*, Manchester: Manchester University Press.
Nietzsche, Friedrich ([1882] 1974), The Gay Science (Die Fröhliche Wissenschaft), trans. Walter Kaufmann, New York: Vintage Books.
Nietzsche, Friedrich (1968), The Will to Power, trans. Walter Kaufmann and R. J. Hollingdale, ed. Walter Kaufmann, New York: Vintage Books.
Okri, Ben (1991), *The Famished Road*, Jonathan Cape.
Oluo, Ijeoma (2018), *So You Want to Talk About Race*, New York: Seal Press.
Osunde, Eloghosa (2021), 'Reality is Plasticine', *The Paris Review*, 6 January. Available online: https://www.theparisreview.org/blog/2021/01/06/reality-is-plasticine/ (accessed 6 February 2022).
Pàlsson, Gísli and Heather Anne Swanson (2016), 'Down to Earth: Geosocialities and Geopolitics', *Environmental Humanities*, 8 (2): 149–71.
Parisi, Luciana and Steve Goodman (2009), 'Extensive Continuum: Towards a Rhythmic Anarchitecture', *INFLeXions*, 2. Available online: https://www.inflexions.org/n2_parisigoodmanhtml.html (accessed 26 February 2022).
Poincaré, Henri (1890), 'Sur le problème des trois corps et les équations de la dynamique', *Acta Math*, 13: 1–270.
Province of British Columbia (2021), [website] 'BC's Curriculum'. Available online: https://curriculum.gov.bc.ca/curriculum/overview (accessed 15 February 2022).
Rancière, Jacques (2010), Dissensus: On Politics and Aesthetics, trans. and ed. Steven Corcoran, London and New York: Continuum International Publishing Group.
Redner, Harry (2015), *The Tragedy of European Civilization: Towards an Intellectual History of the Twentieth Century*, Piscataway: Transaction Publishers.
Reed, Ishmael (2016), The Diabetic Dreams of a Cake. *The Paris Review*, issue 218. Available online: https://www.theparisreview.org/poetry/6810/the-diabetic-dreams-of-cake-ishmael-reed (accessed 25 February 2022).
Retallack, Joan (2003), *The Poethical Wager*, Berkeley: University of California Press.
Rohy, Valerie (2006), 'Ahistorical', *GLQ*, 12 (1): 61–83. Available online: doi:10.1215/10642684-12-1-61 (accessed 8 February 2022).
Rohy, Valerie (2009), *Anachronism and Its Others: Sexuality, Race, Temporality*, Albany: SUNY Press.

Rooks, Noliwe (2017), *Cutting School: The Segrenomics of American Education*, New York: The New Press.

Rovelli, Carlo (2018), *The Order of Time*, trans. Erica Segre and Simon Carnell, New York: Riverhead Books.

Sebald, W. G. (2001), *Austerlitz*, trans. Anthea Bell, New York: Random House.

Serres, Michel (1980), *Hermès. V. Le Passage Du Nord-Ouest*, Paris: Editions De Minuit.

Serres, Michel with Bruno Latour ([1990] 1995), *Conversations on Science, Culture and Time*, trans. Roxanne Lapidus, Ann Arbor: University of Michigan Press.

Shahjahan, Riyad Ahmed (2011), 'Decolonizing the Evidence-based Education and Policy Movement: Revealing the Colonial Vestiges in Educational Policy, Research, and Neoliberal Reform', Journal of Education Policy, 26 (2): 181–206. doi:10.1080/02680939.2010.508176.

Shulman, George, Mark Reinhardt and Romand Coles (2014), *Radical Future Pasts: Untimely Political Theory*, Lexington: The University Press of Kentucky.

Silverman, Kaja (1984), *The Subject of Semiotics*, Oxford: Oxford University Press.

Silverman, Kaja (1988), *The Acoustic Mirror*, Bloomington and Indianapolis: Indiana University Press.

Simondon, Gilbert (1958), *Du Mode d'existence des Objets Techniques*, Paris: Aubier, Editions Montaigne.

Simondon, Gilbert ([1958] 2017), *On the Mode of Existence of Technical Objects*, trans. Cécile Malaspina and John Rogove, Twin Cities: Univocal Publishing.

Slapšak, Svetlana (2016), *Cabbage: A Review of the Historical Anthropology of Food and Sexuality*, Belgrade: Biblioteka XX vek.

Souriau, Étienne (1939), *L'Instauration Philosophique*, Paris: Librairie Félix Alcan.

Spillers, Hortense J. (1987), 'Mama's Baby, Papa's Maybe: An American Grammar Book', *Diacritics*, 17 (2): 64–81.

Springgay, Stephanie and Sarah E. Truman (2019), 'Counterfuturisms and Speculative Temporalities: Walking Research-Creation in School', *International Journal of Qualitative Studies in Education*, 32 (6): 1–13. doi:10.1080/09518398.2019.1597210.

Stengers, Isabelle ([2002] 2014), *Thinking with Whitehead: A Free and Wild Creation of Concepts*, trans. Michael Chase, Cambridge, MA: Harvard University Press.

Sully, James (1895), *Studies of Childhood*, London: Longmans, Green & Co.

Tahta, Dick (1980), 'About Geometry', For the Learning of Mathematics, 1 (1): 2–9.

'Tamil Units of Measurement' (2011), [blog post] *Tamilvaralaru / Wordpress*. Available online: https://tamilvaralaru.wordpress.com/tamil-units-of-measurement (accessed 25 February 2022).

Tarc, Mishra (2020), *Pedagogy in the Novels of J. M Coetzee: The Affect of Literature*, New York: Routledge.

Tarde, Gabriel (1890), Les lois de l'imitation, Paris: Alcan.

Taussig, Michael T. (2020), *Mastery of Non-mastery in the Age of Meltdown*, Chicago: University of Chicago Press.

The Grizzlies (2018), [Film] Dir. Miranda de Pencier, Canada: Mongrel Media.

Time Space Existence (2018), [interview/video] 'Moshe Safide – Time Space Existence', *Plane-site* and *Vimeo*, 2 March. Available online https://vimeo.com/258311086 (accessed 12 February 2022).

Webb, P. Taylor, Sam Sellar and Kalervo N. Gulson (2020), 'Articipating Education: Governing Habits, Memories and Policy-Futures', *Learning, Media and Technology*, 45 (3): 284–97.

Weheliye, Alexander G. (2014), *Habeas Viscus: Racializing Assemblages, Biopolitics, and Black Feminist Theories of the Human*, Durham: Duke University Press.

Whitehead, Alfred North ([1929] 1978), *Process and Reality*, corrected edn [page numbers refer to 1st edn], New York: Macmillan.

Whitehead, Alfred North ([1933] 1967), *Adventures of Ideas*, New York: The Free Press.

Wimbush, Erica J. and Mary Talbot (1988), *Relative Freedoms. Women and Leisure*, Milton Keynes: Open University Press.

Winterson, Jeanette ([1989] 1990), *Sexing the Cherry*, London: Random House Vintage.

Wolfram, Conrad (2020), *The Math(s) Fix: An Education Blueprint for the AI Age*, Champaign: Wolfram Media, Inc.

Woolf, Virginia (1929), *A Room of One's Own*. Available online: https://gutenberg.ca/ebooks/woolfv-aroomofonesown/woolfv-aroomofonesown-00-h.html (accessed 28 February 2022).

Woolf, Virginia (1930), 'Street Haunting: A London Adventure'. Available online: http://s.spachman.tripod.com/Woolf/streethaunting.htm (accessed 18 February 2022).

Woolf, Virginia ([1942] 1974), *The Death of the Moth and Other Essays*, edited by Leonard Woolf, New York: Harcourt Brace Jovanovich.

Yaeger, Patricia (1986), 'Honey-Mad Women: Charlotte Brontë's Bilingual Heroines', *Browning Institute Studies*, 14: 11–35.

Yusoff, Kathryn (2018), *A Billion Black Anthropocenes or None*, Minneapolis: University of Minnesota Press.

Zeldin, Theodore (1998), *An Intimate History of Humanity*, London: Vintage.

Zeyl, Donald J. (2000), *Plato: Timaeus*, Indianapolis: Hackett Publishing Co.

Index

abstraction   35, 64, 70
actual occasions   110, 140
administration   42, 67
adolescence   39–40
adulthood   39–40
affect(ive)   8–9, 15, 30, 38, 52, 92, 103–4, 111, 131
   and happiness   68
   labour   180, 182
   politico-affective   44
agency   31, 43–4
agential   43–4
   intra-agential   111–12
   realism   111
Ahmed, Sara   11–12, 63–4, 68, 78–9, 151
anachronism/anachronistic   44–5, 47–8, 136
   and Rohy   48–51
animal   135, 142, 144, 171, 173
   sororal-/sororanimal (*see* sororal-animal)
*an*organism. *See under* organism
Anthropocene   61, 97–8
apparatus
   biopolitical   98
   extractive   98
   temporal   64
archive   63, 70, 114, 144, 146
   and Hartman   138–9, 141, 185
Arendt, Hannah   133, 135–6, 168, 170, 174. *See also under* condition
Aristotle   34, 69, 154, 183
arrow   1, 76–7, 82, 89–90
   and line   65
   in time-as-arrow   2–4, 6–7, 11, 24, 29, 31, 33–5, 37, 42–3, 45–6, 48–9, 52, 76, 109, 166
art   5–6, 38–9, 57, 129–30, 179, 185
artifice   30, 35, 135–6
   definition of   6
artificial   135
   culture   72

Ashbery, John (*This Configuration*)   136–7
assessment   32, 70, 177
atavistic   12, 30, 58–60, 63, 79. *See also under* culture
attention
   paying attention to   131–3, 178–80, 182
awi   171, 175
   definition of   193
axiology. *See under* epistemology

Baba Yaga   171–3, 175
Bacchae   163–5, 168, 171, 175. *See also* Honig, Bonnie
Barad, Karen   10, 17, 25, 103, 111–12, 151, 168
Battiste, Marie   151
becoming   49, 109, 114, 122, 126, 130, 131, 158, 161–2, 167. *See also* being; change
   and being   12, 38, 153, 154, 179, 184
   and Deleuze   124–5
   and flow   140–1
   molecular   160–2, 168
   and movement   49
   and Parisi   140–1
   and time   35, 63, 154
being   38, 49, 63, 68, 70, 92, 95, 101, 108, 114, 125, 152–4, 179, 184. *See also* becoming
Benjamin, Walter   135, 191 n.5
Bergson, Henri   46, 101, 183, 187 n.5. *See also* duration
bifurcation
   of nature and culture   12, 47, 87 (*see also under* culture)
Big Bang (theory)   121, 132
Biidaaban (The Dawn Comes)   90–2, 101, 180
biocentric
   and biosocial   42

code/artifice 30, 43, 135-6, 142
  loop 135
  power 141-2
  structure of time 134
  temporality 8, 133
biopolitical/biopolitics. See
  under political
biosphere 44-5
black
  as negative numbers 22-3
Black(ness)
  and child/gay/queer 50
  and colonial violence 30-1, 33
  culture 165
  death 135
  female/mothers/women/girls
    (flesh) 133, 160-2, 168-9, 175-9,
    181, 192 n.12
  feminist poethics 101, 154
  with Ferreira da Silva 96, 98-102,
    108-10, 160
  gaze/in *A Black Gaze* 127, 179-82
  lives/life 109, 134-5, 179-80
  noise 140-1, 185
  opacity of 180
  slave labour 41, 97
body
  as captive 167
  as maternal 98-9, 155-8, 168
  as measure of rhythms 127
Boltzmann, Ludwig 121
bourgeois 37, 39, 42, 45-6
breast-feeding 171

Campt, Tina 17, 179-82
capitalist 29, 43, 45, 61, 127,
  133, 138, 177
Carroll, Lewis 14, 122, 190
category 96, 102, 108-10, 144, 159,
  166-7, 180
  definition of 188
Chakrabarty, Dipesh 33, 36-7, 136
chance
  and Nietzsche 123
change 119, and Chakrabarty 36-7
  of curriculum 10, 32-3, 36
  and growth/development 102, 104,
    114 (*see also* development)
  measure of 34-5
  radical 37

Châtelet, Gilles 24, 81
child 28, 44, 48, 72-3, 113
  and childhood 38-9, 50
  and 'le sentiment de
    l'enfance' 38-9, 44
  and mother 155-8
  as Organism 118, 142-3
  as savage 48-50, 102
childhood. *See under* child
chora
  with Grosz 153
  with Kristeva (maternal) 157-9
  and Plato/Timaeus 152, 153, 180
  and space 153-4
  and time 165
chronology 48, 51, 174
chronosporosis 171, 173, 175
chronotypes (of fiction) 72-3, 75
civilising 7, 28-9, 41-3, 46
Clark, Timothy 9, 44-5
clock 8, 28-9, 75, 87, 89, 166, 189 n.6
coeval(ness) 35, 43, 119, 139, 180
cognitive
  development 10, 41, 44, 50, 69, 73,
    102, 113, 124, 132
  deviation/impairment 7, 42
  tool 51, 92
Colebrook, Claire 61-3, 135
colonial 6-7, 12, 15, 29-31, 33-5, 40,
  133, 135, 138, 179
  and civilizing 42-3
  in contre-colonial 180, 182, 193 n.18
  female/subject 99-100, 102, 175
  fort logic 59, 61
  in neo-colonial 30-1, 45, 177-8
  and patriarchy/masculine 4, 42, 52,
    110, 114, 165, 169, 180-1
  and scientific 46, 49, 114
  and Spillers 168-9, 175, 177
  and time 37-8, 42-3, 46, 52, 87, 92,
    142, 165-6
composite 30, 52, 59, 61-3, 79, 82. *See
  also* Glissant, Édouard; culture
condition
  The Human Condition
    (Arendt) 133, 135, 136 (*see also*
    Arendt, Hannah)
  of/on time 12-14, 29, 36, 42, 49, 74,
    87, 114, 119, 142, 183
consumption 44-5, 170-1

continuity. *See also* continuum
   and becoming   125, 139–40
   of discontinuity   15, 38, 141, 185
   of the number line   23
   of time   11, 34
continuum
   and Parisi   140–1
   of time   5, 37, 69, 74, 119, 127
   and Whitehead   139–40
cosmic
   and cycles/cyclical   125, 127, 133
   order   152
   (time) scale   93, 122, 139
counternarrative. *See* fabulation. *See also*
   Hartman, Saidiya
creative   4, 24, 111–12, 122, 132, 158
creolization   30, 59, 70, 142. *See also*
   Glissant, Édouard
Crow   33–4. *See also* Lear, Jonathan
culture   28, 33, 104, 146. *See also*
   atavistic; composite; bifurcation, of
   nature and culture
   atavistic   30, 58–60, 63, 79
   Black   165
   common   69
   composite   30, 52, 63, 79
   European/Western   12, 41, 52, 97
   literary/literate   36, 86
   and nature   12, 29, 47, 72, 87, 138
   school   67
   of time   1, 8
curre   13, 119
curriculum
   change/trouble   13, 25, 32, 36, 37, 144
   decolonizing   30
   and education   6, 7, 10, 13, 33, 36, 37,
     41, 69, 81, 86, 119, 127
   indigenizing   13, 60, 81, 87 (*see also*
     indigenous, *métissage*)
   and rhythm   127, 132
   as science fiction   76
   slow   129–31, 179

death
   and Arendt   136
   Black   135
   as destination   64–5, 72, 79
   and fabulations   139
   in *The Grizzlies* and *Biidaaban*   91–2
   and Heidegger   130
   and life   118, 142, 172, 184 (*see also*
     Baba Yaga)
   and murder/massacre   162–4, 169
   and Nietzsche   120, 123
   and Woolf   42, 49
de Certeau (Michel)   17, 155–6
defer   11–12, 68, 71, 76, 78, 82,
   92, 102, 113
   definition of   75
   time-as   64, 66
Deleuze, Gilles   167, 183
   and eternal return   123–5
   and flow   14
   and rhythm   127
   and Spinoza   131
desire   105, 107–8, 113, 122
   the dynamics of   49
   sexual   99, 135–6, 164
   temporal   11, 51–2, 128
destructive   44, 80, 158, 167
development   1, 104
   alternatives   76, 150, 182
   in education   1, 10, 50, 62, 67, 73, 102
   human/civilization   39–40, 42, 47,
     71, 97, 145
   moral   42, 44, 50, 109, 113
   and Piaget/cognitive   41, 50,
     69, 73, 113
   stages   102
   temporal   40, 43, 46, 72
deviant/deviance   11, 31, 42, 46
difference
   racial   109
   and repetition   124, 127, 157–8
   and sameness   13, 87–8, 101–2
   sexual   154–5
disability (and learning)   25, 42
discomfort   4, 179, 181
discontinuity
   and chora   158
   continuity of   15, 38, 141, 185 (*see
     also* continuity)
discourse   7, 158, 168
   colonial   29, 42–3
   educational   6, 110, 178
   of Man   141, 185
   on space/time   155
disjunction
   temporal   62–3
displaced. *See* dispossessed

dispossessed 136, 167. See also Le
    Guin, Ursula
Donald, Dwayne 17, 59, 62, 72
duration 9, 72, 80, 88, 101, 120, 140,
    183. See also Bergson, Henri;
    continuum; Parisi, Luciana;
    Whitehead, Alfred North
dwelling (feminine) 100, 102

Egan, Kieran 3, 17, 28, 47–8, 63
endless 36, 108, 143, 162, 170, 179
energy
    from the environment 41, 45, 97
    feminine/masculine 157, 162 (see
        also chora)
    and Nietzsche 120
    and rhythm 14, 127 (see also
        Bergson, Henri)
    and slowness 182
Enlightenment 45, 71, 145
environment. See also curriculum
    and child(hood) 39, 44
    human/animal/natural 4, 135
    surroundings in education 62
epistemology
    and axiology 5, 13, 34, 119, 135
    colonial/patriarchal/Western 12,
        43, 87, 175
    and fabulation 139
    Indigenous 81
    onto-, 45, 95, 98–9, 102, 107, 111 (see
        also Barad, Karen; Ferreira da
        Silva, Denise)
    and time 5–6, 13, 34, 73–4,
        92, 119, 135
epoché. See under Irigaray, Luce
equation
    Equation of Value 95–6, 99, 102, 109
        (see also Ferreira da Silva, Denise)
    in mathematics 26
    of time 114
    of value 48, 49–50 (see also
        Rohy, Valerie)
escape
    in fabulations 163–4, 167, 169, 181
    the human condition 136 (see also
        Arendt, Hannah)
eternal return 120, 122–5. See also
    Nietzsche, Fredrich; Deleuze, Gilles
ethics

    of care/paying attention/
        slowness 130, 178, 182
    of chance 123
    in Ethics of Refusal (Mikulan) 33
    in An Ethics of Sexual Difference
        (Irigaray) 154
    of inoperativity 175
    of opacity 171, 173, 175
    in poethics 101, 154, 180 (see also
        response-ability)
event
    in fabulations 138–9, 166, 186
    in time 8, 36, 37, 69, 71, 120
evidence 42–3. See also policy
excess 98–100, 110, 138, 141, 151, 185.
    See also Ferreira da Silva, Denise
extraction/extractive
    and chora 171, 184
    colonial 6, 15, 38, 52, 98,
        135, 165, 177
    geologic/planetary 68, 97–8,
        131, 134
    neocolonial 45, 178
    and slavery 93, 134, 168

fabulation
    and Black gaze 181 (see also
        Campt, Tina)
    counter-, 138, 144, 145
    critical 70, 123, 139, 141–2, 185 (see
        also Hartman, Saidiya)
    quantic/rhythmquantic 137, 142, 143
    as refusal 15, 160–8
    temporal 9, 11, 168
feminist 4, 13, 17, 154, 175
    Black feminist poethics 101, 154
    kill joy 160
    refusal 14, 168–9, 175
Ferreira da Silva, Denise/DFdS 13,
    17, 92–110, 112–13, 143, 151,
    154, 159, 167. See also feminist
    poethic; equation, Equation of
    Value; the Thing
fiction 74, 76, 77. See also chronotypes;
    fabulation; Le Guin, Ursula
figure
    of female/man/child 50, 99, 100, 176
    and ground 80
    organism/anorganism 118, 126, 137,
        141, 143, 184

flesh
  Black female 168, 175–7, 179, 192 n.12 (*see also* Spillers, Hortense; Wynter, Silvia; Moten, Fred)
  as place 156
flow. *See also* Bergson, Henri; Deleuze, Gilles; duration; rhythm
  and becoming 140
  and chora 158
  as duration 101
  as rhythm 126
fort logic 59–62
Franklin-Phipps, Asilia 17, 160–2, 168, 177
Fugitive. *See also* Hartman, Saidiya
  and Campt 181–2
  and Honig 164

gaze. *See also* looking-glass
  Black/*A Black Gaze* 127, 179–82 (*see also* Campt, Tina)
  male 170–1, 173, 180
geist (and Hegel) 40, 97
geographical (story, *there*). *See* Hegel, Georg Wilhelm Friedrich
geologic(al) 32, 43–5, 74, 81, 97–8, 131–2, 134, 136, 179
gesture
  of exclusion 36–7
  le geste rhytmanalytique 131
girl(s)
  Black (*see under* Black)
  as dreamers 185
  and Hartman 138–9
Glissant, Édouard 7, 9, 12, 17, 30–1, 37, 51–2, 58–9, 63, 76, 79, 107, 142. *See also* composite; creolization
Gogh, Vincent van (and *A Pair of Shoes*) 129–32
Graeber, David 144–5
grammar of thought 12, 87, 96, 101–2, 110
Greek. *See also* Plato; Aristotle
  Ancient/classical 22, 41, 170
  words/etymology 24, 106, 126, 192 n.15, 193 n.16
The Grizzlies 90–1
Grosz, Elizabeth 17, 43, 93, 150, 152–4, 156

growth (arc of) 48, 50, 52, 78, 91, 113–14, 136

happiness 68, 78
Haraway, Donna 80, 181
Hartman, Saidiya 14, 17, 79, 93, 119, 133, 138–41, 160, 185. *See also* archive; fabulation
Hegel, Georg Wilhelm Friedrich 17, 40–1, 95, 97, 100, 107, 108. *See also geist*
hegemony/hegemonic 7, 30–1, 47, 136
Heidegger, Martin 35, 95, 101, 129–30, 183
heteronormative/heteronormativity 38, 114, 141, 160–1, 169, 171, 181
heterotopia 164, 170, 173. *See also* Honig, Bonnie
historicism 32, 35, 37, 50–1
history/historical 5–7, 22, 29, 32–3, 35, 38, 51, 58, 64, 68–9, 81, 88, 107–8, 119, 128, 135, 138, 141–2, 144–6, 151–2, 156, 166
  art 129
  counter-history 139
  The Philosophy of History (Hegel) 97
  transhistorical 51–2
Honig, Bonnie 14, 17, 160, 163–5, 168–70, 172–5, 180
human. *See also* child
  and Arendt (*The Human Condition*) 133, 135–6
  being/existence/experience 4, 5, 13, 28–9, 33, 39–42, 44, 47, 61–3, 65, 69, 71–3, 80–1, 89, 92–3, 95, 97, 99, 101, 107, 129, 139, 144–5, 152, 154, 157–8, 163, 166–7, 169, 171, 184
  consciousness 14, 120, 131
  dehumanizing 177
  and inhuman 32, 34, 98, 111, 119, 134, 172
  and nonhuman 62, 68, 96, 157, 162, 173, 184

identity 52, 124, 150, 154, 168
  self- 154, 156, 159
ideology 33, 43, 131, 156, 169
image
  and/of child 44–5, 118
  and Donald and fort logic 60

and Lefebvre 131
of time 2–3, 11, 13, 25, 28–9, 33, 42, 68
imagination 106, 110, 167
and children 74–5, 79
Newtonian 32
immanence 94, 96, 105
impossible
impossibles 113, 139, 142
writing 139 (*see also* Hartman, Saidiya)
index 113, 166
definition of 188–9
Indigenous
films (*Biidaaban*) 91
métissage 59–60
peoples/subjects 31, 36, 42, 59–60, 71, 91, 97
scholars 13, 14, 60, 87, 191–2 n.10
students 30, 91
worldview/temporalities/ideas 29, 34, 43, 72, 75, 81, 132, 145
individual(ity)
as abstract or separate 25, 112
of being/knowing/developing 14–15, 40, 47, 69
of children 43, 45, 48, 73 (*see also* child)
industrial 7, 40, 133, 156
conception of time 29, 31, 34
revolution 133–4, 144
inhuman. *See under* human
inoperativity 14, 164, 169–70, 173, 175, 177–8
instauration 9, 127, 191
institutional 30, 43, 47, 66, 132
Irigaray, Luce/LI 13, 17, 92, 94–5, 98, 103–4, 106–7, 110, 154–9, 168, 189–90, 192
and *epoché* 106

juvenile 11, 29, 38

Kant, Immanuel 71, 107–9, 156, 183
Keeling, Kara 30–1
Kimmerer, Robin Wall 60, 76
kinship 76, 164–5, 169, 176–7
patriarchal 152, 169, 174, 192 n.13
sororal-animal 169–70, 173, 180
knowing
and being/doing 6, 14, 69, 92, 100, 105, 108–9, 135, 166
and ignorance 175, 178
knowledge 30, 32, 36, 62, 69, 78, 107–9
Koch curve 125–6
Kohlberg, Lawrence 41–2
Koselleck, Reinhart 35, 166
Kristeva, Julia 17, 157–9, 163

labour 45, 78, 133, 177, 181
affective 180, 182
as force 39, 97
labourers 28
as slave 41, 43, 97–8, 134
language 51, 159
as colonial syntax 36
as formal/informal 157
as maternal/paternal 159
as semiotic 159
as symbolic/pre-symbolic 158–9
and/of time 6, 28, 92, 128
Lear, Jonathan 33–4
learning 2, 113, 123, 142, 178, 192
Black 161
disability 42
mathematics 63, 65
personalized 77
place- and land-based 81
as school-specific 39
stages 14, 41, 69, 119, 124, 183
temporality of 10, 64–5, 67–9, 73, 75
Lefebvre, Henri 14, 17, 119, 125–7, 131–2, 142. *See also* rhythmanalysis; rhythm
Le Guin, Ursula 1, 75–6
Leibniz, Gottfried Wilhelm 35, 69, 75, 106, 183
life 42, 73, 104–5, 130, 133, 146, 176, 185. *See also* rhythm
after-life 33
artificial 135–6
Black 109, 161–2, 179–81
cycle 142–3
and death 49, 172, 184
and deferral 68
everyday 155, 158
feminist 173–4
good 113, 120–4, 141, 184
Greek 170
human 5, 69, 80

Indigenous way of life 33–4, 151
lifetime 63, 65
modern 167
nonhuman 96
of obedience 78
school 1, 132
social 5
stages of 41, 64, 66
and time 12, 35, 38, 46, 65, 142, 183
line
and arrow 64–5
horizon 56–7
mathematical concept 26–8, 125–6
number 23–5
and time 55, 64–5, 67–9, 72, 74, 76, 113
linear
non-linear 62, 126 (*see also* chora)
rhythms 133–4
time 1, 6, 31, 43, 46, 62, 69, 76, 119, 124, 136 (*see also* time, -as-arrow)
literate/literary. *See under* culture
local 43, 45, 48, 118–19
looking-glass 176–7, 180. *See also* gaze

magic 79–81, 164, 175–7, 180
male/masculine
child 44–5
versus female 49, 161, 163–6, 171, 176
gaze 170–1, 173, 180
subject 96, 154–6
and Sun 163
and time 45–6, 49, 155, 165, 183
mathematics
and (counter-)fabulations 11, 144
and magic 81
and numbers 22–6
in school 12, 63–4, 66, 123, 125–6
matrix of relations. *See under* mereotopology
McKittrick, Katherine 6, 134
memory 35, 77, 119
of a place 156
mereotopology
matrix of relations 110, 113
and Whitehead 13, 110–11
metaphoric
and metonymic 49–50, 157
metaphysical 94, 102, 110

Western metaphysics 98, 169
metonymic. *See under* metaphoric
mimesis/mimetic 158, 162–3, 166–71, 173–5, 178, 180
mind
of child 47–8, 50
and Kant 108–9
modernity 129
White 134–6, 138, 141
molar 160–2. *See also* becoming, molecular
molecular. *See under* becoming
Moten, Fred 136, 192 n.12. *See also* flesh
multicultural 13, 59, 88. *See also* creolization
multiplicity 24, 51
of time 7, 76–7, 140, 166
murder. *See under* death
mythical 30, 40, 58–9. *See also* Glissant, Édouard

Nanni, Giordano 7, 11, 17, 29, 31
narrative. *See also* fabulation
arc 52, 58, 75–6, 91
colonial 28
educational 25, 139
temporal 40–1, 43, 52
neoliberal 7, 30, 33, 37, 122, 127, 138, 177–8
juridico-economic system 13, 88
Nietzsche, Fredrich 17, 123
and eternal return 120–2
and mimesis 163
and *ressentiment* 167
and rhythm 127
nostalgia 35, 150, 156, 165. *See also* memory
number 77, 144. *See also under* line
duodecimal 127
negative 22–5

ocular 171, 175, 180–1
ontogeny 25, 47
ontology/ontological 5, 25, 48, 99, 101, 135–6, 153, 161
Indigenous 81
onto-epistemology 45, 95, 98, 102, 107, 111
spatio-temporal 6, 99, 156, 168, 180
optimism 38, 45–6

organism   10, 41, 46, 113–19, 135, 139, 141, 184
  *an*organism   137, 139, 142–3
other   7, 11, 13, 31, 43, 88, 92–3, 95, 103, 105–6, 158, 181, 184–6
  female   156, 161
  otherness   106, 167–8

paradigmatic
  and syntagmatic   49, 51
Parisi, Luciana   140–2, 185
pedagogy   1, 15, 37, 41, 43–4, 64, 68–9, 78, 113, 138, 146
  of citation   4, 9
  decolonizing   12, 87, 92, 101, 180–2
  ethico-, 138, 142
  intervention   47, 50
  milieu   9
  and opacity   175
  and slowness   178
  time   102, 114
phallic   52, 118, 138, 141, 156, 184
Piaget, Jean   11, 18, 41–2, 47, 69, 102
place   2, 13, 45, 49, 60, 80, 87, 95, 104–5, 108, 127, 151, 154–8, 168, 175
  feminine/maternal   158, 174, 176
  Indigenous   191
  and memory   156
  place-based   50, 59, 72, 81, 89
  as placelessness   156
  as topos   152–3
plane   26, 125
  sororal   169
plantation   28–9, 133–4, 176, 191
Plato   18, 35–6, 40, 68, 151–7, 165–8, 172, 180, 183, 191
play of expression   108–9, 143
pleasure   98–9
  and animal   175
  and erotic   171
  and food   171
  and leisure   165, 171, 178
  and pain   155, 157
plenum   94, 98, 102, 103–10, 112. *See also* Ferreira da Silva, Denise
plurality   25, 36–7, 80
Poincaré, Henri   120–1
point of view   41–2, 56–7, 59, 62, 81, 184
  spatio-temporal   52, 57
policy   36–7, 42–3, 177

maker   32, 43, 81
political   38, 43–4, 51, 63, 93, 97, 136, 141, 185
  biopolitical/biopolitics   44–6, 50, 98
  and ethics   15, 45, 96
  temporalities   130
positioning   160–1, 174
possibles   15, 114, 119, 142–3, 145, 167–8, 180, 182, 185. *See also* impossible, impossibles
  counter-possibles   139, 142
potentiality   92, 180, 192
  and Whitehead   139
power   6–7, 35, 42, 162–3, 165–7, 186
  biocentric   135, 141
  colonial   15, 29, 31, 68
  and Deleuze   183
  discourses   37
  occult   173–7, 180
  of opacity   181–2
  sexual   98
  of time   2, 59, 73, 80, 119, 183
  will to   124
presence   70, 79, 89, 112, 128, 131–2, 181
present   5, 9, 14, 25, 31, 44, 91–2, 105, 127, 131–5, 183
  affective   38
  definition of   128
  equation of the   166
  eternal   104, 143, 150–2
  and past/future   3, 24, 61–2, 77–9, 97, 119, 121, 141, 184
  and physics   89
  speed   32
presupposition of temporality   1, 32, 130
primitive   11, 29, 44, 46–51, 145, 162
  societies   7
production   8, 138
  of child   102
  of desire   141, 184
  of difference   124
  of hierarchies   7
  knowledge   8, 64
  of racial subject   109
  reproduction   5, 69, 125, 169, 171, 181
  of temporality   133, 171, 192
progress   2, 8, 12, 15, 37, 48, 102–9, 128, 138, 142, 145, 166, 193
  definition of   70

evolutionary 46, 71
progressive development 39–40, 44, 51, 69
progressive time 5, 7, 9, 28–30, 46, 52, 72, 76, 145, 166
proximity 95, 98, 102–5, 112
psychology 43, 45, 47, 113–14, 176

quantic. *See under* fabulation; rhythm
quantum 45, 74, 102–3, 111–12, 121, 140
  existence 11
  fabulation 3
  time 90, 93
queer 11, 29, 48–52, 102, 119, 160–2
  epistemology 111
  modes 38
  queering 12, 64, 79

race 48, 50, 180
  racial code 30–1, 42–3
  racialization 46, 49–50, 101–2, 108–9, 112, 141, 168, 187
  racial knowledge 97
  racial violence 99, 151
  racism 46, 48–9, 52, 93, 123, 135, 161, 178–9
Rancière, Jacques 32, 168
rationality 105, 141
reason 12, 24, 36
  age of 71
  bastard 153
  and Necessity 151–2
  and time 1, 69, 72, 118, 138, 154
  and western epistemology 87, 97, 99–101, 105, 159
recapitulation 48–50
  discourses 48
  hypothesis 47
receptacle 31, 152–3, 156–7, 168
recognition 30–1, 108, 164–5, 181
refusal 6, 14–15, 31, 42, 150–82, 193
  choral 184
  definition of 150
  ethics of 33
  of time 92, 129
relational(ity) 43, 94–5, 102, 104, 110
  colonial 168–9
  ethical 185
  intra-agential 112

maternal 168–9
psychosis 72
rhythmic 131
sororal 174
space-time 133
view of time 69
remediation 7, 11, 22–52, 193
  definition of 22
repetition 5, 13–14, 118–46, 155, 157, 183
  and Tarde 191
representation 8, 31, 57, 82, 99, 123–4, 131, 135, 159, 187
  of time 154
research 45, 47, 50, 79, 113, 133
  creation 8, 179
  educational 3, 5, 8, 31, 37, 43, 49, 73, 81, 136
  transdisciplinary 111
resistance 31, 37, 42, 78, 129–30, 179, 192. *See also* Nanni, Giordano
response-ability/response-able 8–9, 44, 168, 174, 182. *See also* ethics
revelation 56–82
  definition of 56
rhythm 2, 36, 126–34, 138, 157–8, 191. *See also* Lefebvre, Henri
  and cyclicity 4, 125–6, 133
  definition of 126
  and desire 99
  micro-scale 45
  and Parisi 140–2, 185
  and repetition 14, 127
  and school 6, 8, 132–3
  secret 132–3, 182
  sexual 119
  and velocity 4, 8
rhythmanalysis 131–2, 142. *See also* Lefebvre, Henri
Rohy, Valerie 11, 18, 48–52, 119, 136
Rooks, Noliwe 7, 122, 188
Rousseau, Jean Jacques 71–2, 144
Rovelli, Carlo 18, 88–90
rupture 12–13, 86–114
  definition of 86
  of semiotic 158, 175

savage 28–9, 42, 48–50, 102, 168
scale 8–9, 28, 50–1, 63–4, 89–90, 93, 98, 112, 135, 139–42, 167

geological 131
intersecting 97
micro- and macro- 3–4, 43–5
school 1, 5–6, 8, 12, 14–15, 28, 34, 38–9, 42, 63–4, 69, 102, 113–14, 122–5, 131–3, 138–9
  bell 64–8
  chronotype of 75
  curriculum 81, 127
  high school 160–1, 177
  monitorial 78–9
  and policy 37
  to prison pipeline 7, 136
  residential 29
  space 43–4
  time 119, 129, 141, 154, 165, 158, 179, 183–4
  unschooling and deschooling 178
science/scientific 42–3, 47, 52, 71, 81, 111–12, 144–5, 161
  and racism 46, 48–9, 108
  slow 129
  and time 14, 69, 74–5
  and western epistemology 12, 62, 87, 97, 101, 135, 187–8
segrenomic 7, 122, 136. *See also* Rooks, Noliwe
sentiment(ality) 184
  and child 38–9, 44–6
  in le sentiment de l'enfance 38–9
  in *ressentiment* 167–8
settler 33, 35, 59–60, 91–2
sex. *See also* sexual(ity)
  and gender 164, 169 (*see also* gender)
  organ 156
  and sexism 123, 161
sexual(ity). *See also* sex
  and child/primitive/race 7, 43–4, 48–50
  desire 136, 190 n.20
  difference 154–5
  erotic 143
  female 98–9, 175
  and food 193 n.17
  in heterosexual(ity) 29, 44–5, 48
  in homosexual(ity) 49
  and otherness 98, 167
  polymorphous 50, 173
  reproductive/reproduction 118, 142, 171, 193 n.16

in *Sexual Pathology* (Kaan) 48
and time 48, 118–19, 142
Shahjahan, Riyad Ahmed 42–3
signification 13, 49–50, 98–9, 119, 157. *See also* Ferreira da Silva, Denise
Silverman, Kaja 49, 159
Simpson, Leanne Betasamosake 91
simultaneity 35, 140
sister 173–4, 181–2. *See also* sororal
skholē 170–1, 192 n.14
Slapšak, Svetlana 171
slave/slavery 7, 97–8, 136, 139, 141, 167–8
  and Campt 181
  as colonial native/female 99–100
  labour 41, 43, 97, 134
  and master 78, 98, 134
  ship 135, 138
  in transatlantic slave trade 134, 168
slow(ness)
  and pleasure/rest 171, 174–5, 179–82
  and rhythm 127
  and schooling 5, 128–31, 178–9
  and time 35, 89
sororal. *See also* sister; kinship, sororal-animal
  -animal (*see* sororal-animal)
  chorus 181
  definition of sorosis 192
  plane 169
  refusal 174, 180
sororal-animal/sororanimal
  kinship 169–70, 173
  mimetic opacity 180
  pleasure 175
  relationality 174
sovereign 98–9, 172
space
  and Bacchae 165, 171
  and chora 152–4, 157, 159, 165
  and feminine/women 49, 154–6
  with Ferreira da Silva 93, 97, 99–100, 102, 108, 112–13
  and flesh 176
  with Irigaray 95, 104–6
  in paintings 56–7
  with Parisi 140
  and rhythm 127
  sacred/of sanctuary/care 181–2

in space-time 25, 27, 100, 102–3, 110, 112–13, 124, 127, 140, 154–6
in spacetimemattering 25
and use 73
and vessel 75–6
speculative 95–6, 181
  fiction 75 (*see also* Le Guin, Ursula)
  as (future) possible (*see* possibles)
speed
  of change 32, 36–7
  and rhythm 131
  and time 10, 11, 32, 77, 89, 129
Spillers, Hortense 18, 98, 151, 165–9, 175–7, 180, 192 n.12
Stages. *See also* development
  developmental 39, 41–2, 47, 69, 73, 119, 124, 132 (*see also* Piaget, Jean)
  of humanity/civilizations 40–1, 47, 71, 97
  and time 14, 102, 144–5, 183
Strong, Amanda 91. *See also Biidaaban*
structure
  colonial/oppressive 150, 165, 177
  of possibilities 108, 110, 112–13
  spatial 155
  of time 7, 40, 49, 70, 96–7, 134, 167
student 11, 32, 42, 50, 64, 66–7, 78, 81, 114, 122–4, 141–3
  Black/Brown 30, 160–1, 177
  Indigenous 30, 91
  and rhythm 132
  White 179
  woman 160, 177
style 4, 52, 143, 167
subject 11, 28, 62, 92, 95, 98, 102, 104, 114, 127
  Indigenous and Black 31, 109, 180
  masculine 96, 154–7
  queer 48
  rational 28, 43, 46, 97
  segregation of 80
  Subjectum 105, 107
  White 42, 100–1, 108
subjectivity 77, 94, 155
Subject-predicate logic. *See* grammar of thought
syntagmatic. *See* paradigmatic
syntax 35–6, 43, 96, 171, 174
  colonial 168

synthesis 125, 127–8, 184

Tamil (time) 88, 90
Taussig, Michael 15, 18, 157
  and mastery of non-mastery 178
  and mimesis 166–9, 174–5, 192
  and trickery 173
  and Woman 162–3
teacher 2–4, 12, 32, 64, 67, 70, 77–8, 81, 119, 123, 127, 142, 144, 178
  pre-service 86–7, 101
  settler 92, 168, 177
teleological 2–3, 37, 43, 61, 145, 184
tempo 2, 4–5, 8, 179. *See also* rhythm
  bacchaeic 168, 171
  inoperative 181
temporality 1, 8, 47, 90, 108, 128, 133
  of Black gaze 179–81
  colonial 30, 37–8
  and daydreaming 125
  fallacy of misplaced 51
  and fort logic 59
  Indigenous 34
  linear 119
  mimetic 167, 170–1, 175
  narrative 40, 48
  primacy of 107
  segronomic 136
theory
  educational 43, 50–1, 177
  theoretical text 49, 51
  theorizing 103
the Thing 96, 98–102, 106, 110, 112–13. *See also* Ferreira da Silva, Denise
time
  -as-arrow 2–4, 6, 11, 24, 29, 31, 33–5, 37, 42–3, 45–6, 48–9, 52, 166
  -as-deferral 64, 66–7
  -as-revelation 11, 12, 63, 78
  deep 43–5, 81, 132, 179
  definition of 4
  Kategoria of 92, 106, 188 n.6
  school 119, 168, 183
transcendental(ity) 12, 94–6, 100, 106, 112, 154
tropism 1–2, 8, 50
  definition of 10

universal(s)/universalism 51, 64, 109, 111–12

and Black/White 96–7, 100, 109
time 6–7, 32–3, 35, 46, 89
use. *See also* inoperativity
  new/re-, 64, 164, 170
  no(n)-use 80, 169, 171, 180–1
  queering 64, 79
  time as 171, 192 n.14
  unproductive 171, 174
  useful 63–4, 78–9
  in *What's the Use?* (Ahmed) 63, 78–9

value 7, 97–100, 109, 113, 175, 177
  equation of (*see* equation, *Equation of Value*; equation, of value)
Venus in Two Acts. *See* Hartman, Saidiya
vessel
  and Le Guin 32, 75
  time as 32, 135
violence 165, 184
  colonial 30–1
  economic 168
  and education 139, 141
  misogynistic 157
  ocular 171
  patriarchal 169, 179
  racial 99, 151
  temporal 32, 178
  and the Thing (Ferreira da Silva) 96, 98–100, 109–10
virtual 92, 98, 100, 130, 141, 185. *See also* Parisi, Luciana
waiting 12, 38, 129, 131
Wengrow, David 144, 145
White. *See also* colonial

and bourgeois 37, 42, 45
child 44–5, 48
fragility 91, 179
gaze 180–2
modernity 134, 136, 138, 141
and neoliberal/neocolonial 30, 37, 178
and patriarchal 169, 177, 180
people (teachers/colleagues/co-workers) 161, 168, 177–9, 183
supremacy 169, 177
time(-as-arrow) 48–9, 136
universality 45, 100
women/mothers 175–6
Whitehead, Alfred North 8–9, 18, 35, 70, 103, 108, 112, 127, 131, 139
  and extensive continuum 140
  and mereotopology 13, 110–11 (*see also* mereotopology)
Winterson, Jeanette 21, 55, 85, 117, 149
woman
  Black (*see under* Black)
  as looking-glass 176
  and mimesis 162–3, 167–8
  and time/space 7, 36, 150, 154–7, 159, 164–5, 169–71, 173–5, 192 n.10
Woolf, Virginia 42, 49, 176–7
Wynter, Silvia 93, 192 n.12

Yugoslavia 34, 130
Yusoff, Kathryn 43, 97

www.ingramcontent.com/pod-product-compliance
Lightning Source LLC
Chambersburg PA
CBHW062224300426
44115CB00012BA/2208